# LITERARY CRITICISM AND CULTURAL THEORY

*Edited by*

## William E. Cain
Wellesley College

A ROUTLEDGE SERIES

# LITERARY CRITICISM AND CULTURAL THEORY

## WILLIAM E. CAIN, General Editor

# BETWEEN PROFITS AND PRIMITIVISM
## Shaping White Middle-Class Masculinity in the United States, 1880–1917

Athena Devlin

Routledge
New York & London

Published in 2005 by
Routledge
711 Third Avenue, New York, NY 10017

www.routledge-ny.com

Published in Great Britain by
Routledge
2 Park Square
Milton Park, Abingdon
Oxon OX14 4RN
www.routledge.co.uk

First issued in paperback 2011

Catalog record is available from the Library of Congress

ISBN13: 978-0-415-97077-8 (hbk)
ISBN13: 978-0-415-51475-0 (pbk)

*for Laura Kesselman Devlin*

# Contents

# List of Figures

# Acknowledgments

I would like to thank Deborah Carlin, Kathy Peiss, Randall Knoper, and Laura Doyle for all their guidance and suggestions; Rachel Devlin for her encouragement and support (both intellectual and otherwise); Andrea Sanders for her work with the images; and Anthony Lacavaro for his enduring enthusiasm, for reading the entire manuscript, and for all the great food.

A portion of Chapter One was first published in *The Columbia Journal of American Studies* under the title "Class and the Imaging of the Male Body in the Age of Efficiency."

# Introduction

Demonstrating the contructedness of masculinity has been the project of most masculinity studies thus far. For instance, both Anthony Rotundo's *American Manhood* and Michael Kimmel's *Manhood in America: A Cultural History*, which laid much of the groundwork for masculinity studies, argue that men "as men" do not have a history. The authors' desire to redress this absence is rooted in the political and critical positions taken by the feminist movement and women's studies, chiefly that gender is an active cultural construction. But there is a tendency in masculinity studies to continue insisting on this point, perpetuating the myth that gender operates transparently for men. In claiming that gender must be "applied" to men, many works presume (and thereby entrench) an unawareness on the part of men—and, until recently, their authors—of the extent to which they are defined by gender. That begs the question, how active can a cultural construction be that impacts transparently? The result is a partial naturalization of manhood at the very moment of its deconstruction. The texts I analyze in this study show that men have mobilized gender constructions repeatedly and self-consciously to position themselves within the culture.

Late nineteenth- and early twentieth-century America was rife with self-conscious discourses on white middle- and upper-class manhood as a cultural production: how it evolved, how one might mold it, change it, live it, cure it and certainly protect it from competing versions of manhood. But while I find white manhood to be a complex and varying construction, I am not arguing that the men I discuss in these pages—often men of great privilege—are now to be understood as less a part of the dominant culture simply because their masculinity is a more complex construct than one might have thought. Nor do I want to make the complexities or what a number of scholars have referred to as moments of "crisis" in the history of masculinity the most important aspects of the study of manhood. To make crisis the central point about masculinity is to lose sight of the ways in which white men controlled culture and society, defined the rights, and very humanity, of others while

protecting their own self-interests and perpetuating the power of their class
and gender over centuries of change.[1] As confused as men might have been
about how to define manhood at various historical moments, they were never
so confused that they lost power, nor, in fact, the sense of being a group.[2] My
work both recognizes how white men of the upper classes promoted and presented a seamless front, *and* inspects "the ultimate provisionality of identities."[3] Aiming to join those who offer nuanced accounts of masculinity, I
investigate the various and changing interests white manhood was positioned
to cultivate and the ways elite men used "their own," so to speak, to promote
larger agendas for their class and race.

   This project has implications for women's social history. The work does not
focus on a masculinity that is primarily constructed through the repression or
negation of a feminine realm. Instead, I am more interested in lines of connection.
Without trying to invade "women's culture," my work will re-conceptualize spaces
that have been defined as part of the female sphere, and investigate men's presence
in these spaces. My models for crossing over the public/private divide come from
women's studies texts themselves, from books like Glenda Gilmore's *Gender and
Jim Crow* which details the ways black women in the South in the first decades of
the 20th century took advantage of the political and very public plans of progres-
sivism, or Kathy Peiss' *Cheap Amusements,* which shows the impact working-class
women and girls had on an emerging mass/popular culture. Undoubtedly women
in the public sphere operated differently than men. But they were there, and they
greatly impacted and complicated, for example, race and class politics. As the feminist theorist Shane Phelan puts it in her book *Getting Specific,* the public/private
dualism "has prevented us from seeing the lines of power in our lives and addressing them as matters of common concern" (xix).

   On this basis, I believe that a re-conceptualization of the body, consumer culture and nervous illness—all considered the special jurisdictions of
women—needs to take place, one that includes men in these areas as a nego-
tiating participants. Because gender is sewed into the fabric of all areas of culture, we must ask: How does the male body participate in turn-of-the-century
re-conceptualizations of the body? How do men use commodities and define
their own consumption? And, how do preoccupations about manhood specifically affect the construction of the subconscious as well as ideas about psychological health and illness? None of this should erase women from these
spaces. It should, however, complicate the patriarchal gaze, upset certain ideas
about the balance of power, and, most importantly, work to free women from
a naturalized relationship to the body, commodities and the irrational.

   Because gender studies still exists in a somewhat uneasy relation to
women's studies and feminism,[4] I would also like to say a few words concerning

what I believe to be the contributions of gender studies to this project. Many feminist theorists, like Judith Butler, Diane Elam and Diana Fuss contend that destabilizing the subject has positive repercussions for feminism.[5] Women, after all, have consistently experienced the downside of essentialism. But the destabilized subject does not, and should not, be understood as powerful enough to destroy sex-based hierarchies, or for that matter, sexual difference. It has been suggested that gender studies, which has a less antagonistic relationship to poststructuralism than women's studies, over estimates the power of indeterminacy. This has caused some friction between feminist thinkers over the definition (and power) of sex.[6] I do believe that sexual difference matters, and that bodies are marked, not blank screens on which anything can be projected. Here I am in line with feminist theorists Moira Gatens and Elizabeth Grosz who contend that "Masculinity and femininity as forms of sex-appropriate behaviors are manifestations of a historically based, culturally shared phantasy about male and female *biologies* and as such sex and gender are not arbitrarily connected."[7] I work from this theory of connection between sex and gender when approaching the male body. Pointedly, though, I do not wish to investigate male bodies *for* their biology. In the words of Rosi Bradiotti, "The body, or the embodiment of the subject is to be understood as neither a biological nor a sociological category but rather as a point of overlapping between the physical, the symbolic, and the sociological."[8] Still, while "gender" has a tendency to evacuate sex, the term does allow for a certain level of complexity and mutability that, I think, resonates with the cultural and historical changeability of being male or female. If one is not born a man or woman (despite being born male or female), but becomes one, we have to pay attention to the discourses that shape this process of becoming. The idea of gender may have a tendency to erase sexual specificity but it necessitates cultural and historical specificity.

Finally, bodies, male or female, are marked by race. And, just as I attempt to discuss middle-class masculinity without erasing the privilege that comes with being middle-class or male, I attempt to investigate the construction of whiteness without losing sight of it as a marker of privilege. However, as Matthew Frye Jacobson notes in *Whiteness of a Different Color,* whiteness has not always been a monolithic signifier. Indeed, the "contest over whiteness—its definition, its hierarchies, its proper boundaries, and its rightful claimants—has been critical to American culture throughout the nation's history, and it has been a fairly untidy affair."[9] In this book, whiteness is a determining part of the masculinity I try to interpret. And, being its "rightful claimant" involved, at the turn of the century, a great deal of physical and psychological work. *Between Profits and Primitivism* surveys the period between the mass immigration that began in the 1840s and the restrictive legislation put in place after World War I. Moving toward a narrower immigration policy, the turn of the century "witnessed a fracturing of whiteness into a hierarchy of plural and scientifically determined white races" (Jacobson 7). Whiteness, then, was a crucial but fragmented racial category. Only by understanding this can the full import of fears about the *Anglo-Saxon* race, which dominant forms of masculinity was so concerned with, be understood.

Several recent scholars have noted that the great majority of the work on masculinity has focused on white, middle-class masculinity.[10] Some have defended this "predictable focus"[11] by citing a lack of source material on black or working-class men. My reasons, however, for focusing on white middle-class masculinity have to do with my interest in the body and, moreover, with showing that we can in fact locate the process through which white bodies get constructed as hegemonic. Indeed, I believe it is not as difficult to "gain purchase on 'Whiteness'"[12] as some scholars make out. While I agree that the white middle-class male body does not "readily appear in mainstream North American society, because it is the ground from which that social space is typically envisioned and practiced,"[13] I do not think that it is always the invisible norm. Ultimately, my work challenges the idea that the white male body is elided through its being made generic because it shows that such bodies are not always unproblematic and, moreover, do in fact "require the work of conscious performance."[14]

## THE BODY IN PHYSICAL AND CONSUMER CULTURE

In her book *Imaginary Bodies,* Moira Gatens argues that "The privileged relation which each individual has to her or his own body does not include a privilege over its construction" (35). Chapters One and Two investigate both who and what cultural changes influenced the construction of white male bodies in the middle and elite classes. Because this group is most often seen as the arbiter of the physiological construction of others, the critical point here is white men's participation, as objects, in cultural projects that determine bodies.[15] I argue, further, that historically specific investigations of male bodies reveal that the "biological body . . . exists for the subject [both male and female] only through the mediation of an image or series of (social/cultural) images of the body and its capacities for movement and action" (Grosz 41). Thus the first two chapters examine the historical understanding of the specific social, cultural, racial and class-bound markers embodied by and through white men.

Being historically specific about the male body not only denaturalizes that body—and the white male citizen's body is always in need of deconstruction—but also makes visible the assumptions that go along with that body, such as, in the case of the middle-class male, efficiency and self-control.

Because "materializations" are never stable, I ask what is behind the socially appropriate white male body of the turn of the century. What "operations of power produce" this body (Gatens 70)? What are the "conditions of its emergence and operation?"[16] Who controls it, or makes sure it represents the values of a specific race and class? What discourses both "materialize its effects" as well as "circumscribe" its "domain of intelligibility?"[17]

To answer these questions, I turn, in Chapter One, to physical education, especially as it is expressed through exercise manuals written by elite professionals for middle- and upper-class "brain workers." I compare this "moderate" and moderating discourse to the more popular physical culture discourse that sold promises of spectacular physical transformation to a more general, and less educated, audience. I find that physical education for the middle and elite classes promoted a healthy, symmetrical body that emphasized efficiency above all else. The "conditions of its emergence" rest in a number of places but I explore the anxiety about the fitness of the white male body most fully as an effect of industrialism and new forms of work. The particular body constructed through physical education was one meant to define itself as different from the manual laborers of the working class. Importantly, these manual laborers were mostly white, and thus we see through this specific middle-class physical education discourse a perfect example of the "variegated whiteness" that surfaced at the turn of the century (Jacobson 41). I argue against many historians who I believe overstate the idealization of the working-class body during this period. I show that the efficient and slim body constructed by elite physical educators was a crucial tool in the perpetuation of class specificity. While physical educators admitted working-class men had strong muscles, they, along with efficiency experts like Frederick Winslow Taylor, never tired of asserting that it was an *inefficient* body. But, not only was the laborer's body inefficient, it was also incapable of self-discipline and needed constant supervision. Thus physical educators and efficiency experts were careful to emphasize the free will of their subjects. In doing so, a specific whiteness is equated with self-mastery and reveals how the transformation of self into an exemplary subject for the middle-class male rested, in part, on an "internal mode of submission" (Braidotti 127).

I also investigate the relations of power between the men who controlled the materialization of this body and their male subjects. If, as Anne McClintock has argues in her book *Imperial Leather,* "Enlightenment metaphysics presented knowledge as a relation of power between two gendered spaces, articulated by a journey and a technology of conversion: the male penetration and exposure of a veiled, female interior" (23), does the fact of the male body, on both sides, change this relation? Are, in other words, the "relation[s] of power" different when both the penetrator and the penetrated are male? I search this not for the effects of biology so much as the effects of sex and gender on visibility, objectification and the scientific gaze.

It is important when investigating the relations of power here that white middle-class men freely submitted to the gaze of those who would revitalize them. But were they feminized by the experience? Mary Ann Doane's work articulates something rudimentary about the gaze: the phenomenon that subjects, "whether male or female, inevitably appear to assume a 'mask' of femininity in order to become photographic . . . as though femininity were synonymous with the pose."[18] Perhaps this is because, as theorists like Luce Irigaray have argued, the scopic drive has been coded as male, and thus there is always an assumed male viewer. Compulsory heterosexuality would, then, feminize a male or female object of the gaze. But because biological differences between the sexes have some bearing on "differentiation within the symbolic process" (Doane 221), I am careful to explore in detail the power dynamics between male trainers and their male subjects. What I find is that the goal of efficiency does a great deal of work here as well. It helped to banish the idea that the body work these men did, under the eyes of trainers among others, was a self-conscious beautification ritual. These men, so invested in efficiency, were not aesthetic objects but smooth running machines (or soon would be). Physical educators (unlike popular physical culture gurus) also did two important things: they always pictured their subjects in the act of doing an exercise (never posing in ways that presented the body as separate from work), and they imported the science of anthropometry, using it, I argue, as a way to chasten their gaze.

Despite the work of efficiency, however, the need to "rejuvenate" the white, middle-class male body did place these men in a discourse that could not fully separate itself from the social scientific discourse that categorized and catalogued the criminal, the disorderly female, the laborer, and the racial "other." Physical education, I argue, was a reformative program and as such delineated a problem in the men whose class-bound and racially specific bodies traditionally represented power. Thus the chapter also notes that the mania for "scientific" categorization at the turn of the century did in fact catch white men in its web and defined them, at least partially, *through the body.* In a chapter on the commodification of women, Irigaray writes that "society requires that the body submit itself to a specularization that transforms it into a value bearing object, a standard sign, an exchangeable signifier, a 'likeness' with reference to an authoritative model."[19] She is talking exclusively of women, it is her body that is split "into two irreconcilable 'bodies': her 'natural' body and her socially valued, exchangeable body, which is a particular expression of *masculinist* values (180, my emphasis). Physical education illustrates some of the ways the male body too is transformed into a "value bearing object" (and a profitable one at that) but also how that body, being male, has a crucially different relationship to the "particular expression of masculinist values" that form the "authoritative model" (180).

While the first chapter takes apart the quasi-scientific gaze of physical educators and efficiency experts, the second chapter uses two ambitious and somewhat neglected works of naturalist fiction to explore the more diffuse gaze of a consumer-oriented society and its impact on the (often self-conscious) construction of masculinity. As many literary critics have argued, scopic drives and the connection between vision and knowledges are central to the realist/naturalist narrative.[20] Some have argued, further, that the narrators of these fictions (either defined or assumed male) are given "unlimited disembodied vision that is the fantasy of phallocentricism" (Braidotti 73). The emphasis on vision in the fiction of the turn of the century has also been understood by critics as part of a reaction to the role materialism and consumerism played in the construction of social reality. This orientation of the culture toward consumerism provoked a shift in literary discourse, which dealt with the new reality by emphasizing the dynamics of the visual. Using two novels by Theodore Dreiser, *The Financier* (1912) and *The Titan* (1914), Chapter Two investigates both the connection between masculinity and scopic power, and the new role played by commodities in the construction of a highly profitable "manliness" written on the body.

I agree with the critic John Ringnall that the "disengaged onlooker has been a common accomplice in the realist project" and that there is a "privileged role ascribed to seeing in the practice of literary realism".[21] However, I also agree with Ringnall, perhaps more importantly, that the masterful gaze is, in the end, illusionary. What I investigate in Dreiser's fiction are the complex networks of relations the male protagonist, Frank Cowperwood, becomes involved in through the act of looking and through being the object of scopic pleasure for both the men and women around him. What this chapter adds, then, to realist/naturalist criticism is a more fluid understanding of the way power transfers between the spectator and his or her object and how, indeed, the male spectator can and quite often does, fall into the position of the observed. Arguing against critics like Jann Matlock in her article "Censoring the Realist Gaze" I also show how, in Dreiser's work, the act of looking for women is *not* always construed as transgressive and that looking itself was not understood to be a solely male erotic and voyeuristic pastime. Nor, for that matter, are women's acts of looking read as a form of eroticism *for* men.

I also use Cowperwood's complex and varied roles within the scopic and market economies to investigate his own relationship to consumer culture. A

great deal has been written on women's elision with the consumer products
they use in the display of self. In realist fiction perhaps no woman is more famous (or infamous) than Dreiser's Carrie Meeber for her entrenchment in
consumer culture. While critics such as Amy Kaplan, Philip Fisher and Walter
Benn Michaels have differing views on Carrie's level of agency, all agree that
she constructs (or is constructed) almost solely through commodities, and,
further, that *things* have more emotive power than people.[22] Less has been said
about the ways men also rely on these same signifiers to be part of any social
exchange during this period. Because an important location of exchange for
men is in the realm of business, I explore, specifically, connections between
men's relationship to consumer culture and new forms of market capitalism.
I find a link in the character of Cowperwood between being *in* the market and
being *on* the market. I show how a less tangible economic system (one based
on stocks and "invisible" wealth as opposed to property) not only forces
women to become signifiers of their husband's success, but also forces men to
use commodities as signifiers in the construction of their own identity. For instance, Cowperwood is unable to establish his manliness (and thus financial
success) through older channels of exceptional individualism; there are no
feats of heroism or tests of character in Dreiser's novels. Instead, Cowperwood
triumphs only through integrating himself into various networks of people
who come to him or rely on him because (and only so long as) his expert use
of commodities and wealth present an image of stability and confidence. In
other words, his own body works as a marker for his success in a newly abstracted economic order.

I draw distinctions, as I do in Chapter One, on the basis of sex (as a cultural category). Obviously there are different social imperatives embodied in
men, though the commodities used as signifiers (clothes, jewelry, the interior
design of homes, etc.) are, in Dreiser's work, the same for both sexes. Perhaps
the most important distinction to be made is that while women take a great deal
of pleasure in looking at Cowperwood, their ability to convert their voyeurism
into some sort of mastery over him cannot compete with Cowperwood's ability
to control women through a mere glance. And yet I do show, as in Chapter One,
that men too are themselves controlled by a specific visual economy that both
shapes their representation in the culture and precludes complete control over
the construction and visibility of their own bodies.

## PRIMITIVISM AND THE GENDERING OF THE SUBCONSCIOUS

The second two chapters of *Between Profits and Primitivism* analyze the gendered imperatives that impacted the construction of the subconscious and the

characterization of alternate psychic experience. While they look at nervous illness and supernatural experiences, they are not divorced from issues of the body. The connection between the two sections of the work is in the theorization of the physical body as open to "psychical meanings" (Grosz 78). The body, in other words, is not the disavowed condition of philosophic knowledge. Rather, following the work of Elizabeth Grosz, I stress the interaction of the body and mind (as turn-of-the-century psychologists and neurologists did) and work from the argument that issues of the gendered body and its capabilities have "figured strongly in [the] psychoanalytic conception of subjectivity" (62). For instance, in Chapter Three I argue that William James's ideas about supernatural or alternate psychological states as described in books like *The Varieties of Religious Experience* (1902), are based on particular fantasies and anxieties about a racialized and class-specific masculinity. My argument about the gendering of alternate psychic experiences rests on the idea that James used hysterical symptomology to characterize the subconscious. That, in fact, hysterical symptomology was what gave the subconscious (and thus altered psychological states) its more strenuous or virile character. I contend that James's ability to use this "female malady" to such an end hinges, in part, on Jean-Martin Charcot's studies of masculine hysteria in France in the 1880s and its further theorization by Pierre Janet and the English psychical researcher Frederick Myers.[23]

I analyze the reconstruction of hysteria in texts by Janet, Myers and James with an eye towards how this reconstruction answered turn-of-the-century gender imperatives for middle-class men. Put as simply as possible, manliness was being redefined in the middle and upper classes at this time as more physical and less intellectual, more competitive and less spiritual, more strenuous and less sensitive.[24] Behind these new ideals was, among other things, an increasing fear that civilization, with all its comforts and luxuries was weakening men from the dominant classes. Perhaps the greatest bulk of studies on masculinity at the turn of the century focus on this shift and discuss as proofs the rise of organized sports, the romanticization of the working-class male (which I try to complicate in Chapter One), the popularity of tales about life in the West, war and imperialism.[25] All of these things, scholars have argued, gave middle-class masculinity a new strenuousness. My focus, however, is on how this new ideal of strenuousness was incorporated into the male psyche itself, and in ways that did not depend on a romanticization of the physically strong male. James's work, I argue, provided his circle of men with an antidote to over-civilization that was based on exceptional mental states.

Hysteria was understood by Janet, Myers and James to be a regressive state. After Charcot threw his weight behind the idea of male hysteria, Janet notes that more serious studies of the disease and its symptomology took the place of myths about the wandering womb and other causes that were essentially female. What was left, then, was an alternate form of consciousness that was more primitive without being necessarily connected to the feminine. Hysteria itself had proven the existence of alternate states of consciousness (a submerged or split self), which contributed a great deal to the idea of the subliminal or the subconscious. Now removed at least theoretically from female biology, common hysterical symptoms, like hypersensitivity to the tactile, were used by James and Myers to theorize the subconscious as more attuned to the visceral, and as a preserved separate part of the self, immune to forces of civilization. Further, because hysterical symptomology included major changes in the actions and strengths of the body, it provided a lexicon for the unconscious filled with physiological capabilities that went beyond the capabilities of the normal, or civilized, consciousness.

Perhaps the most important term James used to describe the unconscious was primitive. The meanings of the term were complicated and manifold, with connotations that varied from the highly positive and desirable to the most degraded. The primitive self lodged in the subconscious of the men whose stories James tells in *Varieties* or in essays like "On a Certain Blindness in Human Beings" is a positive self closer to nature and capable of intense sensorial experiences, which James labels "strenuous." Indeed, the primitive subconscious makes it possible for James's friends to lead what he calls the "genuinely strenuous life" (*Varieties* 211) without playing football, and perhaps more to the point for James, without having to prove their manliness through the imperialist ventures men like Theodore Roosevelt defined as part of the strenuous life. Importantly, however, I also show that *like* Roosevelt, James, at times, entered into conversations about race suicide. James argues, for instance, that the Anglo-Saxon race, specifically, can turn to alternate psychical experiences to maintain its strength and well being.

While Chapter Three focuses on the role hysteria played in constructing a gendered subconscious, specifically one that helped men from the educated classes feel less effeminate, Chapter Four uses supernatural tales from the turn of the century to investigate some of the more complicated implications of having a primitive subconscious lodged within the white intellectual male.

Jack London, Henry James and William Dean Howells all wrote supernatural tales, the majority of which have educated white males at their center. Using theories of split personality or mystical doubling, the male protagonists come into contact with a masculine "other"—either some submerged part of himself or a ghost. Invariably the other presence flaunts a more primitive masculinity and the relationship formed between the protagonist and his other is more urgent and profound than the heterosexual unions that get relegated to the background of the story. That not withstanding, in several works, most notably London's "When the World Was Young" and James's "The Jolly Corner," women, in the end, are the ones to disrupt the homosociality at the center of the story by banishing the less civilized male self.

Perhaps more explicitly than the previous chapters, this chapter engages with the importance and complexity of homosociality in the construction of masculinity. Evolutionary theories about race and progress are important subtexts in these stories about alternate types of masculinity. While the intense homosociality betrays a nostalgia for a more primitive masculinity, none of the stories show a successful integration between the two selves or beings. They show, in other words, "both the positive potentials of male bonding" and the "divisive effects of racial . . . differences between men."[25] While the stories tend to argue that the price of civilized manhood is the annihilation of the primitive man, they portray white men in the dominant classes as ill, incomplete, and lacking something critical. It is this lack that leads to the split or breakdown that makes the "other" manifest. And while the more primitive man is usually gone by the end of the tale, his absence is, I argue, written as a real loss. Unlike earlier Victorian tales, which often express the need to banish completely the "animal within," these stories, while often playing off that script, do not subscribe to its values. Many tales, especially London's, write the loss of the primitive other as problematic for white men and imply that *integration* of other forms of masculinity or a kind of homosocial bond with the "other" is the ideal for Anglo-Saxon men.

In my discussion of the discourses of race, progress and civilization I draw upon Gail Bederman's useful and insightful work, *Manliness and Civilization: A Cultural History of Gender and Race in the United States, 1880–1917.* In it she argues that fears of over-civilization as well as evolutionary theories of race, which fed into the larger discourse on civilization, were highly malleable and could be made to argue for issues and positions as disparate as the condemnation of lynching and the promotion of imperialism. According to Bederman, the flexibility of this discourse was not only contextual; fine distinctions and the multiplication of terms surrounding discussions of race and civilization made it possible, for instance to laude the primitive man while railing against the savage, to fear over-civilization and still use to great effect the category of "uncivilized." In its application to issues of manliness and race, self-control was central. While African-American men at the turn of the century were considered uncivilized because they were "unable to control their sexual desires" (Bederman 46) men like the psychologist G. Stanley Hall argued that educated white male's power was declining due to an over-abundance of sexual self-control or denial. Due in part to Theodore Roosevelt's theories of race suicide, sex drive and virility were now, at the end of the Victorian era, being linked. Thus the space between the dark sexualized predator and the white hysterical male becomes complicated.

I argue that the split male self I explore in these supernatural stories is one outcome, one way of screening, these very issues for white men. Often, for instance, the protagonist of a supernatural tale is an over-educated white male whose nervous disorder makes him unable to marry. The supernatural experience brings the white man into contact with his opposite—in some cases it is the primitive man, in others a more threatening "savage" masculinity. Often he is afterwards able to marry, though the intense homosociality and the sense of loss I discussed earlier gives that marriage a distinctively disappointing cast and thus does not always provide a permanent solution to the problem of feminization and "over-civilization." In other instances the protagonist simply does not survive the ordeal. Either way, these stories show that "the whiteness of hysteria" not only "signaled the specific reproductive and sexual failings of white women"[26] it also signaled both reproductive and sexual failings of white men as well.

The massive cultural and social transitions that rocked the country between 1880 and 1917 denaturalized definitions of manhood and created a national conversation that self-consciously fashioned gender, to a large degree through creating class-specific bodies (expressed through the shaping of the physical body itself or the commodities attached to it) and importing evolutionary theories of race. What I find intriguing is how often this conversation constructs white men of the dominant class as problematic and in need of some physical, mental, or supernatural reconstruction. My work establishes that men can be, and quite often are, the objects as well as the authors of reformative discourses. It also confirms that masculinity can be found, or is constructed, in places scholars have long used (very productively) to think about the construction of femininity. The construction of masculinity can be found in the physical reconstruction of the body, in men's active participation in consumer culture and in the realm of the irrational or supernatural. I have tried to show too, however, that despite existing in these spaces, the way white male subjects negotiate power as bodies, consumers, hysterics and participants in supernatural experiences differs greatly from women as well as male members of different classes or races. Nonetheless, their presence in these spaces should further complicate our ideas about the avenues through which gender is made manifest.

Chapter One

# Managing the Middle-Class Male
# Body in the Age of Efficiency

Beginning with John Higham's 1970 article, "The Reorientation of American Culture in the 1890s," scholars have described American manhood at the turn of the twentieth century as variously in "crisis," "confusion," or, less drastically, in a state of "renegotiation."[1] While patriarchal authority was in no real danger, it has become clear that in the face of a variety of challenges to antebellum notions of manliness, based most explicitly on men's behavior in the public realms of politics and business, many middle-class white men felt the need to re-make manhood. The discourses that took men as their subjects did so in ways that had less to do with character (what the term "manliness" most often denoted) and more to do with the male body (for which the less morally connotative term "masculine" was used).[2]

Issues of class were central to, and consistently informed, discussions of manhood during this period. Two places where class ideologies found voice were in the changing discourses on the nature and meaning of industrialized work—which for the middle class meant bureaucratic work—and proliferating discourses on the care of the body. While many scholars of manliness and masculinity have noted the role both of these discourses played in the new cultural meanings of manhood at the turn of the century, there has been little discussion of the ways in which the two influenced and helped constitute each other. In fact, the thinking and writing on bureaucratic/industrialized work and the body became deeply intertwined during this period and together produced a way of thinking about manhood that was enormously class-conscious and heavily influential in the renegotiation of male middle-class identity.[3]

Discourses on middle-class male bodies contain interesting negotiations and seemingly contradictory positions. For instance, instead of simply eliding the middle-class male body with concerns about the bodies of "others" or an intensified interest in the bodies of working-class males, a specifically middle-class discourse emerged toward the end of the nineteenth century that took middle-class male bodies as its subject and put them into a realm of explicit representation that was potentially repressive in its pursuit of a normative or ideal corporeality. However, despite increased attention to the body during this period, middle-class discourses on men and their bodies were careful not to produce a male identity that was too explicitly wedded to physical perform-ance. In other words, the dialectic between the mind and the body, while being reconfigured in interesting ways, remained and preserved for middle-class men a form of agency through the notion of *self*-improvement, which the bodily regimes placed on women, racial "others" and the working class often lacked.[4]

Attributing importance to the formation of a distinct middle class over the course of the nineteenth century is a fairly recent phenomenon in schol-arship. According to the historian Stuart Blumin, Burton Bledstein's 1976 *The Culture of Professionalism* and Mary P. Ryan's 1981 *Cradle of the Middle Class* are two of the pioneering works that make the development of the mid-dle class central to our understanding of the nineteenth century.[5] The ease, however, with which later scholars assumed the presence of a solid middle class in this period concerns Blumin. Marx, after all, saw only two classes as fundamental to a capitalist society, with the people in the middle constantly in motion—going either up or down. Although Blumin ultimately feels that a middle class does exist, he bases much of this belief on the distinctiveness of the working and elite classes. He characterizes the middle class as

> one that stresses not actively competing ideologies but an essentially pas-sive or even negative class 'ideology,' which requires little in the way of class-based solidarity (primarily because the political system is already structured to meet its demands) and seeks to avoid overt displays of ex-plicit class cooperation that too obviously contradict the individualism that lies at the heart of the middle-class value system. (305)

But what is so interesting about the middle-class renegotiation of manliness at the turn of the century is that it *does* in fact construct what one might call an "active class ideology" in its pursuit of defining manhood: a distinct form of physical education, and with that, a specific bodily ideal.

Understanding descriptions of the body, male or female, as part of an active class ideology forces us look at the body as an important object in the production of ideology as well as a result of it. Here I differ with Foucault, es-pecially in his earlier works, who tends to see the body as lacking any say in the social inscriptions forced (though not necessarily through overt coercion) upon it. In other words, he does not see the body as bringing anything to the equation beyond a place of inscription.[6] My disagreement with him will become important later when addressing the question of how middle-class men's position as objects of the gaze differ from women's, despite a certain degree of feminization inextricable to that position.

Although the nineteenth-century mania for documenting ethnic and racial "types," as well as criminals, the working class, women and the sick or insane, has been amply studied recently,[7] few works note the documentation of "normal" middle-class male bodies during this time period. Leaving them out of the history of this documentation perpetuates the idea that white men have always maintained the position of *controlling* representation as opposed to being, in their turn, the subject of it and subject to it. To talk about male bodies as an historical and ideological process that is in a constant state of negotiation is not only important to the ongoing project of deconstructing any monolithic notion of "Man"—a category still far less self-consciously investigated than the term "Woman"—but also to our understanding of the power dynamics involved in the exchanges made in visual culture. Feminist theorists from all camps (constructionists, difference feminists, egalitarian feminists, etc.) have long recognized that women's bodies have been excessively visible in patriarchal culture. In the mind/body dichotomy that influences Western social order so persistently, women have been coupled with the body and men (of a certain class) with the mind. As Elizabeth Grosz points out in her book *Volatile Bodies*, Aristotle was among the first to theorize this when he described the womb as nothing more than the material container which held the spirit and soul received from the man. Given the connections in Western culture between vision and knowledge, the idea that woman *is* her body—a visible, material substance—makes her subject to all kinds of psychic and legal surveillance.

Foucault, of course, added men to the list of those repressed by the power/knowledge discourse and its modes of representation. But these men have always been the marginalized figures of the insane, the homosexual, and the criminal, despite noting in his *The History of Sexuality* that the "emphasis on the body should undoubtedly be linked to the process of growth and establishment of bourgeois hegemony: not, however, because of the market value assumed by labor capacity, but because of what the 'cultivation' of its *own* body could represent politically, economically, and historically for the present and the future of the bourgeoisie" (25, my emphasis). Further, despite the fact that the middle-class preoccupation with the body certainly derived a great deal of its force from the construction of the threatening body of the "other," the source material discussed in this chapter indicates that many middle-class men involved in physical education saw their *own* location in the new industrial/urban complex as a source of concern.

Finally, it should be mentioned that the late nineteenth and early twentieth centuries provide an especially fertile ground for complicating (though not eradicating) the mind-body/male-female dichotomies. Phrenology and physiognomy, which were concerned almost exclusively with reading character from the shape of the head and size and construction of facial features, were both highly popular "sciences" throughout most of the nineteenth century. In the early part of the century, Franz Joseph Gall formulated the idea that the brain's functions were compartmentalized into twenty-three discrete areas, with the most developed and complicated skills residing in the front. He reasoned that because the skull of a person grew around the shape of the brain, one could realistically read the inner character of a man through the shape and bumps of the exterior skull. Thus, in works like *A Manual of Phrenology and Physiognomy for the People* (1885) by Nelson Sizer and H.S. Drayton, the high forehead is the distinguishing feature of the most "civilized" man. By the end of the nineteenth century however, physical education writers were moving consideration *away* from the head and focusing their attention on the rest of the male body.

This shift from discerning character to assessing bodies not only focused attention on the body in new ways but also created a link between male bodies and more abstract ideas of "fitness" and success. When the educator Francis Walker addressed the *Phi Beta Kappa* society in 1893, he compared favorably the robust body of the college football player to the earlier nineteenth century "college hero" who he sarcastically describes as "apt to be a young man of towering forehead, from which the hair was carefully brushed backwards and upwards to give the full effect to his remarkable phrenological developments" (261). For Walker, the body on which this towering head rested was weak and dyspeptic. He condemns transcendentalism and sentimentalism for their "contempt for physical prowess," and disparages the fact that people in the early nineteenth century believed that "Brains and brawn were supposed to be developed in inverse ratio." He complains that "Affected notions about intellectuality and spirituality had almost complete control of the popular thought" (262–263). He is happy to report that "Better physiology, coinciding with some changes in popular ideals, have driven away the notions about the flesh as an encumbrance, a clog, a burden, a snare" and argues that criminals are not "powerful brutes" but rather "undersized and undervitalized creatures" (267), while good men are robust and attentive to their physical state. Now, he says, the man with a "capacity for action" is revered over the "speech-maker and the fine writer which the nation had once agreed chiefly to admire" (265). Importantly, then, issues of intelligence and "character"—things most often associated with the term "manliness"—were losing some discursive ground at the turn of the century to preoccupations with what had historically been understood as a more feminine domain; the male body did, in fact, matter.

The cultural changes linked to this renegotiation of manhood and their attendant interests in the male body are many. The most common are the birth of consumer culture and mass culture, the waning of small-scale entrepreneurial capitalism, inroads made by women into the public sphere, the growth of commercialized leisure, greater immigrant control over local politics, the official closing of the frontier and labor unrest.[8] All of these are important changes. However, what seems to have concerned middle-class men the most is the nature and meaning of work: more specifically, how the new forms of work deemed appropriate for the middle class, defined by its strident distancing from manual labor of all kinds, affected the body.

As the American economy changed from entrepreneurial to corporate—the number of non-propertied, salaried office workers grew eight times between 1870 and 1910[9]—discourses on work proliferated as moralists attempted to keep alive a work ethic that equated work with both individualism and virtue in a radically different environment of production. In many ways, they succeeded. Work remained, as it does today, imbued with moral value. However, within the new industrial system of factories, corporations and massed wage earners, a more complex discourse on work had to evolve to meet the challenges of mechanization and incorporation bred by the new industrial system. Many of these discourses have been rehearsed by scholars.[10] My central concern is with the ways in which the middle-class male body became an important point of fascination in the new discourses surrounding work. Daniel Rodgers argues in *The Work Ethic in Industrial America, 1850–1920* that the "presumptive tie between work and morality" had to be, by the late nineteenth century, "pitched at a new level of abstraction" to accommodate the highly complex bureaucracy that characterized the working environment (9). The male body, however, provides a concrete, visual place to re-conceptualize and re-realize individualism and virtue in a new industrialized world while simultaneously smoothing away challenges to the new system. Indeed, for all the disparaging remarks made in the popular press and in books on the sedentary nature of modern bureaucratic work and its draining of manly strength, when writings on work connected with those of physical education, the body became, especially for the middle class, a place where the Franklinesque characteristics of individualism, pluck and persistence could be carried out, not only in the gym or on the athletic field but in the turn-of-the-century world of monopolies, bureaucracies and corporations.

Work and physical education were ripe for a merger. Forms of leisure, like work, showed all the same tendencies towards systemization and standardization, or what is generally called in work discourses, rationalization. From ministers and doctors to advice manuals and popular magazines, people began to write and speak of overworked Americans who lost everything from their moral strength to their health because of the new demands of modern work. Thus leisure became, like work, a responsibility, with its own pundits directing the ways in which it should be engaged in properly. However, as nothing short of a way to keep one's health and moral balance, not all leisure activities were equally acceptable to middle-class moralists. Exercise, or more broadly, physical education was appealing, as it turned out, because on some level it avoided certain aspects of leisure altogether and fit with the older, traditional *work* ethic. It was a way to spend the leisure hours afforded by industrialization in a disciplined, self-improving way that recalled older notions of how to succeed in the work force.

But if exercise was a way to throw off the drudgery of industrial work in a manner that aped the work ethic of a pre-industrial model, it simultaneously taught middle-class men how to labor more efficiently in an industrialized workforce. It was, on the one hand, importantly, a form of "voluntary movement" that attempted to bring men outside the constraints of their working environment, which was often harshly criticized by physical education writers. On the other hand, it placed middle-class men right in the middle of a discourse on efficiency that, I will argue, had much in common with movements like Taylor's scientific management, which so constrained the working classes. Indeed, the inclusion of the body in these connected discourses of work and health meant that middle-class men were now pictured, measured, photographed and evaluated in ways that brought them as objects into the visual culture and further circumscribed their freedom by heightening fears about their efficiency. Thus, the physical education discourse drew middle-class men closer to their working-class counterparts through both its objectification and fragmentation of the body and through its use of the body-as-machine metaphor. This is especially ironic given that physical exercise often advertised itself as a way to regain the bodily symmetry and wholeness that industrialized work fragmented through the over exertion of one part of the body to the exclusion of others. In the end, physical education, though often critical of the health effects of bureaucratized labor, actually acts as an aid to adjusting to, and perpetuating, industrialized/bureaucratic work, not dismantling it.

## CLASS AND DEFINING BODIES IN NEED

Physical education has its roots in Massachusetts in the early nineteenth century. It entered the cultural conversation with real urgency, however, just before the turn of the century, at the very moment bureaucratized work was charged with wreaking havoc on the health of the elite white male population. At a conference on physical education in Boston, Dudley Sargent, the director of the Hemenway Gymnasium at Harvard, sold physical education specifically as a way to "resist the destructive wear and waste of American business life."[11] The concerted effort to re-shape these weakened business men was made by the same men who institutionalized physical education at elite colleges and universities; Harvard, Yale and Amherst were at the forefront of the movement that defined middle-class male bodies as enfeebled and sought to re-vitalize them. Indeed, it is in these schools that much of the measuring, charting and photographing went on in an effort to mold efficient bureaucratic workers and professionals of the future. But while many physical educators worked for schools, they most often wrote for "business and professional men."[12]

The boundaries of this discourse are important to establish. Recently, "physical culture," a term that was used most commonly in popular culture at the turn of the century to reference the process of transforming (and commodifying) the body, has received a fair amount of attention from historians.[13] However, what will become clear through a detailed look into what one might call the "educated" or high-brow literature of physical education in comparison with the more popular writings of physical cultural is that the strong links between work or "efficiency" and exercise are specific to the middle-class discourse.[14] Furthermore, the ideal body type painstakingly detailed in middle-class physical education literature is quite distinct from what is pictured and written about in more popular physical culture tracts.

That physical educators were worried about—and displeased with—white middle-class male bodies becomes clear when we look at their dire and anxious language. They also betray a real concern about middle-class men's heightened visibility in the new urban environments at the turn of the century. William Blaikie, author of the book *How to Get Strong and How to Stay So* justifies the need for what he calls "rational physical exercise"[15] by simply looking out his window:

> Probably more men walk past the corner of Broadway and Fulton Street, in New York city, in the course of one year, than any other point in America— men of all nations and ages, heights and weights. Look at them carefully as they pass, and you will see that scarcely one in ten is either erect or thoroughly well built. . . . A thoroughly erect, well-proportioned man, easy and graceful in his movements, is far from a frequent sight. (9–10)

In his book *The Efficient Life,* Luther H. Gulick, then director of physical training in the New York city schools, also calls attention to the wealth of men, specifically here middle-class men, visible on the urban streets—and he is even less flattering than Blaikie: "Many city business men in middle life have bodies that disgrace them. Everywhere you see fat, clumsy, unsightly bodies; stooped, flabby, feeble bodies; each and every degree of dilapidation and inefficiency."[16] These writers and others like them are conscious of the increased conspicuousness of men's bodies in urban environments and are fearful about what they represent—not only in terms of their physical strength, but also, I would argue, their sexual virility. Note, for instance, Gulick's use of the words "stooped" and "flabby," and Blaikie's search for a "thoroughly erect" man.[17]

Although many writers made explicit connections between urbanism and physical degeneration, neither Blaikie nor Gulick, nor any of the other physical educators that could be said to belong to their group, extolled a return to the country or a pre-industrial society. Blaikie, for instance, is at pains to convince his readers that farmers were in just as bad physical shape as office workers, remarking that the farmer's body is "stoop[ed] forward" and "inerect" (10). Gulick, in his consistently blunt manner states that,

> Nothing could be more misleading than the familiar phase, 'healthy as a savage.' The health of the savage is nothing to boast of. He has only a moderate control over his purely physical faculties. His power of endurance is limited, he is helpless in an emergency, he has no power of continued attention. Health such as his is a low-grade achievement. (9)

Such statements are crucial for understanding the class (and the racial) bias found in so many books on exercise from this period. Historians too often look at the more extreme forms of self-consciously staged masculine spectacles of this period—the prizefights, the hunting trips for rich Easterners out west, the literature of Jack London and the speeches and exploits of Theodore Roosevelt. These obscure the ways in which middle-class men were attempting to form their own version of manhood separate from both the rural or pioneer past and, more importantly, from working-class men. The point of exercise, for this group of writers, was conservative—both culturally and physically: to "retain our acquired Health, Strength, and Power under the conditions imposed upon us by modern progress."[18]

The "us" in the above quotation (with its interesting lack of agency) is quite specifically the middle class. Though Blaikie held that *all* occupations tend to favor one part of the body at the expense of others thus making it more difficult to achieve the bodily symmetry physical educators praise, most of the literature focuses on the injurious affects of specifically middle-class bureaucratic work. For instance, in *Health* Sargent argues that it is "Bookkeepers, penmen, typewriters, pianists, telegraphers, engravers" that suffer the most while "The occupations where men are overworked through all-round physical strain are very few" (15). The people in this latter group are named as blacksmiths, iron-workers, coal-heavers and the like. Sargent makes clear that he is also less concerned with the very rich:

> Even men who are subjected to great all-round mental strain, such as government officials, presidents of railroads, colleges, banks, superin-tendents of factories and managers of great manufacturing establish-ments and great commercial houses, do not suffer as much from the stress of working and living as many of their employees, who work along narrower lines. . . . According to health statistics, the class that has been most used up physically by the strain and stress of the times is the pro-fessional class. (15–16)

While Gulick does not show such lack of concern for the very rich, arguing that the "higher the quality of work, the greater nervous cost to it, and the more highly perfected must be the machine that does it," he does dismiss, more energetically than Sargent, the physical needs of the working classes:

> The conditions for efficiency in the case of the ordinary day laborer are not complex. His work is that of a coarse and ordinary machine, turning out, like a grain thresher, a great amount of production relatively low in grade. His efficiency is but little disturbed by constant feeding upon in-digestible victuals, by frequent carousals, by dirty skin and bad air. Low-grade production does not need a high-grade organism. (8)

Gulick, then, completely dismisses the need to provide decent working or liv-ing conditions for the working classes by arguing that the nature of the work they perform constitutes bodies without needs. Finally, Philip Hubert in his ar-ticle "The Wheel Today" notes as an interesting phenomenon in need of expla-nation that bicycle shows attract "all classes." He quickly contains the meaning of the working-class presence by arguing that the bicycle for the workingman is "not . . . a sporting machine" but rather an "everyday necessity," a way to get to work without spending money on car fare.[19] The rest of the article is filled with tales of the author's various trips on his bike—never once mentioning the use of it for something other than sport and exercise. The historian Melissa Debakis has argued that at the turn of the century "representational strategies—visible in painting, and sculpture, as well as in magazines, newspapers and advertise-ments—attempted to invigorate middle-class notions of masculinity through a focused attention on the bodies of working-class men,"[20] Physical education discourses complicate this thesis. Physical educators created their own class-based bodily ideals and held fast to ways to continue differentiating themselves not only from their working-class counterparts but also, as we will see, the wasted vitality of popular culture's strongman.

Ideas about class embedded in the physical education discourse are, not surprisingly, coupled with fears about the general strength and well-being of the Anglo-Saxon race. Beyond the use of coded language like "flabby," "feeble" and "inerect," men like Sargent motivated their students and older readers with appeals to "the sense of duty which each man owes to himself to improve his physical condition and keep strong and well, that he may help advance the average condition of the race."[21] Sargent wanted to see each man desire "to remedy his defects and pride himself on the purity of his skin, the firmness of his muscles, and the uprightness of his figure."[22] Lending urgency to the problem, Sargent argued that his readers were already working at a deficit: "The immigrants who began to come to America about the middle of the last century represented a much poorer quality of stock physically than those who have preceded them. This large infusion of foreign blood of an inferior quality had undoubtedly impaired the physical status of our people."[23] It seems, then, that not only are middle-class men concerned with their bodies, but that these writers construe bodily concern itself as a crucial marker of racial and class superiority.

## FOR WORK OR BEAUTY? CONTRASTS IN APPROACHING THE MALE BODY

Comparing physical education to the discourse of physical culture in more detail will help illuminate the ways particular class concerns inscribe themselves on the body. Considered outside the realm of "brain worker," working-class men were often closely identified with the machines they worked with. It is interesting, therefore, that middle-class physical education writers so often used the body-as-machine metaphor in their writing. In the Gulick quotation about the needs of the "ordinary day laborer," the author makes his distinction between different *kinds* of machines, low- and high-grade, which stand in for different kinds of class-specific bodies. Other writers, like Sargent, also use the body-as-machine metaphor in their writings, especially when describing how the body functions. For instance, Sargent writes that the

> arrangement for distributing blood throughout the body is not unlike that adopted in many cities for distributing water to the inhabitants on their homes, workshops, stores and factories. In this case the heart is represented by a great pumping-engine which forces the water through a system of iron pipes. . . . [24]

Why did these writers use the body-machine metaphor given its associations with the working class? The answer lies in the connection middle-class physical education made between exercise and a type of efficiency for which the machine was an apt model. This is important because, beyond the more obvious ways of distinguishing the plight of the middle-class office or brain worker from his working-class counterpart, one of the most telling class markers in the physical education discourse is its repeated and strident connection of health consciousness to productivity in the work force. The more popular physical culture writers like Benarr Macfadden, editor of *Physical Culture* magazine and the famous strongman Eugen Sandow, in contrast, were far more invested in the creation of individualized specimens of physical beauty and spectacular feats of strength. As a result—and perhaps because Macfadden's audience was in fact largely made up of working-class men—physical culture writers usually stayed away from metaphors of mechanized efficiency.

The way in which exercise itself is discussed in middle-class physical education tracts is also instructive. The warning, echoed again and again by these writers, is that exercise should never be an end in itself, but rather understood "as a means to an end."[25] That end was increased efficiency. According to Sargent, any and "all sports, exercises, and pastimes, pursued as ends in themselves are necessarily limited to a very small class, and constantly tend to degenerate."[26] The degeneration Sargent speaks of is a kind of self-love or over-investment in one's body: "when one devotes too much time and attention to these self-centered movements, he is likely to become, if not vain and egotistical, extremely conscious of his many muscles. . . . Many of the exercises introduced in this book are especially designed to cultivate the power of externalizing oneself, as it were, and of throwing all one's strength and purpose into the work to be done."[27] This message is repeated throughout Sargent's writings. He ends *Health* exhorting his reader again not to pay attention to the muscles that are being worked but "to concentrate all your energy and attention upon the *thing to be done,* rather than upon the muscles that are engaged in doing it" (162). Similarly, when Luther Gulick criticizes his readers for not maintaining their health, he does so not primarily because they are displeasing aesthetically—something the more popular writers consider supremely important—but because by not taking care of themselves, they are "removed from life or from full service, at important and critical times. . . . The pursuit of health is not an end in itself. But to live a full, rich, efficient life is an end."[28] The emphasis on "externalization," "full service" and the concentration on "the thing to be done" illustrate the explicit connection between exercise and work constructed in this literature, and marks this discourse as separate from the more popular ones.

To underline the connection between work and exercise, Sargent focuses on the ways in which exercise can be viewed as an activity to strengthen one's work ethic as much as an activity to strengthen one's body:

> All physical exercise, however pleasant they are at first, tend to become irksome and distasteful when pursued systematically day after day; but the very energy that one is obliged to put forth in overcoming this distaste is a wholesome discipline. . . . The lesson learned in abnegation and self-mastery contributes the most important elements to the formation of character.[29]

Sargent's emphasis on the systematic and the repetitive in exercise rehearse the key features of industrialized work. But, interestingly, he connects this work to notions of self-mastery and character that are solidly within a pre-industrial or pre-consumer culture, middle-class work ethic. In the consumer culture of the turn of the century, "abnegation and self-mastery" did not have such a high premium. Sargent, however, is trying to give his readers some sense of themselves as masters, if not of their own companies, than at least of themselves. This is a crucial part of the class construction at work in middle-class physical education.

Because bureaucratized and industrialized work is central to the physical education discourse, Sargent and his group tend to espouse sports, especially team sports, over the body-building or solitary gym work advocated by men like Macfadden. For example, although many men associated with higher education at this time were concerned with the violence, aggression and unbridled competitiveness involved in sports like football, most of them gave it at least conditional support. Andrew Draper, a commissioner of education for the state of New York, concedes, for instance, that with the way football is presently played the participants can get away with evading rules and that the game often "encourages real battle rather an open manliness and a chivalrous spirit." However, he ultimately comes to the conclusion that the "advantages of the game are undeniable."[30] These "advantages" are telling; they fit nicely with a corporate mentality and mirror the type of work most middle-class men would end up performing. Football, according to Draper emphasizes the "cooperate effort." And further, "it makes for pluck, nerve, endurance, self-control, and alertness in emergencies. . . . It makes for generalship and for *organized effectiveness*" (318, my emphasis). Another educator, Francis Walker, echoes this idea when he says that organized sports "often demand of the contestants the ability to work with others, power of combination, readiness to subordinate individual impulses, selfish desires, and even personal credit to a common end."[31]

The ideal of "organized effectiveness" in the middle-class discourse is felt not only in the specific kind of exercises these writers deemed appropriate, but also in the systematic approach they took to physical education as a whole. Indeed, the writers we have been looking at thus far wanted to turn physical education into a science. As part of this attempt they imported anthropometry, the system of bodily measurement created by Belgian statistician Adolphe Quetelet, which played an important role in creating the "ideal" middle-class male body. This ideal body was physically strong but also efficient, and one that preserved, in important ways, a distinction from the working class bodily ideal. As we will see, it was in the preservation of this distinction that middle-class men found themselves visually represented in the vast "scientific" cataloging going on at the turn of the century.

Middle-class physical educators used anthropometry to create what they referred to, positively, as "average" bodies. Anthropometry is defined by Jay W. Seaver, in an 1896 book on its practical use, as "the knowledge of modern human proportions [that] has been derived from the measurements of living persons of all ages and of both sexes."[32] Although anthropometry was originally developed to be used in anthropological studies, Seaver contends that "the study of the individual for the sake of bringing him up to a high degree of excellence" is now the most "important duty of the educator" (13). Significantly, the individuals picked for this effort to define physical excellence are white students in elite colleges and universities: "We have largely followed the example set by Dr. Hitchcock of Amherst thirty-five years ago, in making physical examination of the students who were admitted to the gymnasia connected with our colleges."[33] Seaver notes approvingly that more recently the practice has greatly expanded to include the "leading colleges and universities throughout the land" as well as "in very many of the better class of secondary and private schools" (14–15). Along with Seaver, both Sargent and Gulick wrote tracts on anthropometry. In all, they stress that the tests determine such things as "latent possibilities"[34] and the capacity for work, not physical aesthetics: "The movement which emphasizes the necessity of testing what a man can do," Gulick argues "appears to be in the right direction. The capacity of a muscle for *work* is more fundamental than its size or shape, and determines its form more than its form determines its capacity."[35]

The middle-class writers' interest in how one compared to an average over the creation of a more individualized body led them to envision some highly complex—and bureaucratic—tracking systems. In "The Physical Proportions of the Typical Man" for instance, Sargent calls for a "uniform system of measurements, and a common understanding among observers as to what point and under what conditions the various parts of the body are to be measured" (15) so that once an individual has been measured he can be "furnished with a book or card in which his measurements at the parts specified [could be] compared with those of the average man of the same age" (26). To help find this "average man" Sargent requested that every student entering Harvard to go to the office of physical education and fill out health forms. The student would then pass "into the measuring room, and [have] his weight, height, chest-girth, and fifty other items taken." Then, Sargent continued, "All the items taken are . . . plotted on a chart, made from several thousand measurements, and the examiner is then able to know the relative standing of this individual as compared with the other from every dimension taken, also his deviation from symmetry and the parts which are in special need of development."[36] Sargent, believed firmly in what he called the "conclusions" of anthropometry, which state that "There is a perfect form or type of man, and the tendency of the race is to attain this type."[37] Anthropometry revealed nature's plan for the Anglo-Saxon race; physical education simply, but importantly, corrected some of the problems civilization produced along the way. Sargent admitted that in civilized races the natural law is "controverted by social laws," specifically, the division of labor "that tend to foster an inharmonious development."[38] In the hands of physical educators, however, anthropometry could chart and foster the body's road back to pre-industrial health and balance. In this way, physical educators could create a strong and healthy body without disrupting the division of labor, which they saw as the earmark of a civilized society.

While popular physical culture writers like Benarr Macfadden also believed in pursuing exercise consistently, it was never taken as far as those involved in the institutionalization of physical education. Macfadden, for instance, shied away from ever calling physical culture a *science*—in part because he was constantly waging well-publicized battles with medical doctors over the use of drugs in promoting health and was fond of invoking "Nature" as the only proper guide for the body.[39] More importantly, though, Macfadden liked to insist that "exercise should admit variety." He urged his readers to get "as much pleasure out of it as possible." "Do not make hard work out of it," he told them, but "Look upon it as play."[40] This idea is repeated again and again in his articles. In an account of his early life and methods for keeping up his physique, Macfadden states:

> I do not believe in having iron bound rules to live by. I follow each day the dictates of my own intelligence and feelings. If everything is done by rule, after awhile the mind is liable to think by rule—liable to fall into a narrow groove from which it may never be able to emerge. . . . I vary my exercise a great deal, as it is much more interesting under these circumstances. . . . I never make work of exercise.[41]

There is, in Macfadden's articles, a more free-spirited approach to the body—one that allows him to talk on a whole range of subjects, including sex—and a kind of individualism that does not fit with the ways in which physical education quickly becomes a standardizing science for those middle-class writers we have been looking at most closely so far.

Gulick, as noted above, sees health as a means and efficiency as an end. Macfadden, though conceding a connection between health and what he calls very generally "success," nonetheless revels in health itself in an almost sensual way and appreciates it as an end in itself. It is "exuberant health," "health of a degree that makes the very act of living, of breathing, a source of exhilaration" that he is after. Health to Macfadden is not about working more efficiently but rather a state of being that can make a person "actually become momentarily intoxicated with the wild joy of merely living and breathing."[42] The generally less didactic and more sensual language of Macfadden's magazine distinguishes it from the self-restraining attitude that was such an important marker of middle-class identity at the turn of the century.

Macfadden also writes articles and stories as well as publishes photographs that make central the beauty and sensuality of the well-built body. Indeed, *Physical Culture* is obsessed with physical beauty and how to achieve it—for both men and women. In articles like "The Cultivation of Physical Beauty," "Strong Men, Past and Present," "Humanity and Health" and "Methods of Physical Culture of Prominent Players" as well as countless editorials, physical culture is the means to attain not only health, strength and power, but also an aesthetically pleasing physique. While many of these articles focus on women, there is much here both praising men with admirable figures and exhorting men to beautify their bodies. The article "Humanity and Health" begins, for instance, by stating that "Everyone is susceptible to beauty. We are all drawn to it. An exquisite woman will attract us more than a plain one; a handsome man draws our attention, and a beautiful child compels our admiration."[43] The author then goes on to meditate on a florist window filled with flowers, implicitly connecting the way in which we are "arrested and enchained by the beauty displayed" there to the attractions of a well-shaped human body. We are told that if "we would do as much for ourselves as Nature does for us, we would become more and more beautiful each day" and to become more beautiful is to "enlarge, to grow into higher, grander types of men and women" (78). While middle-class physical educators often mention the symmetry that is achieved through exercise, which they applaud as beautiful, they never break off to expound on the importance of attractiveness and certainly don't connect it explicitly or implicitly to the joy involved in looking.

But looking was just what Macfadden wanted to give his readers leave to do. Such articles gave Macfadden the opportunity to fill his magazine with highly erotic and aesthetic pictures of men and women.[44] And, unlike the pictures contained in the physical education books, where the man is always depicted in the act of showing the reader how to perform a specific exercise [see fig. 1], the male bodies that grace the pages of Macfadden's magazine are most often not performing any task beyond flexing muscle. These bodies are, quite obviously, meant to be enjoyed as aesthetic objects. Moreover, the aesthetically pleasing man has muscles that far exceeded the necessary requirements of health and brain work. He is set apart as a unique specimen [see fig. 2].

Men like Macfadden and Sandow are also far more concerned with the physical performance of the individual than their middle-class counterparts. In other words, they are not concerned with promoting the body as part of a cooperative or corporate effort. For instance, Macfadden writes articles like "The Development of Great Muscular Vigor" that teach methods for accomplishing "feats of strength, to satisfy love for great physical beauty."[45] In these articles the measured approach of the more institutional physical educators is not argued with, but completely dismissed. While the more solidly middle-class discourse always warns against excessive exercise because it could fatigue the body and make it unsuitable for work (as well as create an unhealthy self-love), Macfadden writes that in training for feats of strength, "exercise should be prolonged until the part of the body affected is thoroughly fatigued" (49). Further, while the middle-class writers like sports that engage the entire body, Macfadden is not against isolating parts of the body for special purposes: "If there is any particular feat of strength which you wish to perform, find out the muscles which are used in that feat and make special endeavors in various ways to strengthen them" (51).

In an article by Eugen Sandow that appears in the August issue of *Physical Culture* (1899) entitled "Familiar Feats of Strength and How to Do Them," the world renowned bodybuilder is eager to talk about "useless" acts of muscular strength and, more importantly, openly discusses the various "tricks" for accomplishing them—something that goes entirely against the "open manliness and chivalrous spirit" middle-class writers hoped team sports would imbue in its participants. In describing the first feat of strength, for instance, Sandow notes that "Properly you should be knee-to-knee with your opponent, but obviously if you grip him with your knees well above his, the advantage of leverage is on your side" (170). In the second exercise he says, more openly, that "Here, the elements of trickery come in a little more. . . . the dodge is a very simple one" (171). The last feat, which involves a seated man lifting the full weight of another man standing on the seated man's ankles, is also accomplished through trickery, though it requires subterfuge on the part of both men. Sandow remarks that "To do this with say, a 140lb man is no mean feat and will probably excite the wonderment and admiration of all who behold it" (173). Clearly, then, these exercises are not about promoting efficiency or health. They are about individualized strength and spectacle.

How do the bodies in middle-class physical education and anthropometry manuals compare to the unique and pumped up specimens in Macfadden's *Physical Culture?* What, in other words, does the middle-class "average" male body look like? He is, not surprisingly, white—although so are Macfadden's models. Beyond the racial specificity, there is little that unites these bodies. Middle-class physical education writers like Gulick, Seaver and Sargent all look for one thing: symmetry. They applaud the body that shows "harmonious development in all directions." A body on which "No point stands out prominently."[46] It is tempting and, to a certain degree, warranted to draw some connections between this love of symmetry and other middle-class values—specifically, to the changing work environment where men needed to be in "harmonious" cooperation with others, to put their interests behind those of the firm or company they worked for, and the need to feel that this did not make them less manly in the process. There is also the issue of self-restraint contained in this idea of symmetry. In order to achieve the type of symmetrical body pictured in the manuals, one could not overdevelop certain muscles or an area of the body—the arms could not be pumped up to a degree that left the legs looking scrawny or vice versa. One needed to keep strict account of the "whole picture" or in Sargent's words, "endeavor to straighten your own line".[47] Once that is accomplished one could then "better the race" by bringing that straight line up to the standard of the ideal and raise the mean discovered through anthropometry's measurement research.

Another important characteristic of the middle-class ideal body as outlined through anthropometry and the more general writings of men like Sargent or Gulick is that it is slimmer than the bodies found on the pages of Macfadden's *Physical Culture*. Again, because the middle class always connected muscle to work, any extra muscle that surpassed the requirements of (non-manual) work was understood as a waste of precious vitality. But beyond characterizing a body built in surplus of the requirements of middle-class work as frivolous, such a body was connected, as we have seen, to a kind of vanity that threatened to turn men into popular spectacles. This, quite certainly, was *not* the goal for men like Sargent who controlled somewhat the way in which athletes were becoming part of popular visual culture by wrapping them in a quasi-scientific discourse.

The differences between figures 3 and 4 are instructive here. Not only is the man pictured in Gulick's text (like those in Sargent's *Health, Strength and Power*) thinner than the man used to advertise Macfadden's serialized novel *The Athlete's Conquest,* (as it turns out, it is Macfadden himself that is pictured) but, more importantly, the arm of the "ideal" middle-class man is encircled by a tape measure to give select readers "scientific" data from which to gauge the body. Macfadden's arm, in contrast, is encircled by a heavy length of chain. The man being measured by the tape is thus not an aesthetic or erotic object but a (willing) subject of scientific research. While the tape measure is a symbol of science, the chain symbolizes a kind of virility that is quite obviously linked to showmanship and display. In looking at Macfadden one is reminded more of Houdini, the proudly muscular master of the popular stage, than an exercise instructor.

In an article entitled "Feminism/Foucault–Surveillance/Sexuality," Griselda Pollock remarks that "what is at stake in representation in not so much a matter of what is shown as it is who is authorized to look at whom with what effects" (15). Macfadden, for his part, loved putting on all sorts of public contests, especially body building and beauty contests. In this way, he located the body as a sight of eroticism and public consumption. The men authorized to look at middle-class male bodies in the anthropometry texts were, on the other hand, usually "scientists" and "educators," far from the general public that Macfadden was catering to. Given that their gaze was supposed to be "disinterested" and their intentions "pure," it worked to contain to some degree the effect of making middle-class men's bodies into commodified and sexualized spectacles. Importantly, however, once in circulation the scientific gaze of the anthropometrists could not thoroughly control either "unauthorized" consumers or the meaning of these images for its middle-class constituents. Nor could they control the logical referent or relation these kinds of representations of middle-class male bodies had to the "others" that were represented in scientific or medical discourses. The business of picturing and measuring middle-class male bodies inextricably connected those bodies, I would argue, to what we now understand to be repressive and oppressive modes of representation. Indeed, many of the young men Sargent measured for his anthropometric texts ended up as models for his "anthropometric statues" which appeared in the Anthropology Building at the Chicago World's Fair alongside other notable "types." It is worth mentioning here that while Sargent publicly praised Eugen Sandow's body, it did not satisfy the requirements for Sargent's "ideal body" statues. If one wanted to see Sandow while visiting Chicago, the visitor went not to one of the "educational" buildings at the fair ground proper, but to downtown Chicago's Trocedero Theater.[48]

## PHYSICAL EDUCATION AND THE BODY ARCHIVE

In using anthropometry to undertake the measuring and cataloguing of white middle-class men, physical education can be linked to the "regulatory science" of criminology. The practice of photographing and cataloguing criminals was common by the 1880s. While it is important to remember Foucault's distinction between regulatory sciences that exercised what one might call a repressive power on the body (prison is one example) and those, like physical education itself, that exercised a more "positive or reformative channeling of the body,"[49] the differences between the punitive and the reformatory regimes are, as many feminists have pointed out in their discussions of anorexia, perhaps less distinct than it would seem on first glance. Alan Sekula has persuasively argued that when turn-of-the-century writers began to assert that criminals would find it more difficult to ply their trade once their "faces and general aspects" became "familiar to so many"[50] through the police gallery of portraits, "a wider citizenry" was implicitly enlisted "in the vigilant work of detection" (9). Thus, he argued, police photographs served to "introduce the panoptic principle into daily life." Physical education literature, in representing men through what its proponents considered a scientific method (anthropometry), helped to insert the middle class male body into the larger "body archive" being constructed at the turn of the century. And, if their representations often functioned honorifically, they also had the potential to act repressively.

Foucault notes that it is the "body of society" as opposed to the body of the King that was the "new principle in the nineteenth century" and that it is "this body which needs to be protected, in a quasi-medical sense."[51] This social body is protected by the "elimination of hostile elements" through such methods as "criminology, eugenics and the quarantining of 'degenerates'" (55). Authors like Gulick and Sargent confirm that inefficient, flabby businessmen, although not cordoned off from society, were considered threatening to it. The "quasi-medical" or quasi-scientific discourses, then, that took these men in hand or treated them were part of the same phenomena as criminology and eugenics. Indeed, in examining the relation between criminals and being below average in height and weight, Sargent wrote that "the question of supplying some artificial means of both mental and physical development becomes one of the greatest importance. It is difficult to see how the stability and integrity of the race can be maintained in any other way."[52] The paranoia of visibility noticeable in the texts of men like Blaikie and Gulick is not, then, *only* an outgrowth of urbanism, but also a result of the inescapable "new principle" of the social body. As such, physical education and the anthropometric representations of middle-class men do not completely escape the mania for detecting and reforming or repressing the more "hostile elements" within the social body. [See figures 5 and 6].

Alphonse Bertillon, the Paris police official who invented the first workable modern system for identifying criminals, is an important contemporary of the middle-class physical educators discussed above. Bertillon also used Quetelet's conception of the "average man" and his system of measurements. Quite simply, men like Sargent, Gulick, Seaver and others who used anthropometry sought, like Bertillon, to ground their work on human subjects in "scientific principles" and believed that in doing so they contributed to a healthier, more ordered, and specifically for their bourgeois audience, a more *informed* society. Bertillon's work has been studied far more extensively, but the work of the pioneers in physical education show that the same principles and justifications used to identify criminals and certain racial or ethnic types also operated to "normalize" and make more efficient the male middle-class citizenry.

A love of anthropometry, however, was not all these men had in common. Physical educators and criminologists such as Bertillon wanted to systematize their work with human bodies. They argued that if anthropometry was to help achieve the goal of human perfection, it needed to be instituted in a systematic way. Bertillon dreamed of an ordered world in which all subjects that had passed through his department would be furnished with a card that contained their photographic images and anthropometric measurements. Like Sargent, Bertillon wanted and (unlike Sargent) finally instigated a system of cataloging that was based completely on Quetelet's notion of the average man, with criminals falling into three groups: average, above-average and below-average. Bertillon ran into many problems along the way, not the least of which was the trouble he had standardizing police methods for taking measurements and pictures. Most early physical educators complained of remarkably similar problems. Sargent, for instance, noted that while

> there is an abundance of data on the height, weight, and chest-girth of persons of different ages and nationalities, and the dimensions of other parts of the body have been taken by artist anatomists, military surgeons, and gymnasiarchs, yet no one system has ever been adopted by any two examiners. . . . What is most needed at the present day is a uniform system of measurements. . . . [53]

So, while the desire to make scientific the project of getting middle-class men into shape is crucial, so too is the desire to handle those men in a systematic and efficient way. These goals resonate deeply with the prevailing ethos of rationalization that marks modern industrial culture.

Both criminologists and physical educators were also quick to grasp the value of photography to their work. In fact, Bertillon started with photographs and only later combined these images with anthropometrical data to help in the cataloging process. Physical educators and trainers of the late nineteenth and early twentieth century began with anthropometry but soon recognized photography as a possible method for furthering their own work. Seaver, for instance, notes that

> The French police regulations require a minute measurement of the ear and the middle finger of criminals if they are arrested a second time. These measurements help in classifying the photographs that are taken so that they can be readily found among thousands. Some anthropometrical tests can no doubt be made more serviceable in establishing identity in a "rogues gallery" than photography. . . . [Still] Photography may be wisely used as an adjunct of anthropometry. Since Professor Muybridge made his wonderful pictures of animal locomotion by instantaneous process the value of a photograph to show physical deficiencies as well as excellence has been established. It makes a record in an artistic way that is made by tape and calipers in a mathematical or scientific way. Already at some of the better equipped gymnasiums photography is made to assist in preserving the record of a man's physical condition.[54]

We can see, then, a more-than-theoretical link between the modes of representing white middle-class men and criminals or various "others" who were included in the effort to make an archive of the body. The differences between the two efforts, however, are also instructive. Notice that Seaver, while obviously seeing the potential in photographing the men he is training, does not want to make too direct a link to Bertillon's work. Instead, when discussing photography he focuses on Muybridge, whose work he significantly calls "artistic." The battle between photography as evidence and photography as art is as old as the invention of the medium itself. Both the elite and middle classes had "honorific" portraits taken by photographers during this period. These types of photo sessions were, according to Sekula, an "attempt to resist the archival mode through a strategy of avoidance and denial based on craft production. The elegant few were opposed to the mechanized many in terms both of images and authors."[55] Seaver did not want his men being photographed by the anonymous photographers one might encounter at a police station. He avoids this by naming the famous "Professor" Muybridge as a sort of stand-in author who does not simply *take* mug shots but rather "*makes*" "wonderful pictures," thus keeping the middle-class men from being pathologized to the extent that criminals, women and racial or ethnic "others" were.

Still, the desire to somehow rationalize and make scientific the project of getting middle-class men into shape remains, as does the desire on the part of physical educators and trainers to develop a systematic way to catalogue the men under their tutelage. While fears over "race suicide" and degeneracy provide a motivating subtext[56] for the rise of physical education, the notion of efficiency both *in* the subject and *the handling of* that subject is crucial and far less discussed. It is this aspect of physical education that most directly relates to discourses concerned with industrialized work.

## WORK AND THE MIDDLE-CLASS BODY: THE CASE OF SCIENTIFIC MANAGEMENT

Criminology's preoccupation with bureaucratic efficiency mirrors the physical education discourse not only in its mission to identify and classify men through their bodies, but also in its search for way of *handling* large populations systematically and "rationally." On both these counts, the two discourses are also connected to a third quasi-scientific discourse: scientific or industrial management.[57] Indeed, when physical educators like Sargent and Gulick made efficiency, the systematic and the science of measurements central to the care of the body, they connected middle-class bodies to industrial capitalism in ways that were both new and significant. Far from trying to dismantle the industrial system that they conceded led to many of the ailments they were attempting to "cure," physical educators were themselves very much a product of that culture and sought ways to harmonize the body with the "progress" they felt industrialism marked. Physical education, then, needs to be seen as laying important cultural groundwork for scientific management, which unequivocally continues the fascination with the rationalized body. [58] What scientific management makes more explicit, however, is the tension between self-regulation and surveillance lurking below the surface of middle-class physical education writings. This tension illuminates the need in middle-class discourses both to address the idea of physical degeneracy among the members of the educated classes and sustain the brain worker (supervisor)/manual worker (supervised) division that is the earmark of industrialized labor and the basis of class distinction itself.

This is not to say that the physical prowess and athletic spectacles so many historians have been discussing in relation to manhood at the turn of the century were not important. It is, however, crucial not to lose sight of the ways in which middle-class manhood retained the hierarchy of the mind/body split. What is possibly new about the turn-of-the-century conception of the body is that it placed the body in a more complete and dynamic *connection* with the health of the mind and the preoccupation with the efficiency of middle-class men. Nowhere is this clearer than in scientific management.

Scientific management rests on two central beliefs: that science could reveal the most efficient motions for the body to perform while engaged in industrial work and that no *laborer* could understand this science. Underpinning this stance toward the working-class employee is the idea that efficiency is a strictly middle-class preoccupation. Just as Luther Gulick saw working-class men as low-grade machines with little need or desire to change their lot, scientific management held as one of its most fundamental beliefs the idea that working-class men, if left to themselves, would never be efficient workers. Although the father of scientific management, Frederick Taylor, believed that inefficiency was the common enemy of both workers and management, and that employers too often rewarded increased production with lower wages, in practice, workers were treated as inherently inefficient. In order to eradicate this problem, Taylor began breaking down the motions of industrial workers, timing them with a stop watch, experimenting with new methods and generalizing from the results. He believed he could discover "immutable laws," which would then be used to systematize and rationalize labor by identifying what constituted a fair day's work.

The effect of Taylor's effort thoroughly dehumanized the worker. But, I would argue, not because it treated the worker like a machine. As we have seen with both Sargent and Gulick the body-as-machine metaphor was freely and frequently used in middle-class physical education discourses as a positive representation. The machine was the model of efficiency after all, and working-class men were often faulted for *not* being "high-grade" machines. What was dehumanizing about the scientific management discourse was that it wrested the control of working-class men's labor from them almost completely and delivered it to elite and middle-class managers and engineers. These managers would discover "the one best way" to do the workman's job and train him to do it according to their specifications. What this necessitated, it soon became clear, was a form of management that watched its workers like never before. As Linda Biggs argues in her article "The Engineered Factory," the new factory was a panopticon of the highest order with, on average, eight functional foremen replacing the one gang boss or overseer.

But, as the name itself suggests, scientific management did not only affect working-class factory laborers. Taylor's work was a critique of management as much as it was a critique of workers. He rationalized, divided, specialized and directed work on *every* level of industrial production, leading some members of the American Society of Engineers to react negatively to Taylor's system and reject it because it so challenged their idea of themselves as "the entrepreneurial elite within shop culture" (Biggs 176). Other engineers, however, not only embraced much of Taylor's system, but expanded on it, coming up with all sorts of uses for efficiency outside industrial work. Both Frank Gilbreth and Henry Gnatt, two of Taylor's most famous and contentious followers, saw the theories of scientific management as applicable to schools, stores, homes and farms as well as, in Gilbreth's case, sports, surgery

and music. William H. Allen, a general agent for improving the condition of
the poor in New York even wrote a book entitled *Efficient Democracy* (1907)
in which he argues for the use of "efficiency tests" in all public schools, hospitals, charitable institutions and government work.

Given my argument that middle-class men had to contend with their
bodies as never before, that they were measured, watched and to some extent
judged and objectified as the culture became more concerned with their physical selves, it would be easy to slide into the argument that they were, in ways
usually associated with women and discussed by feminist historians and theorists, oppressed by their new physical visibility. It is true, I think, that the push
towards *rationalization* that connects physical education discourses and industrial discourses enlists the body in central ways, attempting to standardize and
understand its operations and motions. Industrial engineers, as just one example, were not only the heroes of the new industrial system, they were also "the
system's original product."[59] But it is important to point out that efficiency is
never constructed completely as a problem of the body for the middle and educated classes. As industrialism divided more completely than ever before manual from non-manual work, non-manual work increasingly became the marker
of a higher class status. But how does such a worker retain his physical power?
Certainly, at this point, to make a seamless connection between productivity
and the body would spell disaster for most middle- and upper middle-class male
workers. Thus, despite all the concerns with male health and the male body, it
was the vigilant connection made between two entities (the mind and the body)
held separate that prevented this class of men from becoming static objects and
prevented the male body from being perceived like the female's (useless and aesthetic) or the working class male's (brutish and productive only when forced).

An example of this critical difference comes in the first part of a three-part
series Taylor wrote for *American Magazine* in 1911. Taylor remarks that "The
writer trusts . . . that before leaving this illustration the reader will be thoroughly
convinced that there is a science to handling pig iron, and that this science
amounts to so much that the man who is suited to handle pig iron cannot possibly understand it, nor even work in accordance with its laws without the help
of those over him."[60] Taylor, then, creates a division between mind and body that
is a priori a class division and, simultaneously a new profession. When referring
to any knowledge that the worker does possess, Taylor is careful to characterize it
as intuitive and unreliable. The worker's knowledge is not scientific; it has been
"handed down from man to man by word of mouth, or have in most cases been
almost *unconsciously* learned through personal observation" (575, my emphasis).

It is, then, the worker who possesses the body completely. And that
body, Taylor is careful to point out, is nothing to get too excited about.

Although he concedes that only one man in eight can carry enough pig iron to satisfy what he considers a fully productive day's work—that is forty-seven tons per day, a number arrived at through "the minute, painstaking analysis and study of movements of men to find their quickest and best motions" (574)—such a man is no great creature. Rather, he "merely happened to be a man of the type of the ox—no rare specimen of humanity, difficult to find and therefore very highly prized. On the contrary, he was a man so stupid that he was unfitted to do most kinds of laboring work" (579). The downplaying of physical prowess is important. Echoing the physical education tracts written by men like Gulick, who dismissed the physical strength of manual workers as "low-grade," the pig iron handler cannot be an efficient worker despite his great strength. Efficiency is a matter of mind.

> If the worker had been allowed to attack the pile of 47 tons of pig iron, without the guidance or direction of a man who understood the art, or science, of handling pig iron, in his desire to earn his high wages he would probably have tired himself out by 11 or 12 o'clock in the day. He would have kept so steadily at his work that his muscles would have been completely exhausted. By having a man, however, who understood this law stand over him and direct his work, day after day, until he acquired the habit of resting at proper intervals, he was able to work at an even gait all day long. (579)

Like physical educators, Taylor's engineers will teach men how to use their bodies in efficient ways. What scientific management makes more explicit, however, is a mind/body split in which the mind retains a place of power in the face of any commitment to the importance of revering the physical in its connection to manliness for the middle class.

Biographical sketches of men like Taylor are in fact perfect examples of the balancing act that went on between the prowess of the body and the spiritedness of the mind. In a lead-in article to Taylor's in *American Magazine,* Ray Stannard Baker is careful to build a picture of Taylor that includes both physical and mental potency. He begins by describing Taylor in terms of machine-like dynamism: "A boyish-looking young man, small of stature, he was as close-knit and wiry as a steel spring."[61] Two sentences later, Baker writes emphatically: "This young man Taylor was a thinker" (565). Only once this is established, is the author cleared, in the next paragraph, to shape the other side of Taylor:

> The boy was given two years of school in France and Germany and then a year and a half of travel in Italy, Switzerland, Norway, England, France, Germany and Austria—'All of which,' he says, 'I heartily disapprove of for a young boy.' After this he returned to the healthy outdoor life of Germantown [Pennsylvania], in which sport was the leading idea— 'than

which there is nothing finer in the world'—then two years of really very
hard study, coupled with athletics at Exeter. (566)

Always keeping the two values of a searching mind and vigorous body in dynamic connection, Baker, in summing up, notes that Taylor is both a man of
"wide cultivation" with a "lively and progressive mind, seizing eagerly upon
the problems of the day" *and* that he "always had a keen interest in sport, having in the year 1881 won the national championship at tennis (doubles) in a
tournament played at Newport" and is an "enthusiastic golf player" (569).
The addition of details on sporting championships reside strikingly enough
in an article about a businessman. These details do not, however, exist on their
own. They do act as a complement to a man who could not, under any circumstances, himself lift forty-seven tons of pig iron and effectively undercut
the "unhealthy" "indoor" experiences of his cultivation in Europe—experiences, however, Taylor needed to consolidate his position in society as much
as he needed, in this instance, to disavow them. Cultivation of the body, for
men like Taylor and others who saw themselves as members of the industrial
middle class, did not act only as a pastime which proved their masculinity, but
also, and perhaps more importantly, as a *class* marker that showed commitment to a value system that critiqued the inefficiency and wastefulness of the
leisure class as well as the working class. And it is in this particular critique
that we can find a connection to a wide range of thinkers, from William James
and George Santayana to Thorstein Veblen.

Having *both* a sound body and mind is an issue that appears often in the
business magazines that flourished at the beginning of the twentieth century.
One magazine that took up the cause of scientific management more completely and enthusiastically than most is *System: The Magazine of Business,* which
was published from 1900 to 1929. The advertising sections of the magazine are
a good source of information on what concerned middle-class male brain workers in the industrial sector. One advertisement that occurs with great frequency
is the "Swoboda System of Physiological Exercise." In its advertisements, and
the many others that are like it, the body and the mind are given equal weight
through the notion of a connecting nervous system that controls both. Given
the richness of the language, I quote here at length:

> You have within you the power and ability to be strong physically and
> mentally efficient, free and regular in all the functions of the body. I can
> show you how to develop and use that power as I have demonstrated to
> thousands in every section of the world——Without medicine, without ap-
> paratus, without any demands upon you whatever except that you follow
> the simple, pleasant corrective exercises I give you. You can build yourself

a strong, superb body, a keen, vigorous brain and so revitalize your whole nervous system that you will once more enjoy the clock-like physical regularity of youth—deep, restful sleep, wide-awake mornings, regular bowel-action. . . . I can show you how to easily revive your natural recuperative powers and throw off your weakness by your own efforts, and revive your old vitality—by scientific adaptation to your individual needs The SWOBODA SYSTEM of Physiological Exercise (*System* 1910).

There are several things here worth noting. First, of course, the advertisement makes clear that the Swoboda System is for the mind as much as it is for the body and that the two are connected. The goal is not only a "superb body" but also a "keen, vigorous brain." Secondly, there is an interesting appeal not only to increased energy, which would be expected, but an increased *regularity.* Interest in regularity, both in terms of one's physical workings (the bowels) as well as one's habits (sleep and work) fit in with the discourse of scientific management specifically, and middle-class values generally. Taylor and his followers were convinced that standardization or regularization of everything, from the planning department down to the smallest motion of the workman, held the key to increased efficiency. It was only by being regular in one's work that one could get the most accomplished. Regularity in exercise was also, as we have seen, crucial to men like Sargent. Third, there is the appeal to one's ability to help oneself with limited guidance. Here the class distinction becomes crucial. Swoboda clients are painstakingly enumerated by profession in the advertisement: "Among my clients, past and present, are judges, senators, congressmen, members of the president's cabinet, governors, ambassadors, and thousands of business and professional men" (*System* 1910). These men, unlike the workers under scientific management, are what we might call today self-actualized individuals, for they are *a priori* men invested in efficiency and productivity. Any hint that they are "soldiering" like Taylor's workmen would be untenable. The banner placed at the top of the add thus reads, in bold, "How to Develop Health, Strength, and Regularity–For Yourself and by Yourself." The ad, then, through its valorization of "regularity" supports the rationalization of the body that is going on for all classes in society at this time, and it works to fit the body into the more corporate, cooperative and standardized structure of industrialized work. At the same time, with its call to do it yourself, it appeals to the middle-class ideal of individualism and self-mastery. Importantly, it makes this appeal by placing a new emphasis on the male subject's body.

The barrage of advertisements telling middle-class men that they needed to expand their chests or calm their digestive systems, that they needed to be constantly aware of wasted or lost energy, certainly points to a reformative and consumerist discourse that first fragments the body and then sells its augmentation. It is also clear that this augmentation was wrapped in the prevailing preoccupation with science and technology.[62] But the line of connection between the mind and the body, often achieved through the conception of the nervous system, kept middle-class men from being defined too completely by their bodies.

Indeed, as so many cultural historians have pointed out,[63] nervous disorders, which so complexly intertwine physical and mental phenomena, were diseases that *only* middle-class men and women could contract. According to the cultural historian Tim Armstrong, among others, it was a badge of honor. It meant that you lived to a great extent in your brain. It was also something, importantly, that middle-class *men* could control—through tonics, vacations, exercise, etc. (middle- and leisure class women suffering from neurasthenia, as Mary Poovey and other have pointed out, were sent to bed and lorded over by husbands and doctors).[64] Controlling one's body in a newly commercial and visual culture becomes the *prerogative* of the male middle class and well to do. The many bodily fads of the period, like Fletcherism, which taught men (like Henry James) to chew food a certain number of times before swallowing, was about *self*-regulation or internal regulation—although, as we have seen in the anthropometric manuals, "men of science" still sought a certain degree of control over their (supposedly willing) subjects. Such bodily regimes challenge individualism through the creation of a normative or efficient body without completely eradicating agency. Taylorism, while certainly influencing notions of *middle-class* bodily (self) management, was more overtly about setting external limits on bodies that were assumed to be unruly—that could not be trusted to set limits, either in terms of output or input, for their own bodies.

Ultimately it is the engineer himself who provides the greatest model for self-regulation. He not only figured out a way to control the bodies of the working class but to make efficiency, waste and energy prominent issues for the culture as a whole. For thinkers like Veblen, who was a great supporter of the engineer, the new engineer/industrial manager was a man in the middle, seeing waste both in the excesses of the rich and the indigence of the poor. Further, he was a model not only of self-control but of environmental control. As critic Cecelia Tichi argues, the engineer became a hero in a world newly destabilized by technology. Engineers had the knowledge to harness and use this new energy and it is telling that Ray Stannard Baker ends his panegyric to Taylor thus: "There have been times in recent years when it seemed as though our civilization were being throttled by things, by property, by the very weight of industrial mechanism, and it is no small matter when a man arises who can show us new ways of commanding our environment" (570). This new way of commanding was, importantly, based on the creation of "scientific" bureaucratic systems and through them the engineer controlled bodies as well as environments.

For middle-class and professional men, industrialism brought with it a more prominent concern about their bodies. Yet the "educated" discourses that would take their bodies and put them under the eye of "science" and through various "rational systems" of exercise or motions studies attempted, successfully, I would argue, to keep them separate from physical culture's strongman, the working class and women of all classes by linking their interests in the body to efficiency and brain work. Physical educators created a specific bodily ideal for the middle-class man, one designed not for show, as Macfadden or Sandow might have it, but for his proper place in the divided system of industrial labor, that is, as a thinker whose very "self-division" is the source of both his vulnerability (to exhaustion) and his power. Scientific management appealed to the middle-class man as one who was physically efficient, as one who built himself rationally and intentionally to function at optimum efficiency, and charged him to watch over those it deemed physically incapable of entering on their own into what one might call a *bodily bureaucracy* that it was assumed the higher class of man entered willingly.

The physical education tracts, then, show us the ways in which new interests about the body had the potential to place middle-class men into a larger reformative discourse of bodily regulation and standardization. Scientific management shows us the ways in which these middle-class bodies negotiated a place of power within the new regime through a system of work that displaced much of the regulatory nature of bodily performance onto the working classes, while claiming for themselves either an always already disciplined body or a willingness and desire to reform themselves with the limited guidance of others. That this forces in middle-class men some sort of internalization of the reformative discourse on the body seems likely. It also seems likely, however, that their special and increasingly specialized place in the industrial world of work served to relieve some of the weight of that body.

Chapter Two
# The Male Body and the Market Economy: Valuating Dreiser's Frank Cowperwood

Both middle-class physical education manuals and popular physical culture magazines illuminate the ways white male bodies, in their very size and shape, do important cultural work. But these texts, specifically dedicated to the care of the body, were not the only ones to concern themselves with questions about what the white male body could signify. Literature from this period, especially realist literature, shows a great deal of concern about male bodies as well. Indeed, whether realism's narrative strategies naturalize the status quo, becoming a vehicle for the dissemination of hegemonic ideology, or whether the practice of mimesis inevitably complicates and critiques the society it is trying to represent, realism's preoccupation with voyeurism makes it a very "revealing" form of fiction. Arguably, what turn-of-the-century realism reveals more than previous forms of fiction writing is the body. This chapter will take full advantage of realism's invitation "to *look*."[1] It will, moreover, focus on two novels from a writer in this tradition who was perceived by many to be one of the most revealing of them all, Theodore Dreiser.

The issues discussed in Chapter One are extended here: late nineteenth- and early twentieth-century discourses on work, class, sex, the body and visibility, and perhaps more importantly, the ways in which these terms interact with each other, helping us locate important cultural shifts in the construction of masculinity. The traditions of both realism and naturalism, despite their different positions with regard to causality, attempt to deal with conceptions of the body that add to and complicate the middle-class body physical educators and engineers were trying to fashion through their own social scientific methods. In realism as in physical education texts, the body becomes representa-

tional of the self. Or, to put it differently, the body becomes a powerful signifier of identity. This leads to a level of anxiety about the body that is new in
American culture at the turn of the century. The reasons for this new concentration on the body were outlined in the first chapter. It will be helpful here,
however, to enumerate the issues that realism concerned itself with most often.
In realist fiction the body is linked to at least five momentous cultural concerns: new forms of work, industrialism (specifically mechanization), the
dawning of market and corporate capitalism, urbanization, and the unprecedented growth in consumer culture.

There has been excellent work done in both feminist and literary theory
on the ways in which these changes, especially market capitalism, urbanization and consumer culture, affect conceptions of the feminine self. Luce
Irigaray's chapter "Women on the Market" in *The Sex Which is Not One* deals
especially well with women's bodies in terms of the capitalist market and
Rachel Bowlby's *Just Looking* is a compelling exploration into realism's concern with consumer culture and the ways in which that interest is coded female. In a more recent book, *Spectacles of Realism: Gender, Body, Genre,* Jann
Matlock convincingly argues that in adopting a "quasi-scientific" mode of
looking, coded as male, realism became "a woman's question because the bodies of women were being exposed in radically new ways."[2] Certainly the most
famous literary characters from this period are hyper-embodied females: Lily
Bart, Emma Bovary, Carrie Meeber, Maggie Johnson, Isabel Archer, Daisy
Miller. And much has been said about realism's male observers, characterized
as Baudillarian *flannuers,* detached and knowing,[3] making women their object of investigation and setting up a familiar paradigm in which the woman
becomes object and is placed in mimetic relation to the commodities she apparently desires to the exclusion of all else. In "Real Fashion: Clothes Unmake
the Working Woman," Anne Higonnet argues that a great deal of realist literature supports the contention that, at this moment, "consumer culture organ-
izes itself around a revision of women's roles, establishing new gender
polarities that align femininity with the display and consumption of commodities." What women then become, she goes on to argue, is a "fetishistic
image," ready for exchange between men.[4] But, as Diana Knight observes in
her essay "S/Z, Realism, and Compulsory Heterosexuality," in order for the
system of female exchange to work, men must maintain "their subject position [as detached observers] and . . . cannot allow themselves to become objects of exchange."[5]

The above marks some of the more sophisticated gender readings in realist criticism. However, while I agree that there is a connection between the
observer and the masculine subject, they are not the same thing. Rather, I

would argue that the role of the observer is most often a *desire* of male characters in realist fiction, who only *attempt* to stay out of the commodified exchange.[6] What I challenge in this chapter is the idea that men can be excluded from commodification and the changing ideations of the self in relation to materiality and commercialization going on in this period. Authors like William Dean Howells proclaimed realism a "virile" art form in contradistinction to the sentimental and romantic novels of mid-century.[7] This position, I believe, rests at least partially on the ability (or fantasy) of the male subject to separate himself from the process of embodiment by the consumer culture. Thus it is crucial that studies of realism include a discussion of the effect the new market/consumer economy had on the construction of masculinity, and to show the ways masculinity struggled with the body as part of these new economies.

The novels I examine here are notable for their willingness to see the construction of the male self as dependent on both the commodities and consumerist desires let loose by market capitalism. This discussion, then, will help complicate the scholarship on gender, consumerism and display during this period in American cultural history. Consumer culture may indeed "align femininity with the display and consumption of commodities." I do not agree, however, that this necessarily establishes "new gender polarities," at least not in realist fiction. Men were producers of consumer culture, but they were also consumers themselves. Using Dreiser's work, I investigate men's relationship to consumerism; how they used commodities in the construction of efficacious identities and the ways in which the consumer culture and new market economy incorporated men (differently from women) into the commercial exchange.

The two novels that crucially challenge and complicate received notions about masculinity and its relation to the body, consumption, power, work, and visual culture are often ignored, and when considered, rather maligned. Dreiser's *The Financier* (1912) and *The Titan* (1914)[8] are the first two installments of a trilogy about a financier by the name of Frank A. Cowperwood. Neither is considered a "good book" by most critics. If they are discussed at all, the amount of attention they usually get compared to *Sister Carrie* (1900) or *An American Tragedy* (1925) can only be called paltry at best. Louis J. Zanine's *Mechanism and Mysticism*[9] is typical. In it, he devotes twenty-one pages in his second chapter to one novel, *Sister Carrie,* and the remaining seventeen to three incredibly long novels: *The Financier, The Titan,* and *The 'Genius.'*—the last of which is perhaps Dreiser's most disparaged novel. While the first two books of what Dreiser called *The Trilogy of Desire* do have their champions, Walter Benn Michaels, Robert Shulman and Howard Horowitz over a decade ago and, more recently, Clare Eby, William Moddelmog and Michael Tranter,[10] the reigning interpretations of Dreiser as a writer often foreclose discussions more than they opens them. The bulk of the rather unsatisfying criticism that surrounds these books, is endemic to much of Dreiser criticism in general.

## DREISER CRITICISM

Dreiser is not often seen as an artist concerned with the problems of representing masculinity. Perhaps this has something to do with the way in which *Sister Carrie* so eclipses the rest of his body of work from a critical standpoint. The best Dreiser criticism comes out of discussions of this novel and much of it has informed the most persuasive arguments about the relationship between consumerism and women during this period. But the strongest barrier to using Dreiser novels for the investigation of manhood and masculinity at the turn of the century has been the almost relentless tendency of critics to view his male characters as constructions of Dreiser himself. Over and over again it is argued that Dreiser's male characters are used only as ways for the author to work out his own fears, shortcomings and personality problems. Given this, his male protagonists do not offer any understanding or position on masculinity that is useful beyond understanding the author. In freeing two of Dreiser's "lesser novels" from his personal life, while keeping a sharp eye on his identity as a *writer,* I wish to bring Dreiser into a more expanded conversation on masculinity. As it turns out, he has a great deal to offer.

While the use of biographical information has limited the social and cultural insights brought out in Dreiser's male characters, I am certainly not arguing that biography is useless. I have, however, been surprised that *so much* of Dreiser criticism rests on it. The cause of this critical tendency to go the biographical direction lies in part with Dreiser's writing style. No one, to my knowledge, has ever praised it. The best H.L. Mencken, a long time friend, had to say about it was that it showed a "plodding" patience; most critics have been far more harsh. Contemporary reviewers were especially annoyed at his use of the vernacular. His writing, they said, was ugly, and critics then have persistently complained about his grammar. While I would not argue that Dreiser is a beautiful writer, an elision has been made between valuations of "good writing" style and the author as a self-conscious producer of fiction. The reigning logic in this camp is that Dreiser's "lapses" are to be understood as a lack of control over his work and lack of artistic distance between himself and his writing—thus the only thing that *could* be going on in his work is the writing and re-writing of the self; such a writer is not capable of constructing, in language, something outside himself. According to F.O. Matthiessen, Dreiser was simply incapable of "invention."[11]

Biographical information not only takes the place of other explanatory frameworks but supplies justifications for its use in the first place. Dreiser's background is brimming with reasons for critics to assume his characters are projections of an unruly self: he had little formal education, he was not of Anglo-Saxon stock, he grew up poor in the outback known as the Mid-West, and he was openly interested in all sorts of "pseudo-scientific" theories. Again, Matthiessen's words are instructive, as he, following Lionel Trilling (who disliked Dreiser far more) set the tone for Dreiser criticism in the 1950s—a tone that still finds its echo today: "Dreiser was the immigrant's son from the wrong side of the tracks, who broke through the genteel tradition *by no conscious intention,* but by drawing in a store of experience outside the scope of the easily well-to-do—experience which formed the solid basis for *all* his subsequent thought."[12] Such use of biographical information to explain books that critics see as poorly written by an author many have called outside the American tradition altogether is both condescending and uninstructive.[13]

Given that Dreiser was considered to be lacking in "invention," the forceful capitalist, Frank Cowperwood is explained by Philip Gerber in his book *Theodore Dreiser* as a product of Dreiser's inadequacies, an inversion of "his own personality," someone Dreiser was "driven" to write about "by his own insatiable curiosity about those few favored ones upon whom nature seemed to have lavished all the gifts she had *withheld from himself.*"[14] Similarly, James Lundquist states that Cowperwood is simply "Dreiser as he would have liked to be."[15] Stephen Brennan and Louis Zanine don't even see something as complex as an inversion. Instead they make straightforward connections between the philandering Cowperwood and Dreiser. Brennan comments, rather delicately, that Dreiser wrote Cowperwood to express the "contradictions" in his own "life process" and Zanine writes that Dreiser's "need to explain Cowperwood's numerous betrayals of his wife in terms of a rejection of conventional mores and an embrace of an amoral pursuit of hedonistic pleasure was no doubt part of Dreiser's deeper need to rationalize his own behavior to his acquaintances, his wife, and himself."[16] Finally, a whole host of critics, Zanine and Gerber among them, find the books to be a rather uncritical swallowing of the Spencerian theories that influenced much of Dreiser's philosophy about life. In all, there is little critical distance given to the author: Cowperwood as wish fulfillment; Cowperwood as rationalization of the author's sexual conduct; Cowperwood as transparent mouthpiece for the author's system of philosophic beliefs. Explaining Cowperwood's behavior through the lens of

Dreiser's life, however, unnecessarily curbs important critical questions. It hinders us from exploring the cultural and social significance of writing a character such as Frank Cowperwood, as well as what he and his endless repetition of affairs say about capitalism, consumerism, masculinity, sexuality and the body at the beginning of the twentieth century.

When critics stop making connections between Cowperwood and Dreiser, a rather large proportion of them find the same two problems with the books: the amount of detail Dreiser uses in both and what has come to be known as the "club sandwich" problem in the second. The number of affairs Cowperwood has in *The Titan* outraged contemporary reviewers and still bothers critics today, and (excluding some of the more prudish early reviews) for similar reasons: professed boredom over the repetition of these sexual encounters and what is perceived to be their lack of connection to Cowperwood's business transactions. In a scathing contemporary review published in *The Nation,* Stuart Sherman desrcibed *The Titan* as "a sort of club-sandwich composed of slices of business alternating with erotic episodes" (11) that bear no connection whatsoever. That criticism proved to have enormous staying power. Matthiessen, Pizer, and Gerber all adopted this reading and it has had consequences for the way in which even current critics so easily dismiss these books.[17] Luckily, a handful of recent scholars have seen the Cowperwood books as a significant and unique contribution to the literature of business in the America.[18] Clare Eby writes that the *Trilogy* is "arguably the most sustained fictional representation of economics written by a United States author" (65). But while all these critics contextualize the books through the lens of economic and/or legal discourses as opposed to biographical data, and while they assume a connection between the sexual and financial economies in the books, there has been little sustained discussion of how this economy or its connection to sexual practices influences gender construction, especially masculinity.

The turn of the century in the United States marks the coming of the "combination" and the corporation. And while the rhetoric of rugged individualism dating from the Jacksonian period had not lost its hold on the American imagination, it is probably more accurate at this time to look at networks of people, women and men, constituting their reality in combination and mutual dependency. The incorporation of men and women into newly formed networks—social, financial, spatial, commercial, sexual and professional—calls for an analysis that pays attention to the ways in which the new economic structures eroded the separation of the domestic world and the business world, the aesthetic realm and the professional realm, the realm of high culture and the realm of the commercial or popular culture, and finally, the producer and consumer.

In his now classic text, *The Incorporation of America,* Alan Trachtenberg begins with a 1869 quote from Charles Francis Adams: "'The system of corporate life' [is] 'a new power for which our language contains no name. . . . We have no word . . . to express government by monied corporations.'" Trachtenberg then states that his book is an attempt to "find appropriate words and names for the power which transformed American life in the three decades following the Civil War." More broadly, he is concerned with the "effects of the corporate system on culture, on values and outlooks, on the 'way of life.'" [19] In my opinion, few novels deal with these issues and answer these questions as fully as *The Financier* and *The Titan.*

Through the concept of "incorporation," Trachtenberg means to take into account "not only the expansion of an industrial capitalist system across the continent, not only the tightening systems of transport and communication, the spread of market economy into all regions of what Robert Wiebe has called a 'distended society,' but also, and even predominantly, the remaking of cultural perceptions this process entailed" (3). In so doing Trachtenberg looks at notions of individuality, the west, the consequences of mechanization, class conflict, urbanization, high culture and fiction. While there are moments in which Trachtenberg draws out some of the gendered consequences in all these areas, the book shies away from much explicit or in-depth discussion of gender.

I would argue, however, that one of the major shifts this process of incorporation entailed was the creation of a new kind of manhood that had different concerns, expressed itself in new forms, and empowered itself in ways that were simultaneously more abstracted (i.e. through market capitalism) and material (through the manipulation of commodities).

In Cowperwood we find a complex illustration of how incorporation plays itself out on the male body and in the discourses surrounding it. Cowperwood's life spans an important time of transition, a time when hierarchies were just being established, when the reach of power through incorporation was just being tested, when the language of corporate capitalism was mystifying to the general population, and when the language of individualism and property still held a tight grip on the American imagination. This is the time of incorporation *and* the time of robber barons. Cowperwood embodies both. He operates through networks and sets up combinations—in gas companies, in street-railways—making himself almost invisible; a felt presence instead of a person. At the same time, he uses the increasingly material culture to construct an image of powerful manhood and, indeed, a titan. He is highly visible as a symbol and invisible as an agent. Male power, in other words, rests on successful negotiations between visibility and invisibility, between (hyper)embodiment and complete abstraction.

## IT'S IN THE DETAILS

To say that Dreiser is not a spare writer is of course an understatement. The amount of detail in both Cowperwood books is rather staggering and difficult to assimilate. Both end around the five hundred page mark, depending on the edition, and it is almost impossible to find a critic who altogether approves of their length. Most think the amount of detail ruins the books. Philip Gerber presents a standard criticism when he says that "too much of everything is included, and the author's preoccupation with infinite details of business and sex may finally explain the lack of total satisfaction experienced by his many sympathetic readers and friendly critics." Lundquist simply calls the amount of detail "unjustifiable."[20] Critics more interested in the literary rendering of economics, like Walter Benn Michaels, Clare Eby and William Moddelmog, do not mind the amount of detail given over to the workings of market capitalism in the decades following the Civil War, Cowperwood's most active period in business. All three use Dreiser's description of the market to make sense of late nineteenth-century cultural perceptions of new forms of business, property, and notions of individualism. But while they find Dreiser's exploration of market capitalism worth a careful reading, none go into the question of *why* Dreiser found it necessary to give up so much space to the minutiae of Cowperwood's dealings in the market—after all, according to Howells, "fidelity to experience" has less to do with mimesis than it does "proportion."[21]

Cowperwood's story is not extremely complicated in terms of action. *The Financier* tells of Cowperwood's break into the business of handling stocks and getting rich through a partnership with Philadelphia's city treasurer, George Stener—a puppet for a consortium of powerful business men and politicians. Using the city's money received by Stener, Cowperwood manipulates the stock market to create a false demand for city loan certificates. Investors get a sense that the market is strong and thus the city loans come in on par. Having so much control over the city's stock exchange, Cowperwood begins to speculate with the city's money on the side, for both himself and Stener. The great Chicago fire causes a panic in the market that exposes Cowperwood's financial manipulations and he is eventually convicted of larceny and sentenced to a prison term of a little over four years (though he doesn't stay its full length).

Early in the novel Cowperwood marries Lillian, a widow five years his senior. They have two children and begin to rise socially, in pace with Cowperwood's financial success. However, he soon begins an affair with Aileen Butler, the daughter of one of the businessmen controlling Stener. Cowperwood's role as scapegoat in the city treasury scandal is, in fact, partially a result of Aileen's father discovering their affair. After Cowperwood is released from prison, the book ends quickly, with Cowperwood becoming an overnight millionaire by exploiting another panic in the market (the failure of Jay Cooke), beginning divorce proceedings against his wife, and leaving for Chicago with Aileen.

   *The Titan,* published two years later, follows Cowperwood on his various "ventures" in Chicago. He is an older character in this book, somewhat more hard-edged from his stay in prison. He is also more powerful. But, as in *The Financier,* there is in *The Titan* a consortium of powerful politicians and businessmen with whom Cowperwood must deal; all ventures involve a network of people, and that network includes both business associates and women with whom he has affairs. Now married to Aileen, Cowperwood first sets out on a venture to consolidate the various gas companies in Chicago. His manipulations of the owners of these companies and their stocks are rendered in the same minute detail we became acquainted with in *The Financier.* After that successful venture, he returns to his first love, the street-railway system. It had been stocks in city transportation that Cowperwood had speculated with in the first book and now, in Chicago, he sets about earnestly to control the public rail system. While this would seem to be the most tangible of his ventures, the bulk of the dealings around his bid for street-railway control involve behind-the-scenes political deals for land grants.[22]

   None of these business dealings make him a popular man and Aileen's flashy beauty provokes both jealousy and disdain from other women; thus when they try to enter Chicago society, they fail. Aileen begins a downward spiral—which critics often find the most compelling aspect of the book—and Cowperwood goes about his business dealings and his affairs. For a while, Cowperwood manages to gain control over most of the street-railway system. More importantly, exploiting another panic in the market, this time brought on by the fight over the gold standard, he finally manages to secure for himself enough money to be above the vagaries of the market. In the end, however, Cowperwood loses his bid for an extension on his land grants for the railways and the book closes with him again leaving, this time with Bernice, a girl half his age, in whom he believes to have found his ideal.

   It is important to give a taste of the kind of detail found in these books. (Most of it concerns explanations of Cowperwood's market manipulations, but Dreiser also, as in *Sister Carrie,* gives over a great deal of room to the details of interior spaces. Most of these spaces are, tellingly, what one might call semi-public, such as hotels, business offices, art studios, which tend to underline the permeability between, among other things, business and sex.) The quote below is a long one, but it will set up several things to which I will turn in my analysis. First, the question of why there is so much detail, secondly, what this detail means for Dreiser as a writer and the middle-class population that constitutes his readership, and finally, how incorporation or combinations affect the power and presence of Cowperwood. From *The Financier,* then, here is an example of Cowperwood contemplating his speculations on street-railways stocks:

> His one pet idea, the thing he put more faith in than anything else, was his street-railway manipulations, and particularly his actual control of the Seventeenth and Nineteenth Street line. Through an advance to him, on deposit, made in his bank by Stener at a time when the stock of the Seventeenth and Nineteenth Street line was at a low ebb, he had managed to pick up fifty-one per cent of the stock for himself and Stener, by virtue of which he was able to do as he pleased with the road. To accomplish this, however, he had resorted to some very 'peculiar' methods, as they afterward came to be termed in financial circles, to get this stock at his valuation. Through agents he caused suits for damages to be brought against the company for non-payment of interest due. A little stock in the hands of a hireling, a request made to the court of record to examine the books of the company in order to determine whether a receivership were not advisable, a simultaneous attack in the stock market, selling at three, five, seven, and ten points off, brought the frightened stockholders into the market with their holdings. The banks considered the line a poor risk, and called their loans in connection with it. His father's bank had made one loan to one of the principle stockholders, and that was promptly called, of course. Then, through an agent, the several heaviest shareholders were approached and an offer was made to help them out. The stocks would be taken off their hands at forty. They had not really been able to discover the source of their woes; and they imagined that the road was in bad condition, which it was not. Better let it go. The money was immediately forthcoming, and Cowperwood and Stener jointly controlled fifty-one per cent. But as in the case of the North Pennsylvania line, Cowperwood had been quietly buying all of the small minority holdings, so the he had in reality fifty-one per cent of the stock, and Stener twenty-five per cent more. (140–141)

The decades following the Civil War were some of the most tumultuous economic times in the country's history. The cycle of boom and bust both terrified and mystified the majority of the population ("They had not really been able to discover the source of their woes"), and Dreiser's detailed novels are an unmasking, to a certain extent, of the economic forces controlling the lives of the middle and working classes. At times they actually read like textbooks. Dreiser carefully explains, for instance, what a "bear" market is, what a "bull" market is, what it means to sell short, what it means to sell long. While the market detail may at times become excruciating, it is, in fact, *the* story. It is the story of a new language, a new discourse, a new force (to use one of Dreiser's favorite terms) that challenges both the traditional position of the literary writer as outside of the realm of business, and controls the lives of his middle-class readers. If *Sister Carrie* is, in Robert Shulman's words, "a touching confirmation of Marx on mystification and commodification,"[23] then the Cowperwood books are a look into the actual *process* of mystification and commodification. The detailing of the protagonist's financial manipulations is crucial to this project.

In his book *Modernism, Mass Culture, and Professionalism,* Thomas Strychacz argues that "the literary text would emerge in an age of mass culture as contextual; it would constantly negotiate with other media and other texts; it would have to be situated in some relationship, however adversarial, to the massive production of words, sounds, and images by—in T.E. Adorno's phrase— 'the culture industry.'"[24] The way in which the new language of market capitalism is negotiated in Dreiser's narrative is instructive. Dreiser himself crafts an authoritative relationship toward the professional discourse of market capitalism. As an author he shows off a seamless and encyclopedic knowledge of hidden economic machinations, through both Cowperwood and at other times as the narrator. To be a professional in the age of mass culture is to "manage and guide in expert fashion the social, cultural, and economic systems of America."[25] Perhaps Dreiser's ability to master economic language and knowledge was a mixed blessing for someone whose reputation as an artist was always being questioned. But the manliness of the artist as a leisured gentleman, as a *non*-professional, was also, at this time, thrown into question.[26]

Dreiser's contemporary reviewers often described his style (with some derision) as straight or "photographic" representations. The *New York Tribune's* review of *The Financier,* for instance, contends that Dreiser's "is a reportorial, rather than a literary talent."[27] Strychacz, however, argues that the reporter was fast becoming something of a "cultural hero" at the end of the nineteenth century—when Dreiser was in fact a newspaper writer. The reporter was considered "tough, uncompromising, at once a reporter, investigator, and man of action." Further there was, according to Stychacz, "a surprisingly consistent refrain . . . that the journalist's role in society demonstrated, by contrast, all that was wrong with the traditional literary life," that is, its effeminate reputation.[28] Authors, Christopher Wilson argues, began to "aspire to the ideal of *reportage.*"[29] There is, then, a link between a reporter-like style and a new form of artistic masculinity. Dreiser's rather showy mastery of the professional discourse of market capitalism, written in the form of a "cold recital"[30] that nodded to the journalistic style is a highly masculine enterprise. If, as noted in the first chapter, men at the turn of the century were finding it harder to prove their manliness in the realm of business because of incorporation, a drastically unstable economy, and the new mystifying, intangible world of market capitalism, both Dreiser's ability as a writer to understand the workings of the economic world and his desire to create a character who is able not only to understand it but eventually place himself above the vagaries of the market, needs to be seen as an attempt at reinstating a sense of male mastery, control and power. Clare Eby has argued that Dreiser "doubts his readers' ability to comprehend the subtleties of Cowperwood's business" and that this, in turn, endows Cowperwood with an "intellectual superiority." While this certainly downplays the "dubious morality" of his dealings (87–88), it also critically shapes his dominant masculinity.

But if Dreiser saves the act of easy assimilation for himself as a writer, his two books in fact *highlight* a rough economic transition. The language of market capitalism is not seamlessly enfolded into the narrative. The extensive detail forces the reader to confront his or her lack of knowledge about the market at every turn. The reader is repeatedly made aware of a new language, a new vocabulary, that other books about businessmen and the market written in this period, like Robert Herrick's *The Memoirs of an American Citizen* (1905), which spare the reader too many technical terms, do not. Dreiser's books are shot through with words and phrases like "coming in on par," "note-broker," "inside banker," "sinking fund," "valuations," "receivership," and (my favorite) "hypothecation." This language invades the text in a way that highlights it as a separate, esoteric, discourse that needs explaining—and a great deal at that. In these books we see the awkward beginning of a new economic order taking over, and the new cultural authority of the marketplace. These books are "transformative acts" that reorganize, in Andreas Huyssen's words, "the body of cultural meaning and symbolic significations to fit the logic of the commodity."[31] It's a rocky road and Dreiser successfully problematizes this transformation in the tension he creates between Cowperwood's rugged individualism (and all the different notions about masculinity that encapsulates) and his incorporation into the dependent networks of people he needs in order to become successful ("Through agents he caused suits. . . ." "A little stock in the hands of a hireling. . . .").

## INCORPORATION AND THE LANGUAGE OF INDIVIDUALISM

Cowperwood likes to think of himself as an individual above all else. His motto, we are told repeatedly, is: "I satisfy myself." In many ways he does, but what the books make clear is that it is always a battle and in the end he usually finds himself enmeshed in entangled webs of connection—often of his own making. Cowperwood's belief in individualism and its connection to masculinity is clearly shown early on through free indirect speech: "A man, a real man, must never be an agent, a tool, or a gambler—acting for himself or for others—he must employ such. A real man—a financier—was never a tool. He used tools. He created. He led" (*F* 42). The fact of the matter is, in *The Financier*, Cowperwood is an agent, a tool, and a gambler. He is the invisible agent and tool of the men who put Stener into office as city treasurer (Edward Butler, Henry Mollenhauer and Senator Mark Simpson); he is also a gambler when he speculates with the city treasury money, and both for a time are extremely lucrative.

As a tool of politicians and powerful businessmen, he is able to create his own little combination and discovers not only how to use others himself, but the kind of flexibility afforded by incorporation:

> When he had left the office of Tighe & Co., seven years before, it was with the idea henceforth and forever he would have nothing to do with the stock-brokerage proposition; but now behold him back in it again, with more vim than he had ever displayed, for now he was working for himself, the firm of Cowperwood & Co., and he was eager to satisfy the world of new and powerful individuals who by degrees were drifting to him. All had a little money. All had tips, and they wanted him to carry certain lines of stock on margin for them, because he was known to other political men. (*F* 86)

There is, in fact, no company in Cowperwood & Co. Nothing so encapsulates the paradox of Cowperwood's world than the phrase "now he was working for himself, the firm of Cowperwood & Co." In becoming a firm, Cowperwood, on some level, is no longer an individual. But, as he is the only person in the firm, all the money, power and prestige belong to him. He becomes a personality: the representation of himself as Cowperwood & Co. Self-presentation, then, is crucial, and perhaps more importantly in this instance, a legitimate form of power for a male character. Cowperwood and Carrie Meeber may not be so different. The abstraction of the self into a company erases that self on one level, but it hyper-embodies the self on another. What becomes most important to Cowperwood & Co. is the way, the physical way, in which Cowperwood presents himself, as the obsessive textual referencing of Cowperwood's body, eyes, clothes, mannerisms, and the effect they have on both business partners and women make clear. Interiority ceases to exist in any but a fleeting, uncontrolled way. Cowperwood becomes the marker for the abstracted capital he controls. The self he constructs is, and has to be, a glittering representation of all the invisible manipulations he carries out.

In *Hard Facts: Setting and Form in the American Novel,* Philip Fisher argues that the city is the space in Dreiser novels which the self attaches itself to: "For a man inside the city his self is not inside his body but around him, outside the body."[32] The self is both externalized and dependent, or, in Dreiser's words from *The Financier:*

> We think we are individual, separate, above houses and material objects generally; but there is a subtle connection which makes them reflect us quite as much as we reflect them. They lend us dignity, subtlety, force, each to the other, and what beauty, or lack of it, there is, is shot back and forth from one to the other as a shuttle in a loom, weaving and weaving. Cut the thread, separate a man from what is rightfully his own, characteristic of him, and you have a peculiar figure . . . much like a spider without its web, which will never be its whole self again until all its dignities and emoluments are restored. (96–7)

Fisher argues that Dreiser is the first author to explore the idea of the self created completely through the "dramatic possibilities" of the city. I would argue that, with the Cowperwood books, Dreiser is also the first author to write the construction of a male identity through the "dramatic possibilities" of incorporation, or as in the above quote, the "web," which engages him in the activity of self-production through commodities—an idea usually associated with women. Men are most often characterized as devoid of the consumerist urge, except perhaps when that urge is connected to "possessing" a woman. The above quote, however, establishes a link between masculinity and a consumerism rife with narcissistic identification—and not at a moment when the object is a desirable female. It is a more "subtle connection" because men have greater control over the production of those commodities they attach themselves to. Market capitalism and incorporation, however, make that connection to production in fact *less tangible.* The result is that men such as Cowperwood have to heighten their alliance to visible signs in the form of commodities to establish and confirm their power.

Like Walter Benn Michaels, I do not see Dreiser opposing or approving of the corporate capitalism he describes in these books. Those critics who see Dreiser as "swept up" with the commodities produced by a capitalist culture show a class bias never seen in the criticism of Henry James or William Dean Howells.[33] Some male critics may, in fact, be uncomfortable with the way in which Dreiser shows *men* as creatures reliant on commodities for self-presentation, or, for that matter, that they engage in conscious self-presentation at all and become, at certain moments, commodities themselves. What Dreiser is saying, I would argue, is that the need for physical, material, commodity-reliant self-representation is endemic to a capitalist/consumerist society—and that this must include men. This is his subject matter and he refrains (for the most part) from moralizing over the consequences.

Importantly, Cowperwood's engagement in self-production is in almost constant flux, intimately connected to his financial status and entirely selfish. For instance, Cowperwood has two children early on in *The Financier* and comments that "He liked it, the idea of self-duplication. It was almost acquisitive" (57). He likes "self-duplication" at this moment in his life because it goes so nicely with the other commodities he has recently acquired, like his house, which he both designs and decorates: the "dinner-table with candles upon it (his idea)" (57). Quickly, however, in tandem with his move beyond middle-class financial status, he drops all emotional investment in his wife and children—though not the domestic stage on which they play. References to his house and the art he continues to collect and place on its walls remain a point of plot development; his children themselves are not mentioned again until the end of the book.

When Cowperwood's fortunes begin to rise due to what he refers to as his "significant combination" (93) with Stener, he drops the middle-class facade. This rise also inaugurates the narrative's obsessive preoccupation with Cowperwood's physical appearance. The amorphous body that the corporation constructs requires a hyper-embodied man. This works itself out in specific and interesting ways for Cowperwood. If the shifting ground on which gender identity defined itself led some men into gymnasiums or imperialistic warfare, it leads Cowperwood into rather obsessive fashion-conscious physical display, and later, a compulsive sex drive.

Cowperwood has now become a "front," and he makes himself visible *as* a "safe" (86) stockbroker, and later, once he is indicted, *as* an "innocent man." (He *is* neither.) At his trial, for instance, Dreiser's narrator noticeably separates himself from the voice of Cowperwood and takes himself and the reader off some distance to watch Cowperwood's masterful self-display: "He was really a brilliant picture of courage and energy moving about briskly in a jaunty, dapper way, his moustaches curled, his clothes pressed, his nails manicured, his face clean-shaven and tinted with health" (241). And later:

> When Cowperwood came into the crowded courtroom with his father and Steger, quite fresh and jaunty (looking the part of the shrewd financier, the man of affairs), everyone stared. It was really too much to expect, most of them thought, that a man like this would be convicted. . . . Cowperwood was given to small boutonnieres in fair weather, but to-day he wore none. His tie, however, was of heavy, impressive silk, of lavender

hue, set with a large, clear, green emerald. He wore only the thinnest of
watch-chains, and no other ornament of any kind. He was always looking jaunty and yet reserved, good-natured, and yet so capable and self-
sufficient. Never had he looked more so than he did to-day. (289)

The language in both quotes is instructive. In the first he is a "brilliant picture"
and in the second, he is "looking the part" of the financier and man of affairs.
He plays it well because "everyone stares" and most think that a man *looking*
like this could (should?) not be convicted. His clothes are immaculate, showing wealth in the "heavy, impressive silk" and reserve in wearing "only the
thinnest of watch-chains, and no other ornament of any kind." Cowperwood
is here using commodities to fashion a particular self. That we are meant to understand this as a construction is clear in the language. He was "looking" jaunty
and reserved, and had in fact never "looked" more so than on this day. Not
only, then, is Cowperwood our completely physicalized object of investigation,
but he is also *only* what he can pull off with his appearance.

   Passages like this, strewn throughout the book, have led some critics to
charge Dreiser with playing the overly-enamored "peasant," to use
Parrington's word,[34] to his somewhat cruel capitalist protagonist with his fine
clothes and self-assured airs. But in the complex inter-play between the visible and invisible in the world of corporate finance, it is the clothes, along with
the physical mannerisms, that can make the man. Cowperwood's presence in
the market is not tangible; he works *through* men, like Stener, or as a secret
agent for Aileen's father, Edward Butler. Further, when Dreiser describes
Cowperwood's presence in the market he consistently uses words like "force,"
"threat," and "reputation." Cowperwood the man is, then, the symbolic capital of all that is *not* tangible in his market manipulations. He, like so many of
the women populating realist fiction, is (his) capital's commodified product.

   Cowperwood's only extra-marital affair in *The Financier* is with Aileen
Butler. It is also partially through this affair with Aileen, through her eyes, then,
that Cowperwood is made visible. But in orchestrating so well his own physical
display to get what he wants, he slips, at times, as he does in the courtroom, into
a commodified spectacle. Aileen experiences real pleasure in objectifying her
lover, slowly going over what "attracted her" (*F* 82): "There was something
about his steady, even gait, his stocky body and handsome head" (82). And later,
"He released her arms and went out, and she ran to the window and looked out
after him. He was walking west on the street, for his house was only a few blocks
away, and she looked at the breadth of his shoulders, the balance of his form.
He stepped so briskly, so incisively. Ah, this was a man! He was *her* Frank. *She
thought of him in that light* already" (125, my emphasis).

But if the narrator, the spectators in the courtroom, Aileen and we the readers are all involved in the voyeuristic pleasure of following the physical presence of Frank Cowperwood (which Cowperwood attempts to manage but cannot always control), we must also be aware of the ways in which his subjecthood, while remaining embodied, does not always open itself to objectifying commodification. In other words, we must investigate the ways in which he asserts a kind of male prerogative to deflect the objectifying gaze, even in a novel that so enjoys "just looking" at its male protagonist.

## POLITICS OF THE VISUAL EXCHANGE

Cowperwood's incorporation renders him both invisible and hyper-embodied. As a hyper-embodied personality representing the corporation, the novel places intense attention on his body—especially in its relation to commodities such as houses, art (which he collects through both novels) and clothes. But if the world is watching him, he is most definitely, at times, looking back—and from the very beginning of *The Financier* his gaze is almost always made a colossal force of deflection: "Already his eyes had the look that subtle years of thought bring. They were inscrutable. You could tell nothing by his eyes" (25). Even Aileen finds herself almost ruled by her lover's eyes: "There was a light of romance in his eyes, which, however governed and controlled— was directive and almost all-powerful to her" (123). And later in the same scene when Cowperwood touches her hand upon leaving,

> it was as though she had received an electric shock, and she recalled that it was very difficult for her to look directly into his eyes. Something akin to a destructive force seemed to issue from them at times. Other people, men particularly, found it difficult to face Cowperwood's glazed stare. It was as though there were another pair of eyes behind those they saw, watching through thin, obscuring curtains. You could not tell what he was thinking. (123)

The importance of Cowperwood's eyes to the image of himself as a powerful and willful man within the cosmology of the novel, then, is crucial. Weak men, like Stener, are described as having "vague" or "fishy" eyes, that have a tendency to reveal too much and, like some of women in the books, to fix "on Cowperwood in a rather helpless, appealing way" (137).

This link between Cowperwood's eyes and his power, however, is complicated. When Cowperwood arrives in Chicago at the beginning of the second book, he immediately, and tellingly, seeks out allies, men with whom he will combine to push through the centralization of the gas companies and, later, the

land grants for the street cars. Judah Addison, president of a powerful bank, is
his first stop. Addison is immediately struck by Cowperwood's "face and force"
and asks that he be let in. This opens the door for the narrator to give us another
picture of the protagonist's "force"—all of which hang on Cowperwood's eyes:

> He looked strangely replete for a man of thirty-six—suave, steady, inci-
> sive, with eyes as fine as those of a Newfoundland or a Collie and as in-
> nocent and winsome. They were wonderful eyes, soft and springlike at
> times, glowing with rich human understanding, which on the instant
> could harden and flash lightening. Deceptive eyes, unreadable, but allur-
> ing alike to men and to women in all walks and conditions of life. (*T* 14)

Once in the office, the narrator turns his attention briefly to Addison, who is
also characterized through his eyes: "hard, bright, twinkling gray eyes—a
proud, happy, self-sufficient man" (15). Addison, we are told, "frequently
liked or disliked people on sight, and he prided himself on his judgment of
men" (15). The force of Cowperwood's eyes is then established once again in
the next line: "Almost foolishly, for one so conservative, he was taken with
Cowperwood . . . not because of the Drexel letter . . . but because of the swimming wonder of his eyes" (15). In some ways, of course, Cowperwood has
won the day—Addison will be his most enduring and important ally—but at
the same time the narrator has managed to objectify Cowperwood. Not only
is he compared to two beautiful and domesticated dogs, but through
Addison's "foolish" behavior under the influence of the "swimming wonder"
of Cowperwood's eyes, Cowperwood casts a spell usually reserved for the se-
ductress. The power Cowperwood commands with his eyes is a feminized
power. He lets himself be looked at by the narrator and by Addison and the
language used by both ("soft and springlike," "swimming wonder") is decidedly feminine. Thus, even though Cowperwood's ability to scare, control and
deflect with his eyes can, at times, deter his complete objectification, these
very instruments of defense become part of his attraction as an aesthetic object.
    But perhaps the most compelling and instructive inquiry into the issues
of power brokered through the visual exchange comes in the early scenes of
Cowperwood's incarceration in *The Financier*. These scenes are striking for
the way they lend themselves so completely to a Foucauldian reading. As such,
they contribute a great deal to the scholarship linking literary realism to
modes of disciplinary surveillance.[35] Cowperwood's place of incarceration is
the Eastern District Penitentiary of Pennsylvania. Constructed in 1822, it is

a surprisingly close variation on Bentham's Panopticon, with an emphasis on vision that fits almost perfectly with Foucault's discussion of it:

> The prison proper, which was not visible from the outside, consisted of seven arms or corridors ranged octopus-like around a central room or court, and occupying in their sprawling length about two-thirds of the yard inclosed [sic] within the walls. . . . There were . . . narrow slits of skylights, three and one-half feet long by perhaps eight inches wide, let in the roof. . . . If you stood in the central room or rotunda, and looked down the long stretches which departed from you in every direction, you had a sense of narrowness and confinement not compatible with their length. The iron doors, with their outer accompaniment of solid wood ones, the latter used at times to shut the prisoner from all sight and sound, were grim and unpleasing to behold. (381)

Next we are told that the prison is, following Bentham's scheme and one of Foucault's primary points of emphasis, "nothing more nor less than solitary confinement for all concerned—a life of absolute silence and separate labor in separate cells" (382). Thus we have the central room that commands a view from above that is powerful enough to foreshorten and make containable to the eye the "sprawling" corridors. We also have the individuation Foucault finds particularly important to institutional forms of discipline: "project the subtle segmentations of discipline onto the confused space of internment, combine it with the methods of analytical distribution proper to power, individualize the excluded, but use procedures of individualization to mark exclusion—this is what was operated regularly by disciplinary power from the beginning of the nineteenth century."[36]

It is the narrator, importantly, who gives the reader the (commanding) view of the prison from the rotunda. While the narrator often disappears into Cowperwood through free indirect speech, it is not the case here. This is important because Cowperwood's imprisonment, just as Bentham would have it, must involve a limiting of the prisoner's vision. We as the readers are seeing something Cowperwood cannot—a view from the tower, a description of the whole. We are not given a scene of Cowperwood looking at the prison as he enters, sizing it up, gaining important knowledge from its architecture— something Cowperwood usually does, and does well enough to understand the power of the personalities contained within it. Instead the narrator reports, in lines worthy of Foucault himself, that: "Life enough there was in all conscience, seeing that there were four hundred prisoners here at that time, and that nearly every cell was occupied; *but it was a life of which no one individual was essentially aware as a spectacle. He was of it; but he was not*" (382, my emphasis). The following scenes show Cowperwood's weakest moments in either book and exemplify beautifully the ways in which control of one's exterior self relies on the ever-shifting "see/being seen dyad."[37]

This weakness is powerfully enacted when Cowperwood is first taken to his cell. During the walk there from the inspection room, he is forced to wear a long hood that "was intended to prevent a sense of location and direction and thereby obviate any attempt to escape. Thereafter during all his stay he was not supposed to walk with or talk to or see another prisoner—not even to converse with his superiors" (388). In Foucault's words: "He is seen, but he does not see; he is the object of information, never a subject in communication."[38] Not being able to see has the effect of taxing Cowperwood to his limit: "He felt strange, very humiliated, very downcast. This simple thing of a blue-and-white striped bag over his head almost cost him his sense of self-possession" (389).

The scenes in which Cowperwood *does* have the ability to see in an institution of discipline that works through the implicit power dynamics of vision are more complicated, and show an interesting negotiation on the part of the author. In this specialized arena, Dreiser attempts to both establish Cowperwood's manliness and challenge it—the effect of which is to naturalize a certain kind of stoic masculinity and at the same time reinforce, again, the importance of incorporation.

When Cowperwood first enters the processing room at the prison, he is made to strip and shower—which, it bears saying, is quite a singular moment for a white upper-class male character in realist fiction at this time. Then, every part of Cowperwood's body is measured, even his teeth inspected, giving us an important fictional account of the turn-of-the-century project of constructing a male body archive through anthropometry (see Chapter One). Interestingly, though Cowperwood stands "naked, but not ashamed" (386) during his inspection, he breaks down when forced to put on the prison uniform:

> He felt and knew of course that he looked very strange, wretched. And as he stepped out into the overseer's room again he experienced a peculiar sense of depression, a gone feeling which before this had not assailed him and which now he did his best to conceal. This, then, was what society did to the criminal, he thought to himself. It took him and tore away from his body and his life the habiliments of his proper state and left him these. He felt sad and grim, and, try as he would, he could not help showing it for a moment. It was always his business and his intention to conceal his real feelings, but now it was not quite possible. He felt degraded, impossible in these clothes, and he knew he looked it. (388)

Not only is the connection between the selfhood of a man and his fashionable clothes once again strongly affirmed here, but Dreiser also highlights Cowperwood's vulnerability to the gaze. It is as he steps into the overseer's office that the feeling of depression assails him. He feels "degraded" because "he knew that he looked it" to those watching. The result is that he cannot control his body—it betrays feelings against his will, making him a spectacle against his will. This is very different from the self-display in the courtroom. Later, when Aileen comes to see him in prison "He felt more poignantly at this moment than ever he had before the degradation of the clog shoes, the cotton shirt, the striped suit" (413). Her seeing him this way, a woman seeing him in this way, "in the face of his *physical* misery," momentarily breaks Cowperwood: it "completely *unmanned* him" and he begins to cry. Importantly, at this moment he cannot look at Aileen: "He drew himself quickly away from her, turned his back, clinched his hands" (413, my emphasis). His vulnerability to the gaze of others, when he cannot meet with his own obscuring "glazed stare," has the potential, then, to take away his sense of manliness.

These scenes, however, must coexist with those in which Cowperwood *can* overcome even the circumstances of prison and regain his manliness, through his eyes. Dreiser, it seems, would have Cowperwood be a person who cannot ultimately, or at least completely, be disciplined. When Desmas, the warden, comes to visit, Cowperwood

> looked at him with large, clear, examining eyes—those eyes that in the past had inspired so much confidence and surety in all those who had known him. Desmas was stirred. . . . Say what you will, one vigorous man inherently respects another. And Desmas was vigorous physically. He eyed Cowperwood and Cowperwood eyed him. Instinctly [sic] Desmas liked him. He was like one tiger looking at another. (398)

In prison, then, Cowperwood is at times extremely vulnerable to the gaze in ways he wasn't when he was free—which is of course the point of disciplinary institutions, as Foucault argues it and many of these scenes enact—with my emphasis on the way in which such disruptions of the stereotypical visual economy upset the linkage between masculinity and power. It is also interesting to note, however, that in a fictional account written during a period in which notions of masculinity were being challenged by long-term cultural changes like the centralization of power and new technologies, Dreiser decides to create a character who can occasionally gain the upper hand in Bentham's Panopticon, an early product of these cultural changes. In doing this, Dreiser also confirms a visual economy that hedges male power. Interestingly, it is only in the presence of

Aileen and the regular prison staff who inspect him that Cowperwood breaks down. With men like Desmas, who have the power to control other men, especially the prison staff, Cowperwood's strength shows itself. In other words, his strength is somehow made manifest with the men who are powerful enough for Cowperwood to want to form a profitable "combination." It is through Desmas that Cowperwood is allowed to "build up some sort of profitable business through Stephen Wingate" (396), a broker who will become Cowperwood's invisible agent while he is in prison. Thus Cowperwood's greatest show of personal male power ("like one tiger looking at another") is with the man with whom it is most imperative to form a partnership.

In some ways, to bend Foucault's reading to the larger issues raised in this chapter, the Panopticon penitentiary could not be a more fitting place for Cowperwood. It embodies the paradox of the two books: it is a kind of combination that works through the *threat* of individuation. Like the new world of market finance, the prison, to use Foucault's words "invests bodies in depth . . . behind the great abstraction of exchange." Further, like the corporation, behind this exchange, "there continues the meticulous, concrete training of useful forces" and "the circuits of communication are the supports of an accumulation and a centralization of knowledge." Moreover, in prison, as in the world that Cowperwood circulates in as a financier, it is the "play of signs [that] defines the anchorages of power." Finally, says Foucault, "it is not that the beautiful totality of the individual is amputated, repressed, altered by our social order"—Cowperwood, can, after all appear a very powerful man, a titan—"it is rather that the individual is carefully fabricated in it, according to a whole technique of forces and bodies."[39] This, of course, is incorporation. Like the market, the great punishment of the Panopticon prison is individuation. Cowperwood's strongest moments as an individual both in prison and in his dealings outside of prison come when he can achieve homo-economic combinations with those men he feels are worthwhile. Thus, the prison reproduces the coupling of individualism and incorporation (which is also, to say, visibility and invisibility) at play in both books.

When his time in the penitentiary is served, Cowperwood takes a moment and at "the entrance of the prison . . . turned and looked back." His lawyer, mystified, asks, "You don't regret leaving that, do you Frank?" To which Cowperwood replies: "I do not. . . . It wasn't that I was thinking of. It was just the appearance of it, that's all" (433). Thus we are given a scene that not only connects a certain kind of totalizing vision with power and freedom, but signals what Foucault describes as one of the great problems of the modern age: "To procure for a small number, or even for one individual, the instantaneous view of a great multitude."[40] The narrator of *The Financier* is all too aware of this problem. At the beginning of Cowperwood's imprisonment, the narrator describes the institution as a place within which the lives of over four hundred people play themselves out but "no one individual" within it "was essentially aware as a spectacle" (382); at the end, Cowperwood attempts somehow to master that denied view on which rests the penitentiary's balance of power. Cowperwood attempts what Foucault might call a sovereign view, but the narrator's line: "he was of it, and he was not" (382), remains true. In the modern urban economy, which is the story here, "the accumulation of men and the accumulation of capital cannot be separated; it would not have been possible to solve the problem of the accumulation of men without the growth of an apparatus of production capable of both sustaining them and using them."[41] The prison is not the only such site of accumulation, as Foucault points out. They are also the networks of men, including Cowperwood, in the market economy. Cowperwood's creation of "apparatuses" [sic] such as street-railways (instead of Foucault's factories, schools and hospitals) both sustains and uses the masses. Cowperwood, then, is never truly outside of the disciplinary "apparatuses" which the market economy—with its secret combinations and proliferating webs of connection and accumulation—make endemic.

## WRITTEN ON THE BODY

So far, then, the books have consistently eroded any strict division between the corporeal and the corporate, the subject and the object, and between subjecthood and objectification. As long as Cowperwood is part of the market economy, and he always is, his subjecthood is constituted for public consumption. His image may be manipulated for his own gain or for the gain of others, but he never loses his status as stock.

Some critics have argued that Dreiser's characterization of Cowperwood in *The Titan* is static—that he becomes so strong that, in the words of numerous critics, he becomes a Nietzschean "superman"[42] who can never lose, never grow, and never change. There *is* a static quality to Cowperwood in *The Titan*, but it is not because Cowperwood suddenly loses some interiority he had in *The Financier*. It is part of Dreiser's point—not about supermen, but about the important role of the economic in the construction of self—that Cowperwood goes through fewer "transformations" once he reaches a certain level of wealth. This is the goal of a monopoly (or any smoothly running "discipline"): to reach a level of control over an entire market so as not to have to worry about disturbances in that market. If the incorporation of self into a combination or monopoly makes for a similar stasis in that individual, we have a phenomenon far more interesting than a superman. The self in *The*

*Titan* has not become any less dependent on the material surroundings that construct the self; he has only learned the lesson of the monopoly. Cowperwood becomes like his street-railways running through the city, seeing everything and making his presence felt through agents and emissaries, like the tentacles of the rail lines themselves:

> And now at last Chicago is really facing the thing which it has most feared. A giant monopoly is really reaching out to enfold it with an octopuslike grip. And Cowperwood is its eyes, its tentacles, its force! Embedded in the giant strength and good will of Haeckelheimer, Gotloeb & Co., [Cowperwood's financial backers] he is like a monument based on a rock of great strength. A fifty-year franchise, to be delivered to him by a majority of forty-eight out of a total of sixty-eight aldermen (in case the ordinance has to be passed over the mayor's veto), is all that now stands between him and the realization of his dreams. (483)

Far from being a description of a superman, the above quotation is, once again, an example of that strange rhetorical mixture of powerful individualism and the power of incorporation. Despite the fact that the language of the quote works to make Cowperwood a supremely powerful, physical figure—the actual "force" of Chicago's transportation system—it is a force only constituted through the "giant strength" of the corporation he has allied himself with (Haeckelheimer, Gotloeb & Co.). Further, he is completely reliant, despite all this, on the forty-eight aldermen he convinced to vote his way. When the land grants are in fact *not* renewed at the end of the novel, Cowperwood himself can no longer be abstracted into the very geography of the city—possibly the ultimate corporation—and the book ends with his departure.

The differences between Aileen's and Cowperwood's bodies are also instructive here in terms of power. Aileen's biggest dream for herself in Chicago is to become part of a specific combination: high society. Her failure is written on her body. Described as "plump" (*T* 35) and with a "swelling form" (38), her boudoir a "veritable riot of silks, satins, laces, lingerie, hair ornaments, perfumes, jewels" which end in a "welter of discarded garments" (37, 38), she is not physically fitted for the society she attempts to enter. She is repeatedly described as *too* beautiful, *too* richly done up—clear marks of the nouveau riche, which Aileen is. She is compared early on to a society woman, Mrs. Rambaud, who in a "simple gray silk" defines Aileen as "other" when she describes her as having an "Orient richness" (40). Further, the narrator comments that Aileen knew nothing of the "serious" side of life (39), but was herself a "vibrating *objet d'art*" (40). As such, she does not have even her husband's somewhat circumscribed capacity to limit her own commodification (40).

Hillel Schwartz's *Never Satisfied: A Cultural History of Diets, Fantasies and Fat* notes that there was, at the turn of the century, a connection being forged between fears of excess in the national economy and fears of excess in/on the individual body. New models in both economics and bodies worked on the principles of "clean, lean, [and] purposeful."[43] Home economists, for example, preached "a willful suppression of abundance,"[44] which included not only material possessions, but food, tobacco, and especially alcohol, which became a sort of cause celebre in some circles. Aileen's undisciplined riotous boudoir with mounds of discarded clothes, her plump body and utter purposelessness as a purely aesthetic object, simply do not fit the new model. As with Cowperwood, Aileen's body is representational—it is, for both of them, the most important signifier—and Dreiser makes us know in no uncertain terms that the self that fails is the physical self. Rejected by society and eventually by her philandering husband, Aileen begins to drink. It appears she can no longer regulate her bodily economy and when, in perhaps the most famous scene of the novel she attacks one of Cowperwood's mistresses, the lack of physical self-regulation is elided with a more totalizing self-regulation.

Cowperwood's body presents a more contradictory picture that plays on gender expectations, *both* male and female. Like his eyes, which show both an intense level of self-control and an excess of sensuousness, his body at certain moments fits in perfectly with the new physical economy and in other moments is the locus of a tremendous excess.

Physical education manuals from the turn of the century show that for the middle and elite classes the efficient and thus controlled body is the slim body, and the athletic-looking body the aesthetic ideal. Cowperwood seems a perfect fit. His eyes, for instance, are not only inscrutable, they are also, "incisive" (*T* 114), and he walks with "rich, sinuous, healthy strides" (10). Significantly, the women Cowperwood comes in contact with are all intensely aware—and appreciative—of his body and bearing. His secretary notes his "good clothes, his remote moods, his easy commanding manner" (122). He is "brisk, dynamic" to Aileen, and "healthy and out-of-doorish, so able" to his first lasting lover, Rita (116). Stephanie Platow (his second) finds his presence "forceful and significant" and admires the fact that he is "always . . . so trigly [sic] dressed, so well put together" (189). And, despite Stephanie's relationship with another man of a more artistic type—who is tellingly pale and anemic—she is intensely drawn to Cowperwood's "strong, solid figure" (220). Indeed, in all Cowperwood's interactions, whether with women or with men, his body is forefronted.

The importance of a positive physical presence is underlined through a comparison that is made between Stephanie Platow's father, who is Jewish, and Cowperwood—a comparison that perhaps reveals the representational power of the body more potently than the repetitive adjectives that characterize the protagonist. Lionel Trilling long ago pointed out Dreiser's anti-Semitism[45] and in the comparison between Cowperwood and Mr. Platow, the "trig" and efficient body becomes a weapon in the service of that anti-Semitism. Through free indirect speech Cowperwood reports that Mr. Platow is "a large, meaty, oily type of man—a kind of ambling, gelatinous formula of the male, with the usual sound commercial instincts of the Jew, but with an errant philosophy which led him to believe first one thing and then another so long as nothing interfered definitely with his business" (187). The Jew's body (and thus the Jew himself) is both disgusting and not to be trusted; not only is it large and thus aesthetically unappealing according to the contemporary standard, but more importantly it is "oily," "ambling" and "gelatinous"—not "solid" like Cowperwood's body. His "gelatinous" body makes his "errant philosophy" inevitable.

Cowperwood's "trig," solid and well put-together body, on the other hand, brings him success with women and, as we have seen with the powerful banker Addison, in business. After Aileen's failure to bring the couple into society, Cowperwood comes increasingly to admire the type of woman whose body fits the mold of the successful society woman—he seeks, in other words, an image to compliment his own self-fashioned image. The first woman Cowperwood has an affair with he meets, significantly, at a department store. She is described as the "type of woman which he was coming to admire. . . . She was a dashing type, essentially smart and trig, with a neat figure, dark hair, an olive skin, small mouth, quaint nose" (104). If Aileen represents a kind of "Orient richness," a woman who is catered to, the new woman is "dashing," showing energy instead of luxury. Where Aileen cannot think on serious matters, this woman is "essentially smart." But perhaps most importantly her thin or "trig" "neat figure" (like Cowperwood's) is in complete contrast to Aileen's riotous, showy, voluptuous body.

Similarly, Rita Sohlberg, with whom Cowperwood has a sustained relationship, is described as having a "sufficiency" about her and is attractively attired in "simple white and blue" (110). She also has youth, which becomes increasingly important to Cowperwood—he even comments to himself at one point that he could see her as his daughter. He also repeatedly calls her naive, which for Cowperwood is more than asserting a male dominance of intellect; youthfulness and naivety also translate into a kind of physical state or attitude in women that Cowperwood admires. Schwartz comments that from "the end of the Civil War . . . to the end of the century, American beauties hovered between adolescence and maturity, between seductively naive and the ambitiously seductive."[46] Cowperwood's lovers after Aileen become increasingly younger and increasingly adept at "hovering" between innocence (an attribute never given to Aileen) and a more mature sexuality. Cowperwood compares Rita briefly to Aileen "when she was six years younger" but notes, significantly, that his wife "had always been more robust, more vigorous, less nebulous" (111).

From the moment we are introduced to Aileen in *The Financier*, her passion for life, sex, clothes and Cowperwood are insistently bold. In the beginning this is what attracts Cowperwood. Lillian, his first wife is referred to as "lymphatic" and passive and Cowperwood is taken with Aileen's obvious spirit. In *The Titan*, however, the women Cowperwood finds attractive are increasingly like Cowperwood himself in their ability to dissemble—to create illusions, which is just how Cowperwood makes his money and carries on his affairs.[47] Cowperwood repeatedly thinks of Rita as "elusive" (114, 115) and is tantalized by it; Stephanie is an actress by profession, and Cowperwood remarks to himself that the "bland way in which she could lie reminded him of himself" (217). With Bernice, Cowperwood's last affair in the book, we meet Aileen's opposite: "You would not have called Bernice Fleming sensuous—though she was—because she was so self-controlled. Her eyes lied to you. They lied to all the world" (321).

Cowperwood's first encounter with Bernice is through a photograph of her when she is only fifteen. He is caught by "a delicately haggard child with a marvelously agreeable smile, a fine, high-poised head upon a thin neck, and an air of bored superiority. Combined with this was a touch of weariness about the eyelids, which drooped in a lofty way. Cowperwood was fascinated. Because of the daughter he professed an interest in the mother, which he really did not feel" (316). A little later Cowperwood discovers another photograph of her, which he buys and hangs in his office. In this one he notes that there was "a faint elusive smile playing dimply around her mouth. The smile was not really a smile, but only a wraith of one, and the eyes were wide, disingenuous, mock-simple" (316). Here then is the ideal—an adolescent girl, whose body thus obviously will not be overabundant, combined with an adult capacity to "seem."

Bernice is all image; it is telling that Cowperwood first falls in love with her picture. When he finally sees her in the flesh for the first time, he remarks that "at first glance . . . she fulfilled all the promise of her picture" (321). And a little later: "Bernice was returning, a subject for an artist in almost studied lines" (323). Bernice is the very definition of the "fetishistic image," though the exchange happens not between two men but between Cowperwood and Bernice's mother, who becomes obsessed with what Bernice—with the right amount of money—could become in society. All three players understand their parts. Bernice never loses her "bored air of superiority," her mother dotes and gets money from Cowperwood, and Cowperwood plays the part of the beneficent benefactor until circumstances allow him to pursue Bernice romantically. What I find interesting here—and this is true to some extent in every one of Cowperwood's longer affairs—is that he too is an object of exchange.

These women, then, to greater and greater degrees, understand in their own way the idea on which both novels operate, the idea on which this new market capital economy operates, on which *both* men and women operate: "illusion—the only reality" (354). Aileen's great fault, it turns out, is that she doesn't understand the difference between what Dreiser calls "naturalism" (63) and illusion. In one of the more obvious narrative intrusions into the text, we are told that Chicago society rests completely on illusion and that "Aileen, urgent and elemental" (64) i.e. natural, fails because she does not understand how to orchestrate, on her body, the illusion of placid control—an image that, again, is just as important to success in market capitalism as it is to success in Chicago society.

But if Cowperwood and increasingly the women he sees fit with the prevailing bodily ideal of the day, which rests on a seeming control of excess, Cowperwood's "trig" body is also the locus of an over-abundant amount of sexual desire and energy. As noted earlier, the number of affairs Cowperwood has in *The Titan* has been a point of complaint since at least 1915, with Stuart Sherman's article for *The Nation*. After him, Matthiessen, Pizer, Gerber— many of the biggest names in Dreiser criticism—have had similar reactions. Not only do they complain that there are too many, they also contend that the sexual and business episodes have nothing to do with each other. There are a great many affairs to be sure—so many, in fact, one tends to lose count—and through their sheer number they become unrelentingly repetitive.

Again most critics take the biographical approach and find all this sex little more than a necessary evil in Dreiser—something the reader has to put up with because the author liked to jump around between women, regardless of his own marital status. I would like to put forth a different argument. The compulsiveness with which Cowperwood has affairs, as well as their seemingly endless repetition needs to be discussed within the logic of the novel itself. I would argue that this seemingly endless repetition of affairs is not gratuitous or merely self-serving. Dreiser's use of repetition does become oppressive, even depressing. But instead of seeing this as simply a fault of an author too preoccupied with challenging the sexual mores of his day, we need to look into what this compulsive behavior says about male sexuality in the economy Dreiser is at such pains to illustrate.

First, we need to establish the fact that Cowperwood is not in control of this physical excess so at odds with the strictly regulated figure he attempts to cut visually. During his affair with Rita we are told that "His feeling for her became at times so great that he wished, one might almost have said, to destroy it—to appease the urge and allay the pull in himself, but it was useless" (119). At another moment we are told that "passion . . . was something which he did not pretend to understand, explain, or moralize about. So *it* was and so *ye* was. He did not want to hurt Aileen's feelings by letting her know that his impulses thus wantonly strayed to others, but it was so" (104). Cowperwood's "nature" becomes "chronically promiscuous" (186). Male control, then, *is* compromised by the new culture of consumerism and extreme acquisitiveness created by industrialism and market capitalism. As much as Cowperwood likes to see himself as a powerful individual, above the average run of man, he typifies the problems unleashed by the new culture of desire. Cowperwood's inability to control his sexual desires is like Carrie's inability to control her own yearning; they both, in their own way, rock back and forth going nowhere, destined to remain unfulfilled.

The paradox of the individual man in the incorporated man also affects the nature of Cowperwood's sexuality. After Aileen finds out about her husband's affairs with Rita and his secretary, she comes to the conclusion that "he would have to go on, and she would have to leave him, if need be; but he could not cease and go back. He was too passionate, too radiant, too *individual* and complex to belong to *one single individual alone*" (230, my emphasis). This quotation both captures Cowperwood's inability to control his physical self on some level and the force of an individualism that, in fact, leads to incorporation. In an economy quickly becoming reliant on proliferating webs of connection, Cowperwood's numerous affairs have logic. They mirror his world of business, which rests not on allegiance to one but combinations with many.

## A DIFFERENT KIND OF SANDWICH

Robert Shulman and more recently Michael Tratner are two critics who make a link between the market economy and Cowperwood's sexual economy, although Shulman gives it limited attention. Both, however, focus on *The Financier* and do not attempt to delve deeply into Dreiser's handling of the juxtaposition between business and sex with specific textual references to *The Titan,* where the sexual episodes become so plentiful.[48] There are, however, so many connections between sexual and business episodes in the second book that it is important to move beyond noting the narrative technique of "juxtaposition" which connects them and look at the actual textual mirroring being crafted.

For example, looking again at Cowperwood's first extra-marital affair in *The Titan*, two things are important: the woman is not given a name, but is referred to as a "type" (104), and they meet in a department store. In referring to the woman as a type, Cowperwood is using the same technique he uses to size up his business partners and enemies. It is, in fact, Cowperwood's ability to understand correctly or name the type of man with whom he is dealing that makes him so successful. When picking a partner to do his trading for him, for instance, Cowperwood chooses a man by the name of Peter Laughlin. No one understands the choice—Laughlin is neither young nor particularly successful. But to Cowperwood he is "a typical Chicago Board of Trade operator of the old school, having an Andrew Jacksonish countenance, and a Henry Clay-Davy Crockett—'Long John' Wentworth build of body. . . . Cowperwood could tell from looking at him that he must have a fund of information concerning every current Chicagoan of importance" (26). Thus, just as the woman represents "a type . . . which he was coming to admire" (104), Laughlin is described as one of a kind of "quaint characters" that Cowperwood "had curious interest in" (26).

Once again, Cowperwood's eyes are an important source of information; they provide a good example of the association being forged between business and sex. Early in *The Titan* the narrator describes Cowperwood's eyes as "alluring alike to men and to women in all walks and conditions of life" (14). Cowperwood uses his eyes in the seduction of both his first lover and his first partner. The woman in the department store has "a curious look of current wisdom in her eyes, an air of saucy insolence which aroused Cowperwood's sense of mastery, his desire to dominate. To the look of provocation and defiance which she flung at him for a fraction of a second," Cowperwood "returned a curiously leonine glare which went over her like a dash of cold water. It was not a hard look, however, merely urgent and full of meaning" (104). When attempting to get Laughlin to work for him—a man who is also described as seeming to possess a great store of wisdom when it comes to the workings of Chicago life—we are told that "Cowperwood had a way, when he wanted to be pleasant, of beating the fingers of his two hands together, finger for finger, tip for tip. He also smiled at the same time—or rather beamed—his eyes glowing with a warm magnetic seemingly affectionate light" (28). In both scenes Cowperwood uses his eyes in an alluring way. Undoubtedly, both business and sexual acquisition for Cowperwood are the manifestation of his male vitality. What is interesting here is that he uses it on both men and women, for both business and sex.

Cowperwood's success in business also rests as I have argued on his self-presentation with a particular, almost fetishistic interest in his clothes. The fact, then, that he meets his first lover in a department store while shopping for a tie is striking. As we have seen, image, or what Dreiser refers to as "illusion," is increasingly important to both Cowperwood and, with each successive affair, the women he sees. Image is produced through the commodities available at the department store—indeed, it is the epicenter of capitalism's ability to create desire, a fact *Sister Carrie* shows Dreiser very much alive to. Thus the desire to create a particular image in business and the desire for a woman who embodies "quite a figure for Chicago at the time" (104) are thrown together here, between the aisles of ties and the laces the woman examines. One could certainly argue that placing the "dashing" woman in a department store simply underlines her commodification. It does. But Cowperwood is shopping too and in the series of glances they throw at one another—sizing each other up just as one does ties or laces—they are both commodified.

Finally, Cowperwood's approach to manipulating companies bears a striking resemblance to his approach to conducting his extra-marital affairs. Cowperwood's incorporation of the various gas companies of Chicago and his seduction of Rita Sohlberg, for example, are both achieved through what we might today call a hostile takeover. In bulldozing through the traditional set-up of the numerous gas companies he attempts to consolidate and then sell off at a profit, Cowperwood makes an enemy of one of the most powerful businessmen in Chicago, Norman Schryhart. Schryhart, unused to being backed into a corner and having to cede to Cowperwood's demands, remarks on "What a shrewd, quick, forceful move he [Cowperwood] had made" (94). In the end, Schryhart decides that it is better to take Cowperwood "at his suggestion, raise the money and buy him out, even at an exorbitant figure" (94). Similarly, with Rita Sohlberg, Cowperwood's seduction is written in the language of a takeover, which, like Schryhart, will corner her into accepting his demands: "Beset by his mood, she was having the devil's own time with her conscience. Not that anything had been said as yet, but he was investing her, gradually beleaguering her, sealing up, apparently, one avenue after another of escape" (113). The use of the phrase "investing her" is a telling one, importing the language of market capitalism used in the business world into his romantic acquisition. In the end, Cowperwood's investment of time and energy in the gas company turns out to be "a most profitable deal" (94); the Rita investment also yields valuable returns: "Cowperwood was trained by Rita into a really finer point of view. He came to know better music, books, even the facts" (121). *All* of Cowperwood's investments are, in one way or another, remunerative.

Since Dreiser's consciousness as an artist is often questioned, it is important to show that the twinning of business and sex under the rubric of market capitalism is indeed intentional. Two issues are important here. The first is that while Dreiser followed the life of Cowperwood's model, Charles Yerkes, quite faithfully for the most part, he made one significant change. The lover that Yerkes took while still in Philadelphia was not, in fact, the daughter of one of the men that he worked for as an invisible agent in the market. The woman known as Aileen in both books was actually the daughter of a chemist—a woman, in other words, who had nothing to do with Yerkes business career. Dreiser's model is continued in *The Titan*. Cowperwood has at least three affairs with women who are, either through their husbands or their position as employees, intimately bound with the business partnerships and scandals that take place in the novel. This in and of itself makes it impossible for romance to exist in a world outside business.

The other issue that serves to connect sex with business is that quality which Dreiser makes fundamental to Cowperwood's character: generalized compulsive acquisition, which I have argued is unleashed by market capitalism and its infinite ability to create desire. Few have noted the fact that Cowperwood collects and changes male business partners as much as he does women—and often with the same searching rapidity. Indeed, it is Dreiser's narrator himself who, quite explicitly, makes this important connection: "Truth to say, he must always have youth, the illusion of beauty, vanity in womanhood, the novelty of a new untested temperament, *quite as he must have* pictures, old porcelain, music, a mansion, illuminated missals, power, the applause of the great, unthinking world" (*T* 186, my emphasis). That consumer culture affects white male sexuality is rarely discussed—even by those critics who see connections between Cowperwood's life in business and in the bedroom. The desires unleashed by the new consumer-oriented economy may indeed make women into commodities—as the quote makes clear—but it also makes Cowperwood its slave, and at times, through incorporation, as vulnerable to commodification as women. Through the economy Cowperwood has a hand in building, sexual compulsion becomes part of a larger production of selfhood that is completely reliant on the making of *multiple* "significant combination[s]" (*F* 93).

## CONSPICUOUS MASCULINITY

I have traced here the ways in which the new market economy makes the male body more important. It becomes a crucial part of the exchange in a world where the production of wealth has become more abstracted. That abstraction, or to use Dreiser's term for what Cowperwood most often does with stock, that "hypothecation," necessitates a marker, a placeholder, an embodiment of power. Most of Cowperwood's work is intangible, behind-the-scenes manipulations of stock in the first book and political deals for land grants in the second. The outcome of that work does produce tangible things such as street-railways. But due to the level of abstraction in the work, it must also produce a new male self as an embodiment of that work and the power it yields. Try as he might, Cowperwood cannot, in fact, become his streetcars. He can, however, produce a self that will attract the right kind of partners, like Addison, and the right kind of women, like Bernice, who Cowperwood thinks is "perhaps . . . the true society woman, the high-born lady, the realization of that ideal which . . . many another grande dame has suggested" (317). In order to attract these people he must sell himself, and like any successful adventurer in this new economy—Carrie Meeber, for instance—he does it well and completely.

Still, if there is one thing that Cowperwood knows it is that individuation "in an economy of fluctuating, or failing fortunes"[49] is dangerous. It makes one vulnerable to the vicissitudes of that economy. Security is achieved through monopoly and more often than not, Cowperwood's business transactions (as well as his affairs) are designed to leave no trace of an individual self. But again, this is a time of transition and Cowperwood wrestles with himself over the efficacy of combination, the hypothecation of self and the will to individualism:

> How was it, he asked himself, that his path had almost constantly been strewn with stormy opposition and threatening calamity? Was it due to his private immorality? Other men were immoral; the mass, despite religious dogma and folderol theory imposed from the top, was generally so. Was it not rather due to his inability to control without dominating personally—without standing out fully and clearly in the sight of all men? (*T* 397–8)

In this way, Dreiser dramatizes how the new economy problematizes one of the most common routes to establishing one's manhood: standing out among men as a powerful individual.

What this chapter has tried to sort out, then, is the paradox the books present in the abstraction of male selfhood into combinations and the resulting importance of the male body. In an increasingly abstract market economy Cowperwood exists as a marker, which orients our attention to his body and his expert use of commodities, and can lead to his commodification, intentional (and to his own advantage) or not. Businessmen know his easy grace will make them money and women fixate on how "trigly dressed" and "well put together" (*T* 189) he is. While the chapter has also tracked Cowperwood's methods of deflecting his own commodification, it is, in the end, the only tangible thing he has to bank on. But, again, he is not banking on selfhood as it is conventionally understood, he is banking on his physical presence—on what that presence communicates to those around him. It is a "magnetism" that is created *not* by the force of his character as much as the commodities he attaches that self to. In breaking with Cowperwood after being attacked by Aileen, Rita squarely confirms this: "His charm for her had, perhaps, consisted mostly in the atmosphere of flawless security which seemed to surround him—a glittering bubble of romance. That, by one fell attack, was now burst" (155). What Cowperwood produces, then, is much like what Carrie produces on stage for the old men who come to watch her. They both sell a subjectivity that is not, in the traditional sense, real or stable.

Not only does Dreiser make clear here that there *is* such a thing as male self-production through the use of commodities, he also makes permeable the line between producer and commodity. The argument, then, that the new consumer and economic culture organized itself through the establishment of "new gender polarities that align femininity with the display and consumption of commodities" is simply not tenable in these books.[50] And, just as importantly, the books make clear that the impossibility of this position is not only or simply due to the *results* of mass production (the commodities that so often elide women with conspicuous consumption) but is endemic to the whole organization of production, which rests on a new form of capitalism that effectively captures men in its irrepressible web. For those who wish to be successful in this economy, visibility must be heightened while individualism is incorporated, and the body must remain solidly in view as the self gets abstracted into an intangible market of ceaseless exchange.

The Cowperwood books are an instructive look into the negotiation of male power in a time of great change. The novels undoubtedly attempt to preserve male power, but in the face of new cultural and economic logics, Dreiser must contend with the creation of new spaces and problems that make permeable strictly dichotomous gender roles. It has been argued that women, and especially women's bodies, are "always a point of trouble for the classic tradition of realist writing."[51] But clearly, these books posit the male body as problematic, negotiable and, at times, troubling.[52] The novels considered here produce knowledge not through the male mind, or even, generally, the male view, but through the male body. In realism's invitation "above all to *look* at the world,"[53] the realist writer is hard put to escape the inclusion of men as objects of its gaze, and the male body in the new consumer economy cannot be a stable point of reference. As Walter Benjamin argued of the flaneur, the position of the male observer teeters on the edge of incorporation into the scenes he witnesses. He eventually falls and becomes part of that scene, part of a spectacle that he has had the responsible hand in producing as a commodity.

**Figure 1** "Bowling" from *Health, Strength and Power* by Dudley Sargent A. Sargent (New York: H. M. Caldwell Co., 1904).

**Figure 2** "Once an Invalid—Now a Hercules" *Physical Culture* Vol. 2, No. 2 (November, 1899).

**Figure 3** Advertisement for *The Athlete's Conquest. Physical Culture* Vol. 1, No 7 (September, 1899).

**Figure 4** From *Manual for Physical Measurements* by Luther Gulick (New York: The International Committee of Young Men's Christian Associations, 1892).

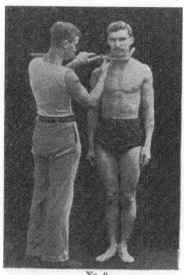

No. 9.

**Figure 5** From *Manual for Physical Measurements* by Luther Gulick (New York: The International Committee of Young Men's Christian Associations, 1892).

**Figure 6** "Measurement of Skull (Full Face)" by Alphonse Bertillon. Archives Historiques et Musee de la Prefecture de Police, Paris (No date).

Chapter Three

# Male Hysteria and the Gendering of the Subconscious

At the same time Theodore Dreiser was creating his robust and tireless capitalist Frank Cowperwood, he was also writing an autobiographical novel entitled *The 'Genius.'* At first glance the two works seem to have little in common. In the Cowperwood books, the male body is defined through the fruits of financial success and its commodification in an astonishingly powerful consumer culture. Cowperwood is a man of great energy and force, and the books record how smoothly that force is incorporated into the logic of a vigorous market capitalism. Eugene Witla, the protagonist of *The 'Genius,'* on the other hand, spends the majority of his time obsessed with his own weakened mental and physical condition. He is usually in a state of indecision, unable to sustain one career or one relationship. He is nervous, unsure, fearful, depleted of energy and unable to participate in any successful economic or social exchange.

Despite such obvious differences between Eugene Witla and Cowperwood, if we look at them in the context of turn-of-the-century anxieties about new definitions of masculinity, especially male energy, strength and the capacity to adjust successfully to a more explicitly competitive cultural environment (both physically and financially), they have a great deal to do with one another. The same anxieties about modern masculinity produced both Cowperwood's almost mythic vigor and sexual prowess, and Eugene's seemingly inexorable tendency toward morbidity. Near the end of *The 'Genius,'* Eugene attempts to explore this tendency. He searches the work of a variety of mind-curists, medical doctors, psychologists, mystics and philosophers, both American and European. Eugene's search reveals the stunningly wide range of discourses that converged around the educated male suffering from nervous disorders at the turn of the last century.

Nervous disorders in the late nineteenth and early twentieth centuries were treated by a wide variety of doctors and lay healers with different understandings of both the causes and optimum cures for nervousness. Eric Caplan has recently traced the growth of psychotherapy in the United States in the late nineteenth and early twentieth centuries through the treatments of such nervous diseases as railway spine and through grass roots movements like New Thought, Christian Science and the Emmanuel movement.[1] Nervous disorders like railway spine, hysteria and neurasthenia, along with alternative approaches to treatment, worked to loosen the hold of the somatic paradigm on nervous disorders, forcing in the medical profession a recognition of the mind's power to transform, or at least impact, the body. As Eugene Witla's case demonstrates, male nervousness in particular became a widespread problem.[2] While in the eyes of the medical profession, women had always been prone to nervousness, many neurologists of the late nineteenth century blamed the fast pace of industrial culture for making men newly vulnerable. According to Lisa Cardyn, this was especially true of nervous conditions, like hysteria, that were brought on by a shock or trauma occurring during work or travel. In reviewing published writings on traumatic nervousness, Cardyn argues that given "the prevailing view that these conditions were a function of modernity, along with the fact of men's continued predominance in the social arenas most susceptible to rapid change, it is not surprising to find in this literature a decidedly masculinist cast. Although cases of traumatic nervous illness in women were frequently detected, late Victorian medicine constructed the typical sufferer as male."[3]

Men's vulnerability to nervousness, in fact, did much to shape the characterization and treatment of nervous disorders generally at the turn of the century. For some, like Pierre Janet, new and more "scientific" treatments and approaches to nervousness rested on the "discovery" of male hysteria. Male nervousness, I will argue, was also responsible for the adoption of nervous symptoms and disorders to explain mental functioning itself and, specifically, to explain the power of the mind to heal. I explore first how nervous disorders, especially neurasthenia and hysteria, influenced the construction of a subconscious or alternate stratum of the mind with unique powers. I then look at the ways the writings of William James and his colleagues in psychical research, especially Frederick Myers, gender this subconscious. In their hands, hysteria becomes the agent in defining the subconscious as a primitive, vital self, unscarred by the feminizing effects of civilization. As such, it located in men—white, intellectual men in particular—a strenuous, curative masculinity.

William James was somewhat ahead of his time, through certainly not alone, in his willingness to look beyond the somatic paradigm in attempting to understand the cause of nervous disorders. But his use of nervous symptoms to characterize the subconscious was not a complete turn from the body, or, as some of his contemporaries might have argued, a turn from science. Indeed, as Jill Kress has recently pointed out in *The Figure of Consciousness*, with "the advent of Charles Darwin's theory of evolution, the exploration of the notion of consciousness became a portion of scientific study rather than the exclusive realm of philosopher." In fact, Darwin insisted that "the mental structures, though they vary according to species, are subject to the same evolutionary nudges as corporeal structures."[4]

For the majority of those within the medical profession, however, nervous disorders, from neurasthenia to hysteria, were understood to have strictly somatic or organic causes.[5] To understand them any other way was to wander into the realm of metaphysics, or worse, spiritualism. For these doctors, nervous illness fell into the category of "functional disorder," meaning that the cause was unknown or rather could not be seen through a microscope. This left a great deal of room for neurologists and surgeons to guess at lesions, minute fractures or concussions of the spinal column as well as a variety of chemical and structural changes in the brain. Caplan has argued that doctors stuck to the somatic paradigm when approaching nervous disorders primarily to maintain their professional status and their authority as scientists. Nonetheless, their attachment to the somatic paradigm in no way prevented neurologists and surgeons from devoting "an unprecedented amount of attention to the psychical symptoms of those for whom there existed no clearly discernible anatomical or organic irregularities."[6] Usually, however, they insisted on cures aimed exclusively at the body, rarely doubting the efficacy of physical treatments. The most popular somatic cures included water, diet and rest cures, electricity and exercise regimens.

One of the first challenges to the somatic explanation of nervousness came out of discussions of the condition known as railway spine. Both surgeons and neurologists treating and writing on this condition in England, France and the United States did much to advance thinking on the possible psychical origins of nervousness, especially male nervousness. Railway spine referred to a disorder in which seemingly uninjured victims of railway accidents, a high proportion of which were men, developed a wide array of physical problems. The condition was first considered to have a physical, though undetectable origin. It was popularized by a British surgeon, John Eric Erichsen, who published the first book on the disease in 1866. He argued that the spine, like the brain, was susceptible to unobservable injuries that caused "'molecular changes' in the spinal cord and gave rise to a wide variety of subjective symptoms."[7] Railway spine was then, according to Erichson a "concussion of the spine"[8] that led to a laundry list of symptoms that would come to bear a striking resemblance to both George Beard's slightly later formulation of neurasthenia in the United States and Jean-Martin Charcot's characterization of male hysterics in France during the 1880s. Symptoms included loss of feeling in limbs, impaired and/or heightened senses, insomnia, and extreme feelings of heat or cold. As Ralph Harrington makes clear, Erichson himself emphasized the *psychological* effects of the disorder and conceded "that there might be a direct connection between the psychological experiences of railway accident victims and their disorder."[9] Indeed, while Erichson never stopped believing in the somatic or organic cause of railways spine, he did come to accept that "a purely psychological influence, in the form of fright" was a "causative agent" in railway spine.[10] As the first author of a book-length treatise on railway spine, Erichson had a strong and lasting impact on medico-legal debates. Indeed, lawyers used Erichson's theories repeatedly in litigation against the railway companies and juries throughout the 1870s awarded heavy damages to victims of railway spine.[11]

By the 1880s, railway surgeons and neurologists began to openly question the validity of a somatic cause of railways spine. One of the first to do this was a Boston surgeon by the name of Richard Hodges whose 1881 article argued that the condition of railway spine was not unique to railway accidents and suggested that traumatic accidents of any kind could result in the symptoms of railway spine. More to the point for those interested in the medico-legal debate, he argued that the reason the symptoms of railway accident victims persisted was due to the litigation proceedings against railway companies and the promise of pecuniary rewards.[12] Two years later, a British surgeon, Herbert W. Page published *Injuries of the Spine and Spinal Cord Without Apparent Mechanical Lesion and Nervous Shock in their Surgical and Medico-Legal Aspect,* in which he argued that nervous shock was responsible for the physical disorders collectively known as railway spine. Page's ideas, along with those of Harvard neurologist James Jackson Putnam, who "regarded the possibility that psychic agency alone might produce the hysterical symptoms associated with railway accidents as highly probably"[13] influenced the work of the man most responsible for institutionalizing male hysteria: Charcot. While Charcot did not himself challenge the somatic origin of hysteria, he did link a psychical trauma to *male* hysterical, specifically.

## MALE HYSTERIA AND THE IDEA OF THE SUBCONSCIOUS

The diagnosis of male hysteria was a crucial one. Not, as it turns out, because it challenged traditional gender roles or belief in the male subject's inherent rationalism. It did neither. Male hysteria did however make possible a re-evaluation of hysterical symptomology. This, in turn, legitimized the use of hysteria in studies of the subconscious. But how did a disease closely associated with women become so influential in the construction of a subconscious gendered male? This had much to do with the specific studies about hysteria carried out at the turn of the century.

The acceptance of the idea of male hysteria at the turn of the century is hard to gauge, especially in the United States. Certainly hysteria was not a term often used in relation to men in America. At the same time, there are an astonishing number of similarities between neurasthenic symptoms, which such a large number of American men were treated for, and what were known in Europe as hysterical symptoms. There was also a certain degree of overlap between the two terms in the literature on neurasthenia in the United States. But while neurasthenic patients were often referred to, in passing, as hysterical, an hysteric, or showing signs of hystereoneurasthenia or hystereoepilepsy, female patients were given these labels far more often than their male counterparts.[14] Further, despite an interesting period in France when male hysteria was considered one of the most cutting edge questions in the study of nervous disorders, the historian Mark Micale, who has written extensively on male hysteria, observes that the diagnosis never "decisively entered the cumulative canon of established medical knowledge."[15] Finally, while some dissertations and articles on hysteria coming out of France in the late 1880s and 1890s put the ratio of hysteria in women to men as low as 5 to 1, the 1910 edition of the *Encyclopedia Britannica* concludes that hysteria: "is much more common in the female than the male—in proportion of 20 to 1."[16]

While several doctors in the mid-nineteenth century remarked on possible stray cases of hysteria in males, including some military surgeons during the American Civil War who reported on hysterical symptoms in soldiers,[17] the first *sustained* study of male hysteria was undertaken by Charcot during the 1880s. Again, like many American neurologists studying nervous disorders at the same time, Charcot believed hysteria was caused by a lesion located on the brain or along the spinal cord which could manifest itself in symptoms throughout the body. This idea, which releases the anatomical seat of the disease from a woman's uterus, is an important condition for its possibility in men. It was, according to Micale, Charcot's fight to disprove "the old genital mythology" that initially led him to take up the idea of male hysteria. Also, unlike many of his colleagues, Charcot shied away from including sexual behavior in his list of primary hysteric symptoms. This is an important change in the characterization of the hysteric. The mid–nineteenth-century hysteric, while no longer considered a witch, was still, according to William James, seen "as a victim of sexual trouble," a person of "moral perversity and mediocrity" or, at best, someone who was indulging in purely imaginary disorders.[18] Charcot argued differently. Importantly, he rejected both the link between hysteria and "sexual continence" as well as "the more recent Victorian image of the hyper-erotic hysteric." When questions of sexual behavior did come up in discussions of male or female hysterics Charcot never considered them primary causes, but secondary "provoking issues."[19]

In freeing the disease from many of the myths that had accumulated around the idea of the wandering womb and the sexually unsatisfied or, alternatively, sexually overindulgent woman, Charcot not only greatly expanded the diagnostic possibilities of hysteria, but more importantly, made an implicit connection between male hysteric subjects and a more scientific approach to the study of the disease. Pierre Janet makes this crucial connection explicit. In his Harvard lectures he discusses the myth of the wandering womb and then argues that as "hysteria required an uterus, its existence was not admitted in men, and *the first serious discussions bore on the existence of masculine hysteria. The recognition of this disease in men changed the old conception of hysteria and determined an ensemble of more precise clinical researches.*"[20]

One of the most fascinating aspects of Charcot's work, and one that would have important consequences for some of hysteria's enduring symptomologies, is that it did not attempt a "masculinization of the hysterical concept" itself.[21] Like many doctors treating nervous disorders, Charcot was interested in all the "morbid phenomena" that repeated, especially "motor impairments and sensory derangements."[22] He did not, however, alter their character to include distinctive data from his male cases. For instance, one of the oldest symptoms of hysteria is "acute ovarian discomfort."[23] Given the ancient connection between hysteria and a woman's reproductive system, this is not surprising. What is surprising is that Charcot applied the same idea, which, crucially, he considered a symptom and not a cause, to his male patients. One way to determine hysteria in men, according to Charcot, was to palpitate points on their abdomen where women's ovaries would be; tenderness there would suggest hysteria.

The great majority of Charcot's male patients were from the working class. While nervous disease ultimately spread to all classes in the United States, the working class was not considered at risk until after the beginning of the twentieth century. With the exception of class, however, there are a great many similarities between diagnosed male hysterics in France and male neurasthenics in America, especially when it comes to symptoms. Charcot's male patients and American male sufferers overlap in a large majority of complaints, such as: insomnia, pallor, loss of appetite, unspecified fears, and somatic symptoms, like numbness or periodic paralysis in extremities, total loss of sensation in certain parts of the body or, alternatively, hypersensitivity to stimuli of any kind, loss of voice, contractions of the visual field, diffuse sweating, headaches, ringing in the ears or hyper-sensitivity to sounds, chest palpitations, increased sweating, an array of digestive disorders and upper respiratory problems. Most importantly, both neurasthenia and hysteria were disorders in which the body's ability to simulate an organic disease was a primary feature. The only common symptom in Charcot's hysterics that appears very rarely in the literature on American males with neurasthenia is intense convulsions or what Charcot would call a "violent paroxysm" (42).[24] Interestingly, this hysterical fit or convulsion, made so famous by Charcot's female patients and, according to him, found in both men and women, is dismissed by Janet almost immediately. I would argue that while Charcot, for a whole host of reasons, which must have included the desire not to contradict himself, applied the same symptomology across gender lines, the unseemly nature of this particular symptom, which compelled the complete loss of bodily control, could not survive long in a disease to which men were now vulnerable. Other kinds of somatic manifestations, however, would remain very important—even as the disease itself was increasingly understood as having a mental, as opposed to physical, origin.

While hysterics and neurasthenics tend to share a lot of symptoms, the causes and/or precipitating events of nervous disorders have important differences, some of which rest on sharp gender distinctions. For female sufferers in the United States diagnosed with either neurasthenia or hysteria, heredity was believed to play a bigger role than it did for men. Heredity counts for more in women because biology counts for more. In *Before Freud: Neurasthenia and the American Medical Community, 1870–1910,* F.G. Gosling argues that the "higher incidence of nervous heredity discovered in women was undoubtedly due to physicians' common belief that women were biologically predisposed to nervousness" (46). This is not to say, however, that heredity did not factor in at all for men. But here we run into national differences as well. Heredity is a highly significant part of discussions of nervous illness until at least 1910, but always more intensely for women *and* men in Europe; it forms the basis for all the more dire predictions of degeneration that swirl around nervous illness. Even though some American doctors talked about race suicide and degeneration in their work on neurasthenia, most were less willing to give heredity as much power over their male patients as European doctors.

While doctors like Charcot felt strongly about the impact of heredity regardless of gender, other issues of bodily predisposition and precipitating events were as gendered in France as they were in the United States. For most men in the United States and France, the workplace was crucial. For Charcot's working-class male patients, hysteria was usually thought to be brought on by bodily overexertion or an accident at work, i.e. a traumatic accident.[25] For American men of the middle and upper classes, nervous illness was also most often a result of work-related traumas, in the form of psychical shocks, exposure to dangerous levels of over-stimulation and/or mental over-exertion. The only men for whom the workplace did not supply the precipitating event were American working-class men—a good indicator of the low value elite classes placed on the worth and possible dangers of their work. Most health problems among working-class men in the United States were thought to be the result of over-indulgence in a substance (frequently alcohol) or in sex.[26]

In discussing their female patients, on the other hand, American and European doctors were far more likely to talk of "emotional disturbances" such as romantic rejection or the loss of a child as the precipitating event. Generally, though, women did not need much of anything to "set off" their nervous disorder: "Women were susceptible to the disease because of their natural fragility and hypersensitivity." There was an "explicit understanding that women's natural, healthy state differed not in kind, but only in degree, from their diseased state."[27] Indeed, many doctors in the United States were so invested in seeing female nervousness as inherent that they often failed to look into precipitating causes at all.[28]

One of the most important differences between American and French conceptions of nervous disorders in men turns out not to be their symptoms, then, but ideas about cures, a subject on which Charcot had very little to say. According to Micale, the most striking thing about Charcot when it came to the subject of positive cures was his silence. He mentions hydrotherapy, electrotherapy and hypnotism, which Janet and the French School of Nancy would take up more enthusiastically, but little else. His major impact on cures in Europe stemmed from his career-long battle against almost any form of surgical intervention. This in particular was a boon for women. American doctors, on the other hand, had a far more optimistic view on the treatment of nervous disorders. There are, of course, the famous rest cures of S. Weir Mitchell, but there was also a great deal of faith placed in changes in diet, new habits of rest and exercise, and prolonged travel. Finally, much stress was placed on the will, which was discussed by everyone, from neurologists to general practitioners and philosophers like William James.

Cures bring up a great many issues. Anita and Michael Fellman argue that a "thread of 'hygienic utopianism,' of belief in moral and social perfection through reform of the body" runs through, and is specific to, American culture.[29] Because doctors in the United States did not place much emphasis on hereditary dispositions to nervous disorders in men, hygiene is an especially important element in the connections made between masculinity, self-control and health. The emphasis on mental and physical hygiene (along with various other lifestyle changes) found in so many popular books on nervous disorders, like J. H. Kellogg's *Neurasthenia or Nervous Exhaustion,* not only frees men up to try a myriad of cures but also implies that their powers of self-control have not been permanently or completely destroyed by nervous illness. Cures, in fact, were often platforms for expressing manliness. For instance, one of the most popular cures for nervous illness placed sickly urban men in explicitly masculine cultures in the "untamed" (and "unspoiled") West. Owen Wister, Theodore Roosevelt and Thomas Eakins are among the many white men from elite classes who made prolonged visits to ranches in the western part of the United States.

Ideas about hygiene, however, should not be understood to be completely free of hereditary determinism. Despite many books which promised health to anyone who adopted the author's hygienic rituals for diet, wardrobe, baths, rest and exercise, notions of how to practice hygiene were easily adopted for use in racial discourses. An American work on neurasthenia, for instance, discusses hygiene as a way to battle the hereditary taint, not through dietary measures or exercise but through putting into effect "legislative measures" to insure what the author calls "sanitary marriages."[30] As late as 1910, when the psychological origin of hysteria had been fairly popularized by Janet among others, an English neurologist wrote for the *Encyclopedia Britannica* that certain "races are more liable to the disease than others; thus the Latin races are much more prone to hysteria than are those who come from a Teutonic stock," and, like women, "in more aggravated and complex forms." The writer also notes that in "England it has been asserted than an undue proportion of cases occur among Jews."[31]

Charcot's ideas were widely disseminated throughout Europe and the United States. Several American doctors went to Paris to study with him, including, early on, George Beard; far more read articles produced by his disciples.[32] The negotiations that American doctors made to accommodate Charcot's ideas about male hysteria are interesting and telling. For instance, Dr. Albert Abrams, who suggested the "sanitary marriages," constructed, in the same book, a specific kind of neurasthenia called Splanchnic Neurasthenia, which occurred in men. It shared common symptoms with hysteria and was discernable through the same abdominal palpitations Charcot used on both male and female hysterics. As Janet himself noted, then, American neurologists and psychologists often simply adopted Charcot's symptoms without calling them hysterical. And while Charcot's ideas on the organic causes of hysteria lost their currency, his "demystification" of the disease through his work with *male patients* paved the way for hysteria to play a crucial part in theories of the unconscious coming out of Europe and the United States.

In France the study of hysteria was carried on most famously by Janet, whose development of pathological psychology centered itself around his work with hysterics. In England, hysteria played a major role in explanations of supernatural phenomena explored by the Society for Psychical Research. This is especially true in the work of one of its founding members, Frederick Myers, whose theory of a subliminal stratum of consciousness, lying beneath the ordinary threshold of consciousness, was based on the capabilities of hysterics while in dissociated states. In America, William James's work on hysteria helped him orient his study of psychology around the idea of consciousness as a "plurality of states"[33] and provided specific cases from which to pursue his interest in issues of the mind-body connection. Most importantly, all three men re-evaluated hysteria's symptomologies, transforming them, in many cases, from morbid or debilitating defects to the extraordinary powers found in alternate forms of consciousness.

## NEW APPROACHES TO NERVOUS ILLNESS

There are important parallels between the changes initiated by the possibility of male hysteria and late nineteenth-century transformations in psychical research—both of which would have a significant impact on the turn toward psychological explanations of nervousness. As we have seen with hysteria, male patients brought with them a certain level of scientific acceptance. At a crucial moment in the medical profession male hysteria worked as a validating force and helped to legitimize experimental or abnormal psychology. A similar argument can be made for studies in psychical research, the new, more scientifically valid way of studying spiritualism and supernatural phenomena. Until the last decades of the nineteenth century, spiritualism—like hysteria—was largely connected with women. Mediumship, the form spiritualism usually took before 1880, centered on invisible forces that spoke primarily through young women. Often their "controls," that is, the spirits they spoke through, were men. Importantly, however, they were dead men. Ann Braude argues in her book, *Radical Spirits,* that this form of spiritualism provided a platform from which many women found an opportunity to speak on a variety of reform issues, such as female dress code, abolition, and women's suffrage.[34] Interestingly, many mediums had neurasthenic illnesses prior to the discovery of their power. All of this changed in the 1880s with the creation of the Society for Psychical Research (SPR), first in England in 1882 and soon after in America in 1885. The Society was, with one exception, a group of male scientists who were dedicated to applying scientific approaches to unexplained phenomena. The female mystic was soon displaced in favor of clinical studies on telepathy, automatic drawing and hallucinations—and the number of male subjects jumped dramatically.[35] In the end, mediumship did not disappear altogether, but it was greatly transformed by the presence of male "researchers" who, very much alive, placed all sorts of test controls on their female subjects.

These changes were, in part, a result of controversies surrounding the study of nervous disorders that took place a decade earlier when neurologists were attempting to carve out a place for their own practices. Several American doctors in the 1870s, Beard among them, announced that those who practiced spiritualism were suffering from a disease called "medio-mania."[36] Much like later incarnations of nervous disorders, the etiology was both physical and hereditary, and the symptoms mirrored those common in hysteria. But at this time neurologists defined themselves and their practices by criticizing the approach of psychological medicine; and their attacks on psychological medicine mirrored their attack on spiritualism. Neurologists argued that, like spiritists, psychiatric doctors lacked an "empirical method," the right skeptical attitude and experimental approach.[37] The SPR, which was made up of many psychologists, including William James, was certainly a response to these criticisms.

The success of the SPR, I want to argue, was predicated in part on the male hysteric subject. The Society imported current ideas about hysteria from France, something they would not have done without Charcot's rehabilitation of the disease through his work with male patients, and used them as proof of the existence of another stratum of consciousness unlike our normal, everyday consciousness. This alternate stratum became crucial to explanations of psychic phenomena. Importantly for psychical researchers, this stratum was considered morbid only in some cases and the gateway to the supernatural in others. This subconscious was also, as we shall see, a highly gender-inflected concept.

The use of hysterics as subjects for psychical research shifted the character of psychic phenomena. Telepathy and hallucinations, which became more common in the literature of spiritualism at the end of the nineteenth century, placed more emphasis on phenomena that could be explained through modes of consciousness rather than the actual presence of a spirit. Or, to put it another way, the new supernatural experience existed more as an extension of the individual as opposed to a force originating outside that individual. This type of phenomena is clearly more suitable for the autonomous male subject now appearing in the SPR's literature. With these new types of supernatural phenomena, explanatory frameworks became far less concerned with religious debates (often considered the more feminine realm) and more immersed in psychological ones (the scientific male realm). This claim is supported by the simultaneous (and scientifically respectable) studies of hallucinations taken on by the International Congress of Experimental Psychology and the SPR in the 1880s.

However, instead of eradicating spiritualism through pathologizing it like earlier neuroscientists, the SPR incorporated it into theories of alternative consciousness that, being less demonized, could be reconstructed as something called psychic phenomena. The Society's ability to "encompass the unorthodox"[38] via abnormal psychology shows how far psychological medicine had come between the mid-1870s and the end of the1880s, again, a period marked by the appearance of the male hysteric, and with him, a legitimized scientific discourse.

The link between a rationalist scientific discourse on spiritualism and masculinity was explicit. William James, for instance, praises a magazine that dealt with exceptional religious states by writing that they "strike the right balance between over-criticism and over-credulity" and that the "invariable manliness and straightforwardness of tone of its original matter are most refreshing."[39] There are two important things to be noted here. First of all, psychical researchers defined themselves against a kind of narrow scientific materialism in order to accommodate more marginal forms of consciousness—which is why "over-credulity" is important. However, because their research was marginal, they felt the need to constantly stress their skepticism. This makes the use of a "rational" discourse crucial. In the quotation above, James praises the manliness of the writing, using the term as a synonym for the rational, the plainspoken, the un-dramatic, and the scientific. This, James argued, was the kind of language one must use to study the supernatural. Theories of the subconscious provided the scientific discourse; the subconscious itself provided the unknown.

Psychical researchers and experimental psychologists, then, turned simultaneously to the construction of new theories of consciousness coming out of the study of hysteria and made more appealing, according to my argument, by the presence of male subjects. British psychical researchers used French theories on abnormal psychology; French psychologists cited cases recorded by psychical researchers;[40] William James extended and shaped the work of both in his own writings. The most important issues at stake here, I believe, are the characterization of the new alternate stratum of consciousness, i.e., the subconscious or the subliminal, and how this characterization assuaged anxieties over the intellectual man's ability to meet the more physically strenuous definitions of masculinity.

## GENDERING THE UNCONSCIOUS

### Frederic W.H. Myers

Frederic W.H. Myers was a close friend and colleague of William James in England, and one of the founding members of the Society for Psychical

Research. In 1905 his major work, *Human Personality and its Survival of Bodily Death,* was published posthumously. Although Myers never considered himself a psychologist, and the main purpose of his book is to argue for access to the spiritual world through the subliminal, this incredibly detailed work maps out new theories of the unconscious and abnormal psychology. Indeed, much of *Human Personality* reads like work by Janet, early Freud, and the later work of James, especially *The Varieties of Religious Experience.*

At the beginning of his book, Myers adopts psychological terminology to explain supernatural phenomena. A surprising number of these terms are the same as those used to describe symptoms of nervous disorders, especially hysteria. For example, the first term in Myers's glossary is "aboulis," which is defined as the "loss of power of willing." Both neurasthenia and hysteria were often described as diseases of the will, especially in the United States.[41] Myers also includes a host of terms for conditions, again usually found in treatises on hysteria, in which human faculties become *more* powerful or effective. For instance, "analgesia," which is "the loss of the sense of pain" or "hypermnesia," which is a heightened faculty of recall in which memories normally lost to the regular consciousness are brought forth with great vividness. Myers also includes "heteraesthesia," which is defined as a "form of sensibility decidedly different from any of those which can be referred to the action of the known senses" and "hyperaesthesia," which is "unusual acuteness of [all] senses."[42] As will be seen in the next chapter, all of these symptoms play crucial roles in turn-of-the-century fictional accounts of the supernatural experience as well.

Myers constructed a theory of the mind based on two terms: the subliminal, which is comprised of "thought, feelings, etc., lying beneath the ordinary *threshold (limen)* of consciousness," and the supraliminal, what we would call consciousness, and he defines as "lying *above* the threshold." The supernormal or the supernatural is any "faculty or phenomenon which transcends ordinary experience."[43] The subliminal, according to his argument, is the gateway to the supernormal.

The term supernormal encapsulates something important to the definition of the psychical phenomena at this moment in history. Myers wants to make clear with this term that he is not "assuming that there is anything outside nature or any arbitrary interference with natural law" (xvii) in these types of experiences. One can see here, again, the importance of the psychological discourse, which James defined as a natural science. Defining the supernormal in this way keeps it within the realm of the scientifically explainable. Certain fiction writers, especially Henry James, found this aspect of psychical research to be appalling—basically taking all the mystery out of the mystical. Fiction writers only used the term "supernatural." But for the men involved in psychical research, a marginal scientific field, the discourse of natural science was a life preserver for their reputations.

Myers connected his work on supernormal phenomena to the study of hysteria because, he argued, both dealt "with instabilities on the threshold of consciousness" (28). The region of the subliminal is often referred to as the "hypnotic stratum." Supernormal experiences come through, so to speak, by using this hypnotic stratum, which Myers argues is a "strangely mingled" region of "strength and weakness . . . a faculty at once more potent and less coherent" than our regular consciousness."[44] Myers believed that a supernormal experience was simply the subliminal breaking through a subject's consciousness. He (along with James and Janet) also believed that the hysteric's hypnotic stratum or subliminal was more readily accessible and volatile than a healthy person's, breaking easily and repeatedly into his or her consciousness. Seemingly, then, the supernatural experience and hysteria are one and the same. Myers, however, does distinguish between the person who has access to his or her subliminal through hypnosis or what he calls an "uprush" from the subliminal, and the hysteric whose subliminal will burst forth in ways that cannot be incorporated into the conscious self. For non-hysterics who have supernormal experiences, the subliminal and the supraliminal (or regular consciousness) are connected through memory—even if the memory is not always immediately available to the conscious self. Hysterics, on the other hand, *can* be missing this memory or link, in which case a complete "break" (32) between the supraliminal and the subliminal is the result. The hypnotic stratum (the subconscious) itself can be healthy or sick. The *sick* hypnotic stratum is completely unstable and lacks any, even unconscious, integration with the rest of the self. For some suffering from nervous disorders like hysteria, hypnotism can help re-integrate the two strata. In severe cases, the two remain forever divided.

Still, it is also important to point out here that Myers's conception of hysteria was far from negative. Both he and Janet argued for hysteria's special connection to life's more profound questions. In his first Harvard lecture, Janet boasts that every "time we want to throw some light on the mysteries of our destiny, to penetrate into the unknown faculties of the human mind . . . to foresee the future or to talk to the dead," we appeal *not* to "an *ordinary* person" but rather so someone whose "sensibility is overexcited in a certain direction" a person who is "*medically speaking* . . . a hysteric person."[45] Further, while Myers argued that he was in fact looking for the "*converse* of hysterical changes. . . . for integrations in lieu of disintegrations; for intensifications of control [and] widening of faculty, instead of relaxation, scattering, or decay," he was always careful to point out cases in which hysterical second personalities were helpful to, or improvements on, the primary personality. He also reminds his reader that "There are in hysteria frequent *acquisitions* as well as losses of faculty. It is not unusual," he comments, "to find great hyperaesthesia in certain special directions—of touch, hearing, perception of light, etc.—combined with hysterical loss of sensation of other kinds."[46]

Beyond hyperaesthesia, the subliminal or hypnotic stratum, according to Myers, has the power to visualize with "added acuteness" (96) and store memory better. There is also, in the subliminal region, an "extension of conceptions" (22) and "mental concentration" (60). Overall, Myers paints the subliminal as space containing an amount of force and perceptiveness unprecedented in the conscious strata, and with characteristics—like the complex thinking and the higher levels of concentration—which are usually associated with the successful (male) subject.

The use of hysteria as a model for a more powerful mind, however, is tricky. Nervous disorders supplied psychical researchers with a way of looking at changes in the self through the concept of "thresholds" which James describes in *The Varieties of Religious Experience* as "a symbolic designation for the point at which one state of mind passes into another" (119). Though "symbolic," this idea actually relied on the physiological fact of brain fragmentation, which had already been materially proven in experiments with animals. The mental and physical instability found in nervous disorders convinced many in both the United States and Europe that such diseases were forms of degeneration. Indeed, James discusses thresholds in his chapter "The Sick Soul." But Myers and other psychical researchers, including James, attempted to show that activity in the subliminal region, though not the same as our normal consciousness, could in fact be called "evolutive" in many cases and "dissolutive" only in some. In their attempt to reconfigure and revalue the subconscious region (and, through that, what constituted a "sick soul") members of the SPR imported theories about genius, which became extremely useful in gendering the subconscious male.

### Theories of Genius

A great deal was written at the turn of the century, in both Europe and the United States, on the why and wherefore of genius. Like the psychic, the genius, while considered exceptional on some level, was embroiled in theories of degeneration and morbidity. The discourse on genius assumed a male subject almost entirely. Cesare Lombroso, whose writings on the topic were discussed more than anyone else's at the turn of the century, argued that genius was very rare in women because they "are, above all, conservators. Even the few who emerge have, on near examination, something virile about them. As Goncourt said, there are no women of genius; the women of genius are men."[47] Myers's

connection of the psychical discourse to the discourse of genius, then, makes
masculine the subject "capable" of having a supernatural experience.

Like theories of hysteria and other nervous disorders that remained popular into the early twentieth century, genius was thought by some, Lombroso
most famously, to be caused by an "irritation of the cerebral cortex"[48] or a
"want of balance in the cerebro-spinal system."[49] Genius was believed, also
like nervous illnesses, to be part of a chain that shared common elements with
epilepsy, which, on most neurologists' charts, was once removed from out and
out insanity.[50] John F. Nisbit, whose book *Insanity of Genius* was first published in the United States in 1891 and went through numerous editions, argued that genius was a mechanical function having to do with the
"localization of the functions of the brain, and, secondly, the established kinship of an extensive group of brain and nerve disorders, of which insanity or
paralysis are the more obvious expression, and gout, consumption, malforma-
tions, etc., the more obscure."[51] From these descriptions, one could persuasively argue that genius was in fact a form of male hysteria. But while almost
everyone writing on genius linked it to nervous disorders, there is a major split
between those who found it to be a degenerate condition, and those, like
Myers, who believed it could be seen as progenerate. William James was one
of the few who took a middle ground, claiming in his Lowell lectures on exceptional mental states as well as in *The Varieties of Religious Experience* that
while genius was not "an advanced stage of evolutionary progress," it was not
a form of degeneration either.[52] In fact, any degeneration associated with genius, in James' view, came from medical science which "denigrated" any non-
quantifiable mental process "to the level of pathology."[53]

Lombroso is perhaps the most famous writer to connect genius to degeneration. He argues that men of genius, when they do procreate, which
thankfully due to their morbidity is rare, have offspring who are insane; there
is no conservation or increase in genius down the line. "This fact," he concludes, "confirms *a posteriori* the degenerative character of genius."[54] Boris
Sidis's book *Philistine and Genius,* published in 1911 and obviously taking advantage of the work being done in psychology, comes to a different, and far
more Jamesian, conclusion. Sidis argues that "psychotherapeutics" has taught
us "the principle of stored up, dormant, reserved energy" in the subconscious
that we "are not able to reach." Instead of being scared that this energy is
pathological, we need to use the "medical psychopathologist" to show us how
to harness it. It is only with the help of these medical men, he continues, that
we can achieve the goal of becoming "a great race of genius with powers of rational control of . . . latent, potential, reserve energy."[55] While both
Lombroso and Sidis see the issue in neurological terms, Sidis's discussion of

genius, like Myers's of hysteria, suggests that, with the help of psychologists, control could be gained over the potent nervous energy of the subconscious. Myers describes *both* the inspiration of genius and psychic phenomena itself as a "large infusion of the subliminal" in one's "mental output."[56] In this way, the capacity for genius and having a supernatural experience become almost the same thing.

There is a specific symptom found in both hysteria and genius that Myers uses to debate the issue of degeneracy. The "fixed idea" is a recurrent theme in almost all literature on nervous illness in the United States and Europe. Doctors concerned with any type of nervous disorder warned about the evils of "morbid obsessions" in their patients. Myers defines the fixed idea as "the persistence of an uncontrolled and unmodifiable group of thoughts or emotions which from their brooding isolation,—from the very fact of deficient interchange with the general current of thought,—become alien and intrusive" (33). For Lombroso, the fixed idea in the genius was the root of the problem—he developed abnormally in one direction, losing that all-important balance in his "cerebro-spinal system." Undoubtedly what his obsession revealed was profound; the price, however, was his own health. Janet talks of a similar problem in hysterics who could "abstract" themselves to a remarkable degree, focusing only on one thing and becoming completely indifferent to everything else.[57] In Myers's conceptualization, however, the genius's fixed idea is only temporarily isolated in the subliminal—it is an obsession, but the subject is ultimately capable of integrating what is in his subliminal, which Myers characterizes as especially powerful nerve force, with his everyday consciousness.[58] The ability to integrate what happens in the subliminal with the supraliminal is the earmark of health. Myers argues, as he does for the psychic, that "Genius . . . should rather be regarded as a power of utilizing a wider range than other men can utilize of faculties in some degree innate in all;—a power of thought;—so that an 'inspiration of Genius' will be in truth a *subliminal uprush*."[59]

### William James

The potential strength of the subliminal, as sketched out by Myers and others working on this hidden stratum, reconstructs the value and the meaning of hysterical symptomology. We see this in the work of William James as well who wrote to a friend just before his Lowell lectures on exceptional mental states that he wanted to re-shape thoughts about "decidedly morbid subjects" toward "optimistic . . . conclusions."[60] In his lecture on hysteria given as part of the Lowell series, James cites professors at Princeton and the University of Pennsylvania who characterized the unconscious as an intelligent region of the mind.[61] But James goes beyond them. Using the work of Janet, Alfred Binet and Myers, James sees hysterical symptoms as proof of "the *exalted* sensibilities of the secondary intelligence." According to Eugene Taylor's reconstruction of the lecture, James argues that the "subliminal stratum is supersensitive, and even the weakest stimuli are experienced with great intensity. Normally inaudible sounds are clearly heard; distant objects can be seen in clearer detail than usual; faint heat or cold applied to the skin is felt as extreme."[62] As we shall see in James's *The Varieties of Religious Experience* and essays like "On A Certain Blindness in Human Beings," the ability to experience the sensory world with this kind of intensity is a highly positive and, for that matter, highly masculine quality.

There is, however, one idea that separates James from Myers. After his discussion of genius, Myers goes on to argue that "one characteristic of the subliminal . . . is that it is in closer relation than the supraliminal to the spiritual world."[63] James was never able to positively affirm this particular capacity in the subliminal, though he does make room for the possibility in *Varieties*. It is on this subject that the most useful distinction between the terms subliminal and subconscious can be made. Both James's view of the subconscious and Myers's view of the subliminal held that these strata "express themselves in purposeful actions and . . . bear all the marks from which we are accustomed to infer conscious cognition and volition, but of which nevertheless the subject or normal personality has no knowledge or awareness." But whereas the subliminal, for Myers, could be connected with the spirit of another (often dead) person, James's subconscious was usually understood more strictly as a form of cerebral dissociation. Myers's beliefs about the subliminal led him to conclude that the soul could exist independently of the body and that the subliminal's general development was distinctly *away* from "the activity of the organism."[64] James's ideas on the subconscious kept a more causal relationship between states of consciousness and physiology.[65]

In part, he differs from Myers here because, as a highly experienced turn-of-the-century psychologist, James understood the need to connect theories of the mind with physiological theories and the legitimizing force of the somatic model. James believed that a great deal goes on in our subliminal region, that because it is more open to suggestion, it is more open to the recuperative powers of sleep, of hypnosis, of the self-abandonment of prayer or religious self-surrender, and *perhaps* even "spiritual agencies." He argues, with telling use of italics, that "it is logically conceivable that *if there be* higher spiritual agencies that can directly touch us, the psychological condition of their doing so *might be* our possession of a subconscious region which alone should yield access to them."[66] But James stops short of saying the subconscious is necessarily, or even usually, spiritually connected. As we will see, however, he does consistently connect the subconscious to physical health. What interested James most are the ways in which the special openness of the subconscious could energize and make us more physically healthy. In other words, while James was ready to explore the supernatural possibilities of the subconscious, he was more focused than Myers on the *physical* benefits of extraordinary states of consciousness.[67]

James's work with the Society of Psychical Research was close and enduring, though not without its problems. His involvement with the society spans the period between 1884, a year before the American branch was officially established and 1909, a year before his death. He served as president of the American society for two years, and as the vice-president for seven. As we have seen with Myers, there was a close connection between British psychical researchers and French theories of abnormal psychology. While in America the German model of laboratory psychology was dominant, James did differ from many of his Harvard colleagues in his enduring intellectual connection to the French school. According to Eugene Taylor, this connection dates back to at least 1866 when James was in medical school and under the tutelage of the French-trained professor Charles Edouard Brown-Sequard. This, in turn, set the stage for James's interest in abnormal psychology, especially the work being done by Janet on dissociated states of consciousness. James's early work with phenomena such as automatic writing, in fact, shows that he was less interested in spiritualist hypotheses than working with Janet's theory that such phenomena show the existence of a double personality or that "true dissociation of consciousness" was possible. More than anything, it seems, James used "the paradigm of psychical research" to study scientifically the relationship between the mind and body and to help him in "the development of dynamic theories about the subconscious."[68]

While James credits the founding members of the Society in 1892 with proving "with Janet and Binet . . . the simultaneous existence of two different strata of consciousness, ignorant of each other in the same person,"[69] James himself had already theorized the existence of alternate brain states in several chapters of his *Principles of Psychology* published two years before. This is not to say that James was the first to posit such theories, rather, that theories of abnormal states of consciousness were part of the American psychological discourse and grew in conjunction with ideas coming out of France and England, despite the fact that they are usually only associated with James in his later work. While *Principles* maintains its continuity through its commitment to seeing psychology as a natural science, and while it relies heavily in places on the laboratory work coming out of the German tradition, especially in its discussion of localized brain function, James also attempts a discussion of brain capabilities beyond what was provable by experiments using physiological measurements. In doing this he enters not only the murky waters of abnormal psychology but also the possibility and problems of mystical phenomena.[70]

James agreed that hysteria was rightly conceived as a disease of the hypnotic stratum, or the subconscious, and like Myers, did not want this region itself to be seen only in terms of a pathology or as James puts it as "only . . . a dissociated part of the normal personality."[71] James wanted the workings and manifestations of the subconscious to be part of the study of mainstream psychology. And, he also agreed with Myers on the evolutionary possibilities of this more hidden stratum of consciousness. In a review of Myers's *Human Personality and Its Survival of Bodily Death*, James argued that

> Those more directly intuitive faculties which it [normal consciousness] lacks, and of which we get glimpses in individuals whose subliminal lies exceptionally open, can hardly be vestiges, degenerations of something our ancestors once possessed. We should rather regard them as germs of something not yet evolved for methodical use in our natural environment, but possibly even now carrying on a set of active functions in their own wider 'cosmic' environment.[72]

The subliminal here, as in Myers's writings, is a receptacle of capacities or physiological sensitivities that might, in fact, be more evolved than our standard conscious abilities.

The idea, however, that the subliminal may be, in some ways, more evolved than our conscious stratum becomes more complicated when we look at yet another defining characteristic of the subliminal: its "primitive" quality. Janet, Myers and James all saw what they called a more primitive element operating in the subconscious. Janet had noted in his work with hysterics that action separated from consciousness "retrogrades in a manner and assumes an appearance that recalls the action of the visceral muscles, the action of the lower animal."[73] Myers, for his part, argues that "one characteristic of the subliminal . . . is that it is in closer relation than the supraliminal to . . . the primitive source and extra-terrene initiation of life."[74] James argues in "On a Certain Blindness in Human Beings" that the cure for sickly and feminized intellectuals who are "stuffed with abstract conceptions" was to "descend to a more profound and primitive level" through divorcing oneself, for a time, from one's regular consciousness and opening up to the subliminal self, "with its irrationality."[75]

The characterization of the subliminal as "primitive" has particular relevance at this moment in history, when industrialism and consumer culture were thought to have made white men of the upper classes effeminate. The tropes of this discourse, furthermore, are distinctly racialized. The "pure sensorial perception" that one experiences "when brought down to the non-thinking level" is explained by two characters in "Blindness": "a chieftain to his white guest" and an English traveler roaming the shores of the "Rio Negro." James recognizes the "primitive difference"[76] by quoting the chieftain. However, beginning in the very next paragraph, he appropriates that difference for white men by relating (and prioritizing through text space) the experience of the European traveler. The traveler describes himself on his wilderness trip as one who had "undoubtedly *gone back*" to a "state of intense watchfulness or alertness." What's more, in the "suspension of the higher intellectual faculties," he experienced "the mental state of the pure savage."[77] A similar scenario unfolds in a case about automatic drawing that James reported to the SPR. The subject is a male bookkeeper who, after an elevator accident, finds himself able to produce automatic writings. The bookkeeper testifies that the early experiments yielded little but that gradually "my hand moved with more regularity and the pictures produced became interesting. Among these were dark-skinned savages, animals and vases of ancient type."[78] Again the subject is a white male. Like Charcot's male hysterics, he has experienced a physical trauma, and, not incidentally, an accident of a modern character. The trauma has, it seems, opened up a doorway into his subconscious. He begins to experience what Myers labeled "subliminal uprushes." What the man produces on the page confirms that *within himself* resides, just as it does in the English traveler, the primitive self many thought men were losing at this time. The subconscious, then, provides a perfect solution to the fear of over-civilization and the loss of what was thought to be the more virile male self. It ingrains within each man the possibility, and the memory, of a pre-industrial self. The primitive, thus appropriated as part of the white male subconscious, reinvests white male power.

James's valorization of "primitive" experiences had much to do with both a larger critique of scientific thinking and an attempt to recast his work in psychical research. James believed that science had to be redefined to include more marginal experiences. James also believed that these marginal experiences needed to remain marginal and not completely explainable by the narrow "mechanical rationalism" of the day. In his resignation speech to the American branch of the SPR, James warned that science had become too entrenched in mechanical explanations of natural phenomena. In its present form, he argued, this type of science committed a "violent breech with the ways of thinking that have until our own time played the greatest part in human history."[79] This form of scientific thinking did not take into account "Religious thinking, ethical thinking, poetical thinking, teleological, emotional, sentimental thinking;" all of which, he argued, were "the dominant forms of thought," though they were "outside of well-drilled scientific circles" (134).

However, after criticizing the narrowness of a certain kind of scientific thinking, James turns, in the same speech, to setting his own boundaries, using racist and sexist stereotypes to distinguish his position. In discussing the study of supernatural phenomena he argues, "we must all admit that the excesses to which the romantic and personal view of Nature may lead, if unchecked by impersonal rationalism, are direful. Central African Mumbo-jumboism is in fact one of unchecked romanticism's fruits" (134). Here the feminine ("romantic") and the racial "other" are put together to form an unacceptable excess that only the masculine discourse of "impersonal rationalism" can keep contained. What James wants to make clear is that his work on supernormal experiences and abnormal psychology will not allow the superstitions of the African or the irrationality of the feminine to take over. In James's mind, as long as these forces can be kept at bay, the Society for Psychical Research can heal "the hideous rift that Science, taken in a certain narrow way, has shot into the human world" (136).

James makes a similar argument in "The Will to Believe." Here, James writes that he does not blame "the rugged and manly school of science" for its disdain of the "little sentimentalist who comes blowing his voluntary smoke-wreathes . . . from out of his private dreams."[80] However, he does criticize the narrow "doctrine of objective certitude"[81] which that manly school of science follows for leading men to fear error more than desire truth. James admits that "For my own part, I have also a horror of being duped."[82] But in a revealing simile that now claims the manliness of his position, he tells his reader that putting the fear of error before the pursuit of truth "is like a general informing his solider that it is better to keep out of battle forever than to risk single wound."[83]

The manliness of a more daring science comes up again in "Reflex Action and Theism." But to the issue of the virility inherent in reckoning beyond one's powers of observation, James adds the question of Anglo-Saxon racial vitality:

> But if the religion of exclusive scientificism should succeed in suffocating all other appetites out of a nation's mind, and imbuing a whole race with the persuasion that simplicity and consistency demand a *tabula rasa* to be made of every notion that does not form part of the *soi-disant* scientific synthesis, that nation, that race, will just as surely go to ruin, and fall prey to their more richly constituted neighbors, as the beasts of the field, as a whole, have fallen prey to man. I myself have little fear for our Anglo-Saxon race. Its moral, aesthetic, and practical wants form too dense a stubble to be mown by any scientific Occam's razor that has yet been forged."[84]

For James, everything is a balancing act; what hangs in the balance is not only our souls, but also the manliness and strength of the Anglo-Saxon race. It is crucial that James ties both his concern for manliness and his race to the pursuit of the unseen, the mystical, to that "something that gives a click inside of us,"[85] and to powers, like telepathy, which he discusses in "The Will to Believe" as a phenomenon scientists are too scared to examine because it "would undo the uniformity of Nature."[86]

## GIFTS FROM THE SUBCONSCIOUS

The realm of the subconscious for James must be primitive without being "degenerative," mystical without being feminine, energizing without morbid excitements. Myers believed, perhaps more strongly than James, that with practice we could take only the most desirable traits from the subliminal. On a physical level, Myers argued, the hypnotic state can help us "to develop . . . inhibition of pain" and the "reinforcement of energy;" on an intellectual level, it can help with "concentration of attention;" and on an emotional level, make more potent one's "sense of freedom, expansion, [and] joy."[87] A powerful subliminal, then, clearly promises a great deal. It promises a cure to almost every common complaint of the neurasthenic—all the somatic disorders, the aches and pains, the lack of energy or force, the loss of concentration and the depression that deflates manliness. Again, all of this is based on what the *hysteric* can do: "It is enough to hope that we may inhibit pain, as it is inhibited for the hysteric; or concentrate attention, as it is concentrated for the somnambulist; or change the tastes and passions, as they are changed in alternating personalities."[88]

While James was less comfortable than Myers with the connections that still existed between the supernatural and morbid conditions, he also clearly used and re-valued hysterical symptoms in the construction of the subconscious. One reason he so energetically supported the mind-cure movement, which preached the power of certain mental states to heal the physical body, is that they made such "unprecedentedly great use of the subconscious life"[89] and did so in a positive way that took advantage of its suggestibility—a quality usually considered injurious—and brought health to the individual. A mind-curist whom James particularly liked was Annie Payson Call, whose 1891 book argued that nerves could be completely trained "to enable the body to be an obedient servant to a healthy mind."[90] Call believed in the inherent goodness of Nature. If one were to only use Nature as a "guide" or "chief engineer," she argued, its "wholesome laws" would free the individual entirely from the morbid.[91] Following Nature is not just the way to health; it is the way to God. Because Nature can never be morbid, the powers originating from the subconscious get reconstituted as almost completely beneficial components of the self.

Physical cures are just one example of what the subconscious is capable of when harnessed by a strong mind. In *The Varieties of Religious Experience*, James gives an example of what an evolved subconscious can achieve for the man most often discussed in documents on neurasthenia: the business man in industrial culture. James takes the story from a mind-curist book entitled *In Tune with the Infinite*:

> 'One of the most intuitive men we ever met had a desk at a city office where several other gentlemen were doing business constantly, and often talking loudly. Entirely undisturbed by the many various sounds about him, this self-centered faithful man would, in any moment of perplexity, draw the curtains of privacy so completely about him that he would be as fully inclosed in his own psychic aura, and thereby as effectively removed from all distractions, as though he were alone in some primeval wood. Taking his difficulty with him into the mystic silence in the form of a direct question, to which he expected a certain answer, he would remain utterly passive until the reply came, and never once through many years' experience did he find himself disappointed or misled.'[92]

There are several important things to note here. First of all, the tale is set in an atmosphere that, beginning with Beard, was understood as a primary cause of nervous illness in men. The modern office with all its new ideas, gadgetry and noise, was thought to tax the nerves and intensify one's mental susceptibility, which was one of the most common characteristics of a hysterical personality.

Secondly, as James' *Principles* makes clear, much of psychology's focus at this point was on the relation of the senses to mental states. It had only recently been discovered that the body registered sensations the conscious mind did not. The control of stimuli in an industrial society was severely challenged. The man in the story is able to control the excess stimuli produced by such a society. He goes into his subconscious, to the same "non-thinking" place as the traveler on the banks of the Rio Negro. This is a segregated consciousness, but one that produces results that the conscious self can use in the modern world of business. The neurasthenic and the hysteric are controlled by their subconscious. This man, on the other hand, is able to use his without becoming its slave. The use of the word "mystic" in the story is important. As discussed, James and Myers believed access to this realm, when it can be re-integrated into conscious life, signals a healthy supernatural (or supernormal) experience. Many of the mystical experiences James relates in *Varieties* similarly require control over random stimuli in order to achieve connection with something in the "wider 'cosmic' environment."[93] The supernatural experience, then, far from being one of abandonment is, in many cases, about self-control and control over environment.

Finally, the detail of the man being able to mentally remove himself from the modern world and place himself in a "primeval wood" is important. It adopts, in its own way, the rhetoric so romanticized by politicians like Theodore Roosevelt or fiction writers like Owen Wister about pre-industrial culture. And it does so in a remarkably similar way. The business man, just like Roosevelt's or Wister's ideal man, is effective in the modern culture and does not wish to turn back the clock, instead he is able to remain productive in an industrial setting *and* tap into a past believed to require and instill more explicitly manly talents.

While uncontrolled over-stimulation could leave one vulnerable to nervousness, James was careful to point out that strong stimuli itself was not the problem; rather it was something to be sought after: "all sensations, how- ever unpleasant, when more intense are rather agreeable than otherwise in their very lowest degrees. A faintly bitter taste, or putrid taste, may at least be *interesting.*"[94] Indeed, in James's work, a mystical experience is quite often one of intense sensation.

Importantly, for James's intellectual audience, these strong sensations do not always have a material cause; more often they emanate from our con- sciousness, from our ability to exteriorize an abstract idea or principle. And al- though the experience is non-material, it is sensational. In fact, it is suprasensational. James argues that there is "in the human consciousness a sense of reality, a feeling of objective presence, a perception of what we may call 'something there,' more deep and more general than any of the special and particular 'sense' by which the current psychology supposes existent realities to be ordinarily revealed."[95] (Myers called this heteraesthesia.) This special sense is present in the mystical experience and James offers as proof several ex- amples of people's encounters with hallucinations. In all, the most important point is the intensity of sensation, both of the feelings and of the senses, in- volved. I quote at length one man's tale because his narrative is representative of many stories found in *Varieties:*

> 'After I had got into bed and blown out the candles, I lay awake awhile . . . when suddenly I *felt* something come into the room and stay close to my bed. . . . I did not recognize it by any ordinary sense, and yet there was a horribly unpleasant 'sensation' connected with it. It stirred something more at the roots of my being than any ordinary perception. The feeling had something of the quality of a very large tearing vital pain spreading chiefly over my chest, but within the organism. . . . At all events, some- thing was present with me, and I knew its presence far more surely than I have ever known the presence of any fleshly living creature. . . . the cer- tainty that there in outward space there stood *something* was indescribably

*stronger* than the ordinary certainty of companionship when we are in the close presence of ordinary living people. The something seemed close to me, and intensely more real than any ordinary perception."[96]

Here, as in so many stories of the supernatural, the mystical experience is more real than any "real" experience. Further, at such moments, when people show all the major symptoms of hysteria: hallucinations, hyperaesthesia, delusion, etc., they are experiencing, according to James, "the genuinely strenuous life."[97] The Rooseveltian language is crucial. The concept of the strenuous life, made famous by Roosevelt's 1899 speech about America's rough and ready pioneer past and imperialist future, conceptualized manliness through physical strength. In using the term, James emphasizes the bodily experiences involved in psychical phenomena. And at the same time, because there is much evidence to suggest that James thought Roosevelt's idea of the strenuous life too narrow and anti-intellectual,[98] he complicates the more secular, muscular ideals about manliness by connecting them to mystical and/or psychical experiences he conceptualizes through the lens of psychology. This well served men from the educated classes.

Throughout this chapter, I have been looking at the implicit concerns about modern masculinity embedded in the psychological discourse on the subconscious. At the end, here, I would like to look at some explicit comments James makes about masculinity in *The Varieties of Religious Experience*. Myers argued that the conscious self developed in "relation to the external world"[99] while the more primitive subliminal grows away from the materialism that influences the conscious self. While James's ever-present concern with the body kept him more interested in *connections* between the physical and the mental, he does see the subconscious as a possible antidote to the materialism of modern culture. Interestingly, this leads him to connect the concerns of the conscious self to feminization: "Does not . . . the worship of material luxury and wealth, which constitutes so large a proportion of the 'spirit' of our age, make somewhat for effeminacy and unmanliness" (289)? While this "danger" as he puts it, does not go unnoticed by the population, most "would point to athletics, militarism, and individual and material enterprise and adventures as the remedies" (289). In doing so, they are partially right, for these "contemporary ideals," he goes on to say "are quite remarkable for the energy with which they make for heroic standards of life, as contemporary religion is remarkable for the way in which it neglects them"(289). Through his construction of the subconscious, however, James revitalizes this neglected aspect of the religious experience. What militarism or war brings, he argues, is intense feelings, physical changes and most importantly, the annulment of "customary inhibitions," along with "ranges of new energy . . . and life . . . [on] a higher plane of power" (289). But every one of these "heroic" feelings, James argues, can be found in the mystical (which is to say, hysterical) experience; all these things can emanate from the *sub*conscious region of the self: "The beauty of war in this respect is that it is so congruous with ordinary human nature. Ancestral evolution has made us all potential warriors; so the most insignificant individual, when thrown into an army in the field, is weaned from whatever excess of tenderness toward his precious person he may bring with him" (289). In other words, it could be said that the more primitive, ancestral subconscious takes over; its evolution in a "separate direction from a parent stem," away from the daily activity of preserving the organism,[100] will be ready to change, in James's words, the self-indulgent and effeminate "insignificant individual"[101] into a fighter.

But James does not want war to "be our only bulwark against effeminacy."[102] He wants to find something just as heroic for men, something that will be "as compatible with their spiritual selves as war has proven itself to be incompatible" and he speaks of asceticism as a possible solution.[103] But, I would argue, he has been shaping another alternative all along, an alternative that does not necessitate a rejection of a modern (and consumer oriented) life. The alternative to war (and even asceticism) here *is* the experience of exceptional states of consciousness that *The Varieties of Religious Experience* has been so insistently cataloguing. Like the case quoted above, all the stories here tell of a more intense sense perception and form of contact with the emotions that are stronger than everyday feelings, whether they are feelings of fear, disgust or happiness. Mystical experiences are, like war, experiences in which the physical self is transformed, for moments or forever, and in which faculties are heightened in new ways. Exceptional mental states stir "something more at the roots." This is the strenuous relationship with the self—something every thinking man now has within his power to experience.

## CONCLUSION

Charcot's "discovery" of male hysteria had lasting consequences, though not as a direct challenge to gender stereotypes. Rather, the central role hysteria plays in the construction of the subconscious would not have been possible without a highly respected neurologist claiming its existence in men. After Charcot, hysterical symptoms became the basic features of the subconscious. In the process, much of that symptomology was reassessed and revalued with an eye toward addressing male gender anxieties.

While the disease itself never truly lost its special connection to women, hysterical symptomology, ironically, gave men several important attributes thought to be challenged by a society characterized as "over-civilized" and feminizing. Hysteria infused the subconscious with the sensory acuity of a great hunter, "uprushes" worthy of a genius and a primitive self lodged safely within every white man's nature. And, it did so without necessarily making him unhealthy. Instead, nervous illness in men could be redefined *as* a strenuous experience—which, in turn, secured the subject's manliness. Thus, while nervous disorders were indeed disruptive to the stability of *male roles,* psychologists and psychical researchers (and, as we will see in the next chapter, fiction writers) constructed nervous disorders in ways that ended up securing their subjects' *masculinity* according to new gender definitions.

Much of what James suggested in his more popular lectures relocated the cure of nervous illnesses in this mysterious and potent strength found in the region of the self thought to be causing the trouble. In fact, he argued at the end of his Lowell lectures on exceptional mental states that "The result" of his work was "to make disease less remote from health. . . . The line of health is not narrow! A particularity . . . when it is recognized, should be welcome if it can be made useful."[104] Myers, for his part, argued that his work on the subliminal proved that nervous degeneration was simply "nervous change or *development.*"[105] This was far better than any cure. Hypnosis, automatic writing, having a supernatural experience, these were all ways to get in touch with a self that was always already healthy—*because* it was more primitive, *because* it was a self more sense oriented and less inhibited. This logic makes it possible to discuss nervousness in men without upsetting notions of male self-control. Women displaying the same attributes were thought both sick and "disorderly."[106] By encoding the subconscious with the qualities of an idealized "strenuous" masculinity, men's unruly self, on the other hand, was naturalized.

Chapter Four

# Shapes That Haunt the Dusk:
# Masculinity and the Supernatural
# Experience in Fiction[1]

Reconstituting alternate psychological states, male hysteria or irrational male behavior as forms of strenuous masculinity was not limited to the literature of psychology. The "primitive" self that the subconscious revealed, or was made to reveal, had a broad cultural usefulness, speaking—as physical education and many naturalist novels did—to concerns of over-civilization, the consequences of increased leisure, new forms of labor, heightened consumption in an urban environment and, attendant to all these things, a perceived feminization of men and culture. In this chapter, I discuss the use of new theories of the subconscious and alternate psychological states in late nineteenth- and early twentieth-century supernatural fiction. I argue first that the psychological frame around the supernatural experience provided a space for white men to evaluate homosocial bonds and, in some cases, sort through anxiety over romantic attachments.[2] In the second half of the chapter, I discuss more specifically how the construction of a primitive subconscious was instrumental in mapping the "other" both *in* and for white men, establishing a comforting but complicated way for them to enact and, at times, embody different forms of masculinity.

While tales of the supernatural from the turn of the century and the gothic fiction of the eighteenth century share an interest in the occult, the earlier gothic stories were often set in lands far from the homes of its writers and readers, with plots that took place in a distant past. Supernatural tales from the late nineteenth and early twentieth centuries, on the other hand, insist on their modernity—through contemporary settings and through the special erudition of their characters, which is most often a kind of occult scientific/psychological knowledge. The result is the adoption of a "discourse of empiricism . . . to describe and manipulate supernatural phenomena."[3] This, along with the insistence that such tales, in Henry James's words, "must be connected at a hundred points with the common objects of life" leads to "the textual confrontation of two models of reality"[4] and, according to common arguments, one of the most important tensions in turn-of-the-century supernatural fiction.[5] This tension between the comforting scientific frame (not to mention the patently real parlor drapes) and supernatural phenomena also uniquely challenges—and makes malleable—male gendered identity.

Discussions of gender in supernatural fiction, however, have usually focused on women generally and female sexuality specifically.[6] According to Allan Gardner Lloyd-Smith, women themselves generate an "uncanny effect" because there is a 'slippage' between woman as sign and the discontinuous expression of the 'something else,' or woman-as-other, that exists within the sign."[7] The space between what Woman stands for and who she "really" is, is most often explored through her sexuality—thus the multitude of readings of *The Turn of the Screw* (the most critically assessed supernatural tale from this period), which focus almost exclusively on the governess's sexuality. Both historically and in fiction, women are also represented—along with Africans and African-Americans—as *possessing* supernatural powers. Almost all the famous mediums in the United States were women, and as William Dean Howells' *The Undiscovered Country* (1880) and Henry James' *The Bostonians* (1886) demonstrates, fiction followed suit. However, by the turn of the century, the popularity and prevalence of psychical and psychological discourses re-framed supernatural fiction. At this moment men begin to populate these stories as the "subjects" of supernatural experience. Their relation to the supernatural is quite specific. While women often possess supernatural powers, men rarely do, unless it comes in the guise of occult scientific knowledge. This difference is hard to overstate. Looking at constructions of masculinity through the lens of the supernatural tale would seem to yield little because of the naturalized connection between women and the irrational or the unexplainable. As long as men themselves do not *possess* the unexplainable powers, however, they are not in danger of over-identification with the irrational. By making men, in a sense, *victims* of the supernatural, they retain their kinship with the rational while participating in the irrational in ways that restructure identity in interesting and, at times, culturally attractive ways.

The investigatory stance taken up by a great many male protagonists of supernatural tales references the Society of Psychical Research, which was comprised almost completely, in the United States and England, of the male educated elite. In an 1884 letter, William James wrote: "we are founding here a

'Society for Psychical Research,' under which innocent sounding name ghosts, second sight, spiritualism and all sorts of hobgoblins are going to be 'investigated' by the most high toned and 'cultured' members of the community" (xxxiii). In fictional tales of the supernatural from this period, the protagonists are indeed invariably "high toned" and highly educated. These stories, like the experiences William James tracks in his own writings, attempt to create for this educated male a strenuous experience—one that is both physically and mentally challenging and which will fulfill new expectations of manliness.

In his essay "On a Certain Blindness in Human Beings,"[8] James argues that educated men need to experience the "mystical," which, crucially, he connects to the primitive and separates from practical capitalist or materialist concerns. Inextricably bound to this conviction is the idea that white men need a new awareness of, and relationship to, the "other." So, not only do "the highly educated classes" need "to descend to a more profound and primitive level" (642), but they also need to recognize that the "savages and children of nature, to whom we deem ourselves so much superior, certainly are alive where we are often dead" (642). While tolerance of difference is certainly an aim of James's essay, it also clues us in to the important connection being made between the supernatural and primitivism. Like the men James talks about in "Blindness," the male protagonists of supernatural tales are intellectuals or businessmen who have become detached from the "mysterious sensorial life" (644). Their supernatural experience becomes the mode through which they make contact with—and in some cases assume—"'the mental state of a pure savage'" (642). While this experience provides them with the reassurance that they are indeed both special and manly men, the ultimate effect of their encounter with the primitive is clearly more complicated.

In talking about the primitive selves that so insistently populate these stories, race is critical. While the "other" in supernatural tales might be understood as a ghost, quite separate from the protagonist, more often the presence exists as another part of the subject; his hidden self. White men travel back and forth between savagery and the enlightened, scientifically-minded gentleman with great freedom in these tales. According to Collette Guillaumin, who writes about racism and power, white men have "escaped the process of substantivization which has befallen those whom they dominate."[9] It has been my project throughout this work to substantiate white manhood, to discover its outlines, constructedness and borders. Thus in looking at the hidden, primitive self in these stories, I look at the ways in which a racialized contrast stabilizes privileged identity—how in other words, the supernatural tale ends up stabilizing a specific racial manhood through transitory experiences with male otherness that only the white male is afforded. [10]

Often, however, the exclusionary practices used to reconstitute white manhood at the end of the tale, happen, quite obviously in some stories, to the detriment of the protagonist's own *homosocial* happiness. In other words, while an acceptable form of white masculinity is more often re-established and reaffirmed in supernatural tales, many stories are accompanied by a sense of loss. This loss of affinity with a male other, in some cases, demonizes white *women*. For while the primitive other (who is, in these tales, very occasionally genderless but usually specifically male) can be understood as having highly evocative powers, both spiritually and physically, which white men would like to associate with, women in the stories tend to be seen as the ones who "tame, reduce, and finally betray her man's true character."[11] Moreover, when heterosexual bonds do survive supernatural experiences (and they usually do) their intensity compares poorly to the intimacies of supernatural homosociality.

Here again, as with the discussion of the changing nature of work for middle-class men at the turn of the century, or male commodification in the new market economy, or male illness in a fast-paced modern culture, the body is central. Indeed, like many of the trends discussed in this work, supernatural tales usually accomplish their re-definition of white male identity through the transformation and trials of the body.[12] Whether the trial of the body is the physicalization of nerve tension (an hallucination, for instance) or an actual physical feat, the test is ultimately about the "virility" of the male subject, a virility often associated with aggressive capabilities or the needs of a more primitive society. However, despite the fact that the highly physical nature of the supernatural experience becomes grounds for a transformative gender experience, it is a tightly scripted one that generally ends with a unified psychological selfhood that is class-bound. Many of the experiences in the tales, for example, are treated as special events, an occasion so to speak, which makes it possible for these men to distinguish their savageries from the working classes as well as racial others. Moreover, a great many of the tales are played out in domestic settings, which further solidifies the middle-class status of the individual: the young man who goes through supernatural psychological growth in the home is the man who can afford to stay out of productive life, at least for a time. The more time he has to spend in the domestic sphere, "the greater his value as a marker of class status."[13] In this way, some of the tales are reminiscent of the new boyhood fiction that dates from this period. Like the stories of Tom Sawyer or Huckleberry Finn, masculinity in supernatural fiction is formed through violence but is also bounded by the differentiation of life "stages" and/or a domestic setting that secures class status while perhaps also showing an aggression toward the female sphere in general. And just as Twain and other writers of boyhood fictions tend to end their narratives abruptly, sustaining the separation between manhood and boyhood, so too do the supernatural tales, keeping forever separate "real" life from one informed by the insights and capabilities of the more pluralistic selfhood often experienced in the supernatural encounter.

Some stories, however, do offer a critique of this transformation from split self to acceptable unified middle-class male subject through their very valorization of the supernatural experience as intense and rewarding. Moreover, while the middle of the nineteenth century saw the emergence of middle-class professionalization with its attendant directives to "'establish universal standards for moral and civil behavior,'"[14] some turn-of-the-century ghost stories project a sense of uncertainty that is modern in its challenge to the "self-confident positivism and empirical realism" of the late Victorian period.[15] We see this most often in the stories of Henry James. Importantly, however, this challenge is always measured against the benefits of belonging to the "scientific priesthood" of the Anglo-Saxon community[16] and the desire to retain a connection between women and the irrational.

## THE SUPERNATURAL AND THE QUESTION OF HETEROSEXUAL FULFILLMENT

Both W.D. Howells and Henry James wrote supernatural tales that set up an opposition between homosocial bonds and heterosexual unions, using the supernatural experience as a stand-in for the protagonist's sexual and/or romantic anxiety. At times, especially in the work of Howells, the tales engage in fairly standard parallel dichotomies between the rational and irrational and the male and female. Indeed, Howells is quite careful to retain a place for male fraternity within a rationalist discourse in his supernatural fiction. In some cases, however, both Howells and James configure the standard oppositions differently, using the supernatural as a way of complicating the subjecthood and desires of the male protagonist in highly suggestive ways.

Howells' 1903 short story, "His Apparition" [17] is a fine example of the way in which a supernatural occurrence can, quite neatly, stand in for the transition from bachelor to husband. For Arthur Hewson, the protagonist of the story, seeing a ghost brings about an identity crisis and inaugurates a relationship that will end in marriage. An educated member of the leisure class, Hewson is vacationing at an inn in upstate New York when, on his first night, he sees a "figure"—whose gender, interestingly, is never disclosed but whose appearance coincides with the arrival of Roasalie Hernshaw, the woman Hewson will eventually marry. Hewson's embarrassment at seeing an apparition is immediately cast in gendered terms and he qualifies his hallucinatory experience obsessively. First, he establishes that it was an "incident . . . of a dignity which the supernatural has by no means always had" (5). Second, he notes with pride how "very little agitated" he had been at the moment of confrontation, and that even though he later felt some discomfort "when the conflict between sense and reason concerning the fact itself arose" he maintained "a sort of central calm, in which he noted the particulars of the occurrence with distinctness and precision" (5). As dawn approaches, Hewson fantasizes about how he will tell the other guests at the inn about his apparition in "matter-of-fact terms . . . with a serious regard for the integrity of the fact itself, which he had no wish to exaggerate" (7). But while Hewson clearly wants everything surrounding the incident to reveal his credibility as a rational (i.e. male) witness, he also wants to make an impact and, tellingly, to do so feels he should wait to tell his story at the moment when the greatest number of *women* are at the breakfast table: "he should need the sympathy and countenance of women; his story would be wanting in something of its supreme effect without the electrical response of their keener nerves" (11). From the beginning, then, Hewson's experience pulls him into female company.

A factual and plain-spoken account of the supernatural, however, does not come as easily to Hewson as he expects. To begin with, he soon realizes that telling his story to the other guests would be bad business for the inn and is forced to keep quiet. Later, when he returns to New York City, he tells the story compulsively, leaving out only where the occurrence took place. From the moment Hewson begins to tell his story, he feels conflicted and is repeatedly dissatisfied with the way he handles the narrative. He is especially worried that he is telling his tale too often. He is most insecure at his all-male club, where he begins to feel that the story of his apparition has compromised his homosocial bonds. For instance, Hewson wonders if he has told "his story too often, and that perhaps the friend who suggested his doing so, was playing on his forgetfulness. He wondered if he were really something of a bore with it, and whether the men were shying off from him at the club on account of it" (26). Becoming increasingly paranoid he soon thinks the "circle at the five-o'clock cocktails [at the club] gradually diminished" because of him. Like a man boring his bachelor friends with his love for a woman, he feels his experience quite literally pushes him outside the circle of men. Hewson simply cannot integrate such an experience into the mostly male society that makes up his bachelor life.

Howells, in fact, is at pains to connect Hewson's experience at the inn with Miss Hernshaw whenever possible. When Hewson sees her at a social gathering, he immediately connects the two: "had he been suddenly confronted with his apparition he could not have experienced a deeper and stranger satisfaction than he felt as the girl lifted up her innocent fierce face upon him" (33). Further, Hewson values Miss Hernshaw herself in the same terms as the apparition: "she, with his vision, formed the supreme interest and equally the mystery" (33).

At this particular gathering a psychologist by the name of Wanhope, a staple character in Howells' supernatural fiction, makes his appearance. A cool and detached man of science, he is often the most authoritative male in the stories. When the issue of ghosts comes up during dinner, Wanhope claims that he has never yet spoken directly to a man who has seen an apparition. At this, Hewson decides, once again—though for the first time in front of Miss Hernshaw—to tell the story of his sighting. After recounting his experience, Wanhope "fixed his eyes on him with scientific challenge as well as scientific interest" (41), and puts Hewson through a series of questions at the end of which his only remark is "Curious." Hewson thinks that the psychologist "seemed rather annoyed by the encounter" (45). Conversely, Miss Hernshaw finally takes some interest in the protagonist. Not only does she believe that it happened, (and guesses correctly *where* it happened) she also shares his deeper feeling that the experience is made vulgar by the telling.

Though Miss Hernshaw makes Hewson feel more keenly the shame of his repeatedly telling the story in society—as if for some cheap thrill—Howells finally makes Miss Hernshaw guilty of the greatest folly: she (accidentally) tells a female journalist the story and includes the name of the inn. Because of her actions, the inn gets a reputation for being haunted and loses all its business. Hewson, then, feels compelled to buy the place. This, of course, greatly disrupts the lifestyle he has chosen for himself:

> Hitherto he had been able to live up to his ideal [of a leisured gentleman] with sufficient satisfaction, and in proposing himself never to marry, but to grow old gradually and gracefully as a bachelor of adequate income, he saw no difficulties in his way for the future, until this affair with the apparition. It now incurred the chances of an open change in his way of living. . . . He must not only declass, he must depatriate himself. (60–1)

A supernatural event, like love, disrupts a certain kind of class-specific homosociality. In this story, one might argue further that the anxiety of falling in love gets illustrated *through* the telling of an apparition sighting, which, due to its "nature"—that is, its connection to the irrational—challenges Hewson's very citizenship in the land of men.

While in this tale Howells has associated women with elements of the supernatural and characterized heterosexual union as a disruption of sorts, he ultimately finds that disruption positive and marriage productive. Hewson and Miss Hernshaw marry and live happily together at the inn upstate. Howells has simply used the supernatural to tell a love story and this is itself quite telling. The supernatural conveniently brings up, and can act in the place of, male anxiety about changing his associations from homosocial to heterosexual. The problem of the supernatural in the world of science—its challenge to empiricist foundations and rationalism—works perfectly as a metaphor for "letting a woman in your life." Indeed, the supernatural here engages and constructs clear oppositions between homosociality and heterosexual attachments. Given its connection to discourses on the subconscious, however, the supernatural can also now confront the limitations of "consciousness-centered" models[18] when discussing the sexual or romantic longings of a male character. In other words, it provides a way of talking about repressed desire.

In most of Howells' stories where the psychologist Wanhope appears, the supernatural tales are narrated in the "Turkish room" of his all-male club. Wanhope's relation to the stories is similar to that of psychical researchers like Frederick Myers and William James, men who also attempted to frame the supernatural experience in the scientifically grounded discourse of psychology. The all-male club is amply suited to the almost strident homosociality found in the stories. The exoticized "Turkish room" moreover is perfectly in tune with the primitivism associated with supernatural experiences or altered states of consciousness. Clubs like Wanhope's, for elite professionals in urban settings, began springing up in the 1840s and attempted to provide a place for men to experience fraternal sameness outside of professional hierarchies. However, according to Dana Nelson, who writes about fraternal spaces in the nineteenth century, this was rarely achieved. As a matter of fact, most clubs had rather elaborate rituals (many of which drew on primitive or occult traditions) that reinstated hierarchies. In Howells's stories, Wanhope, due specifically to his "scientific" training and his profession of psychologist, is at the top of the pyramid. The men who make up Wanhope's circle are usually, like Wanhope himself, bachelors, and comprise a sort of second tier of listeners, whose comments are heard but never given the value of Wanhope's interpretations. The men they discuss—the one's who *have* supernatural experiences—are connected to the feminine in that they are either married or going through a process that will end in marriage. As objects of detached interest they are perhaps farthest from the center of male homosociality.

The importance of the psychologist Wanhope and the all-male club as a frame for the supernatural tale is particularly revealing in "The Eidolons of Brook Alford." Like "His Apparition," the story is concerned with the transition from bachelor to husband. In this tale, however, the question of the protagonist's real desires is far from clear and the heterosexual union itself is made questionable. An eidolon, most simply, is an apparition or phantom. The term comes from "eidos" which refers to knowledge that comes in the form of vivid images. More than any other Howellsian supernatural tale, this one, in both style and content, is reminiscent of tales by his friend Henry James. It is a story about repression, about an unspoken threat lying just beneath the surface in Brook Alford. While this threat is never named by any of the characters, clues abound.

The frame of the tale itself brings up the idea of multiple readings, levels of narration and obfuscation. The unnamed narrator of the story is a member of Wanhope and Alford's club and opens his narrative by commenting that he is not simply trying to recount the actual tale of Alford, but to recreate the narrative of Brook Alford's eidolons as constructed *by Wanhope*, to "give the story of Alford's experiences just as Wanhope told it."[19] This is not, as one might suppose, because Wanhope's version of the events is so thorough, but rather, because it is so selective. The narrator remarks that: "there were certain other commonplaces of our knowledge of Alford which he [Wanhope] could omit without omitting anything essential to our understanding of the facts which he dealt with so *delicately,* so *electly,* almost affectionately, coaxing each point into the *fittest* light" (65, my emphasis). The reader is not part of this shared homosocial club knowledge, but the narrator makes it clear that there is a select group of men who might truly understand Alford's predicament. Hints as to what that might be lie in the narrator's specific understanding of what is so "right" about Wanhope's narrative. For instance, on the most superficial level, the story is about a man (Alford) who, being in a somewhat run-down state, goes to a health resort. While there, he meets a widow named Mrs. Yarrow whom he eventually marries. But, while this sounds like a romance, the narrator notes with approval that Wanhope "dismissed" the "love-affair which was supposed to have so much to do with Alford's break-up . . . to its proper place in the story" (65–6). One reading of this approach is that Wanhope would simply prefer not to see Alford's life in romantic terms or himself a narrator of a romance; this certainly fits Wanhope's general character. But the dismissal of the love affair can also read as a clue about the nature of Alford's hallucinations and thus his real motives for marring Mrs. Yarrow. I read Alford's hallucinations as manifestations of anxiety over his status—economic, physical and sexual: he is educated but poor, he has his work but is sick and thus unable to accomplish it, and, perhaps most importantly, he is an older bachelor. Given this set of anxieties, the *romance* or love-affair may be banished from a central place in the story, while Alford's dependence on Mrs. Yarrow for a stable identity can still be understood as both crucial and central.

Alford's first hallucination, or rather, his ability to externalize "a mental vision" (70) with such an intensity that it blots out whatever reality is in front of him, occurs for the first time while sitting across from Mrs. Yarrow. This first vision, which is a sort of re-enactment of a target practice he had been watching earlier in the day, is understood by Alford as merely a "mental process" he can't explain (67). While entranced by his vision, he loses all attention to what Mrs. Yarrow is saying. When the vision or eidolon is gone Mrs. Yarrow's face re-appears and she laughingly charges that he had not been listening to her. Alford has to assent, and in the "joking that followed" (68) a relation between the two begins. Although first upset by the vividness of the image he conjured, he soon, like many male characters in supernatural fictions, begins to feel "proud of what had happened to him as out of the ordinary, as a species of psychological ecstasy almost of spiritual value" (68).

Alford and Mrs. Yarrow spend the rest of the afternoon and evening together. Later, upon turning in for the night and at the very moment Alford "realized" that Mrs. Yarrow was "a very pretty woman" (69) he turns on the light in his room and "in the first flash of the carbon film he saw her sitting beside the window in such a chair as she had taken . . . in the parlor" (69). He is suitably shocked to find the upstanding widow in his bedroom, but when he asks her what she is doing there, her image suddenly dissolves. This time Alford is more unnerved by the vision and wonders how often his thoughts would report themselves in such startling images. On a train returning from Boston a few days later, after an unsuccessful attempt to see his doctor, Alford is accosted by hundreds of swirling eidolons: "Whatever had once strongly impressed itself upon his nerves was reported there again as instantly as he thought of it" (72–3). The visions are made up of both the dreadful and delightful: sitting at the death-bed of his little sister; the "pathetic, foolish face of the girl whom long ago he had made believe he cared for, and then abruptly broken with" (73); the proud face of his mother when he graduated college; the "collective gayety [sic] of the whole table on a particularly delightful evening at his dining-club" (73). He is aware that, transfixed as he is by the images, he looks "queer" (74), but what upsets him the most is the knowledge that the images are subjective, coming, uncontrollably, from inside his own head—and forcing him to look.

Feeling a "deep and hopeless dread" he gets off the train and walks straight "into the arms of Mrs. Yarrow" (74). His reaction is instructive: upon seeing her he feels "glad of heart, as if he had been saved from something, a mortal danger or a *threatened shame*" (74, my emphasis). Mrs. Yarrow saves him from his own thoughts, thoughts that had become so powerful that they "externated" (70). With Mrs. Yarrow the eidolons stop: "Not one, fair or foul, showed itself, and slowly he felt a great weight lifting from his heart. In its place there sprang up a joyous gratitude towards Mrs. Yarrow, who had saved him from them, from himself" (76). There is room to read some sort of sexual repression or confusion here. Alford's thoughts are being externalized and he is fearful of some unnamed shame that they might "out." Being with a woman calms that fear, makes the externalizing stop, and what he feels for her first and foremost is "gratitude," not love. Indeed, a short time later over dinner Alford thinks to himself that "It was not passion, it was not love, he perceived well enough; it was the utterance of a vital conviction that she had saved him from an overwhelming subjective horror" (78). Moreover, despite his attentions to her, Alford does not ask Mrs. Yarrow to marry him. We are never given a real explanation for Alford's not doing so but at this point in the story, the narrator states that "Wanhope here permitted himself a philosophical excursion in which I will not accompany him" (81). Its placement in the narrative suggests that this excursion might have something to do with Alford's "psychology" when it comes to women and marriage, and it is notable that the narrator does not make the reader privy to it.

After Mrs. Yarrow leaves the spa, Alford has a complete collapse and the visions return. It is finally on the advice of his doctor, to whom he confides, that Alford goes back to see Mrs. Yarrow and asks her to marry him. Before Alford proposes, however, he tells the widow of his visions. When she, rather jokingly, asks him what he sees when he looks at her, Alford gets at the heart of his reason for wanting to marry her: "I could never see any one else while I looked at you!" (88). The narrator comments that Alford was "only half aware" of the poetry of this remark, and really meant "what he said very literally" (88). While the narrator says that poor Mrs. Yarrow "took only the poetry" (88), she ultimately understands her position well enough. "Then I am a prescription!" (88), she pointedly tells Alford in the same conversation. Furthermore, when Mrs. Yarrow pays a visit to Alford's doctor before agreeing to marry him, she half-heartedly argues that women "have no right . . . to expect the ideal in life. The best they can do seems to be to make the real look like it" (89). For Alford, she is willing to take part in marriage that is, on some level, a masquerade—and with a full understanding, it seems, of its social necessity. When one of the club members asks Wanhope if they do in fact marry he replies: "Oh yes. At any rate, they were married that fall. They are—I believe he's pursuing his archeology studies there—living in Athens" (90). The syntax here is a bit confusing and another club member, known for his cynicism, "smoothly inquire[s]": "Together?" (90). The voluble Wanhope doesn't answer.

Alford is a man fearful of his own thoughts and has no desire to have them vividly manifested in front of his unwilling eyes. His desire *not to see* is paramount; Mrs. Yarrow and marriage are the means to the repression he is after. It is not critical to see this in sexual terms, but his marriage, painstakingly painted by *both* Wanhope and the narrator as pragmatic as opposed to romantic, does have the result of moving Alford outside the club's circle of men and the liminal identity of "bachelor." As an object for their discussion, he is no longer one of Wanhope's boys, though (and this is crucial to the story) his previous membership affords him important considerations in the retelling of Wanhope's narrative to the reader. No longer sick, and thus no longer experiencing "a species of psychological ecstasy almost of spiritual value" either, he is able to pursue his archeological work again—to dig into Grecian history and not be bothered by his own.

Henry James's "Sir Edmund Orme" is a similar tale of "heterosexual fulfillment" thrown into question by the supernatural experience. Edmund Orme is the name of the ghost that haunts Mrs. Marden, a widow who had, many years previously, broken off their engagement. Mrs. Marden went on to marry and have a daughter. When the story begins, that daughter, Charlotte, is of marrying age herself and has a host of suitors, one of whom is our narrator. While it is the wrong done to Orme by *Mrs. Marden* that conjures the ghost, the story insistently focuses on the relationship between Orme and the male narrator/suitor.

That Orme is visible to the narrator raises him above the pack of Charlotte's suitors in the eyes of Mrs. Marden, who has been the only one to ever see Orme. Not unlike Alford's early feelings about his hallucinations, the narrator is delighted by his ability to see Orme: "I . . . felt I had a part to play. So far from dreading another encounter with the 'perfect presence,' as she called it, I was affected altogether in the sense of pleasure."[20] Indeed, the narrator's desire to know Orme quickly becomes more important than courting Charlotte. After his first encounter with Orme, the narrator takes a walk with Charlotte and some of her other suitors. He notes that Mrs. Marden

> remained invisible all the afternoon, but this was a detail to which I gave as little head as I had given to the circumstance of my not having Charlotte to myself, even for five minutes, during all our walk. *I was too much taken up with another interest to care;* I felt beneath my feet the threshold of the strange door, in my life, which had suddenly been thrown open and out of which came an air of a keenness I had never breathed and of a taste stronger than wine. I had heard all my days of apparitions, but it was a different thing to have seen one and to know that I should in all likelihood *see it familiarly,* as I might say, again. (159, my emphasis)

These sensations, most often used in the description of heterosexual love, are in this case reserved for the young man's experience with Orme.

The narrator quickly becomes a sort of authority on Orme (condescending even to Mrs. Marden on the topic) and feels that a certain kind of relation to the ghostly is called for, one that preserves the mystery of the event and, perhaps more importantly, the ambiguity of the relationship between Orme and the suitor. According to the narrator, Orme is so "fine and . . . sensitive," so "thoroughly honorable" that "I should no more have thought of *taking a liberty*, of practicing an experiment, with him, *of touching* him . . . or of addressing him, since he set the example of silence, than I should have thought of committing any other social grossness" (167, my emphasis). This "etiquette" nicely illustrates Henry James's famous distaste for the kind of experiments performed by the Society for Psychical Research on supernatural phenomena.[21] Such an approach, however, also works to ensure that the narrator's connection with Orme is special and, quite tellingly, more elaborately coded and thrilling than his courtship of a (living) woman.

Like any good suitor, the narrator is alive to the way Orme looks and carries himself: "He had always, as I saw, more fully later, the perfect propriety of his position—looked always arrayed and anointed, and carried himself ever, in each particular, exactly as the occasion demanded" (167). And while the narrator finds Orme "strange, incontestably" he also thinks of him "as right" (167) and adopts Mrs. Marden's description of him as a "'perfect presence'" (158). His obsession with Orme becomes strong enough to excite in him thoughts on life's most poetic subjects: "I very soon came to attach an idea of beauty to his unrecognized presence, the beauty of an old story, of love and pain and death" (167). Ultimately, the narrator's feelings for Orme affect the believability of the depth of feeling he professes to have for Charlotte. In a telling moment the narrator comments that "After our visit to Trenton Sir Edmund Orme gave us a holiday, and I confess it was at first a disappointment to me. I felt myself by so much less designated, less involved and connected—all with Charlotte I mean to say" (169). The narrator's need to clarify *who* he feels less connected to reflects how easily we could mistake his professed love of Charlotte for the interest he has in the far more romanticized figure of Orme.

In the end, the only thing stronger than the narrator's interest in Orme is his desire to keep Charlotte from ever seeing him. While the narrator explains this duty as one of keeping "an adorable girl" from being "menaced and terrified" (170), it also maintains the secrecy and exclusivity of the narrator's decidedly romantic supernatural relationship. In the final scene of the tale, however, Charlotte does see Orme. This is a complicated moment of loss for the narrator. The narrator's response to Charlotte's sight is to "cover her, to veil her face" from Orme (172). It seems now, incontestably, that the narrator has his full attention on Charlotte. And yet, when the story closes he is thinking of Orme. At the same moment that he hears Charlotte "shriek" at the sight of Orme, he reports "another sound, the wail of one of the lost, fell at the same instant on my ear" (172). The last lines of the story find the suitor trying to figure out whether that sound, in competition with and which he describes as "more tragic" than Charlotte's shriek, was the "despairing cry" of Mrs. Marden or "the articulate sob" of Orme (173). Thus the tale of "heterosexual fulfillment" ends on a note of loss, and the supernatural has provided a new stage on which to enact the "homoerotic ritual of heterosexual exchange."[22]

In both "The Eidolons of Brooks Alford" and "Sir Edmund Orme," the moment of commitment to a woman is also the moment at which something significant comes to an end for the male protagonists. While this brings real relief to Alford and, supposedly, contentment to the narrator of "Sir Edmund Orme," the intensity of the supernatural experience has altered the dynamic of heterosexual fulfillment. Given that Orme made the narrator feel a "keenness I had never breathed and of a taste stronger than wine" and that Alford's eidolons gave him, however briefly, an "ecstasy almost of spiritual value," we are left to wonder at the desires of the protagonists and to question if married life will ever measure up. Whatever the answer, it is true that in fictional tales of the supernatural, women like Mrs. Yarrow and Charlotte not only effectively end intense experiences for the men, but also foreclose any new perceptions of self found within the supernatural experience, making heterosexual union seem rather narrowly scripted by comparison. The supernatural experience has hinted at the possibility of "something more" in these men—something vital, though repressed, something as beyond rationalism as it is beyond the pleasures of heterosexual commitment.

## MANLY ANCESTORS AND THE LESSONS OF PRIMITIVE MASCULINITY

As Chapter Three illustrates, the literature of experimental psychology and psychical research linked the subliminal self to a more primitive self through nervous diseases like hysteria. Such a link is taken up in some form in an extraordinary number of supernatural tales at the turn of the century. In other words, new ideas about alternate states of consciousness made it possible for supernatural fiction to engage in "scientific" understandings of the self that not only allowed for the exploration of submerged desires but suggested a submerged self that was linked to a more "primitive" masculinity. Jack London's "Who Believes in Ghosts?!" (1895), "When the World Was Young" (1910) and "Planchette" (1906) as well as Henry James's "Owen Wingrave" (1892) are all tales in which the male "other" is an out-of-time specter, inhabiting the primitive through his timelessness and/or "savage" masculinity and who supplies an alternative masculinity to the modern, educated white man.

Primitive societies, as well as certain races,[23] were thought of as existing (for the dominant culture) outside of linear time. This "temporal illusion" of an "eternal present" is, according to Marianna Torgovnic, "among the most persistent aspects of primitivism in the West."[24] Thus, to construct the subliminal or unconscious as a more primitive part of the self is to also permanently embed in every man a primal nature, timeless and unscathed by over-civilization. The primitive, as it was now being used in supernatural fiction, naturalizes, for white men, the idea of a more elementary, essentially instinctual masculinity—covered over perhaps, but fundamental and thus secure.

"Who Believes in Ghosts?!" was London's first piece of supernatural fiction to be published and, like so many from this period, it brings together the educated "rational" male with his opposite, that is to say, his "primitive" self. The story's three major characters are educated, scientifically-minded young men and we meet them as they are politely debating the possible existence of disembodied spirits. Of the three friends, only George believes in ghosts, while the other two, the well-named Damon and Pythias, find the idea patently ridiculous. In defending himself, George echoes the line of argument often used by William James, which, among other things, shows a popular awareness of the connections between psychical research and experimental psychology. In trying to convince his friends of the existence of ghosts, George asks the psychical researcher's standard question: "Can you, with this great mass of evidence staring you in the face, say that it is all the creation of diseased brains and abnormal imaginations?"[25] Interestingly, when George explains to his friends what can happen when you see a ghost, he focuses on the bodily trials and ends up reciting many of the major symptoms of hysteria: "these evil spirits have the power to deprive you of one, two, or all your senses, if they so wish. They can burst your ear-drums, sear your eyes, destroy your voice, sadly impair your sense of taste and smell, and paralyze the body in any or every nerve" (14).

As a "scientific experiment" Damon and Pythias agree to spend the night in the town's haunted house. Bored after a couple of hours, they begin a game of chess. Soon, their bodies, and eventually their minds, are taken over by the spirits of two dead men and the "symptoms" described by George begin to manifest themselves. Unknowingly, the two young men are reenacting an old and violent struggle that took place generations earlier between an uncle and his nephew. The nephew had repeatedly cheated his uncle out of his fortune and when there was nothing left but the house, they decided to play a game of chess, with the winner retaining possession of the house. When the nephew wins, the older man strangles him in a state of dementia. The possession of Damon's and Pythias's bodies do not come all at once. There is a great struggle to resist, which importantly they fail: "their faces were distorted in an idiotic gibber. This so horrified them, that they quickly brought their wills to bear and their faces resumed the expression of bewilderment" (15). But will is not enough and within minutes Damon realizes "he was undergoing a reincarnation. He felt himself rapidly evolving into someone else, or some one else was rapidly evolving into him. His own personality disappeared and as in a dream, he found another *more powerful* personality had been projected into, or had overcome—swallowed up his own. . . . As these strange things had happened to Damon, so happened they to Pythias" (16, my emphasis). Once the two men are possessed, the game becomes, according to the narrator, "a mighty duel" (16–17): "Damon boldly opened. . . . Pythias responded. . . . Damon's attack was brilliant and rapid; but he was met with combinations so bold and novel, that by the twenty-seventh move it was broken up" (16). And thus it goes on, with each losing, then gaining, the edge over the other. The feelings of the two players are now anything but gentlemanly. Damon feels an "implacable hatred and horrid desire for revenge" and "a thousand devils seemed to urge him on to the consummation of his desire" (16). Further, it is no longer rationality but deception that has the highest value. Pythias "felt endowed with all the cunning and low trickery of the world" and the "exultation to overthrow, to cast him down, rose paramount" (16).

Perhaps the most important thing worth noting here is the permeability of the male subject—the utter vulnerability of Damon and Pythias—and the fact that the two young men cannot sustain enough "will" to remain themselves. Their rational selves (not to mention their legendary friendship) are no match for the power of the charged personalities of the two dead men. Secondly, London imports the language of abnormal psychology—specifically, the split personality. In this way, the story can retain its connection with the scientific, while the behavior of the young men becomes barbaric as they reenact both the game and then the violent fight.

Here, then, in the place of the civilized man, is the savage competitor. In her book *National Manhood,* Dana Nelson argues that one of the most important trends over the course of the nineteenth century is the creation of an imagined fraternity among white men whose aim, in the words of Burton Bledstein, was to "eliminate wasteful competition and to establish universal standards for moral and civil behavior" (14). As Nelson goes on to argue, however, this connection between white men is "always at risk of being lost between the clashing imperatives of fraternity and competition, brotherhood and self-interest" (16), a tension the story captures. The denial of difference within the white, scientific fraternity is here safely disabled through the supernatural projection of savage competition onto the men's ghostly ancestors. But this is not the only job the supernatural takes on; it has also simultaneously placed the virility of white manhood on display.

At dawn, as Damon realizes he will lose the game, he attacks his friend "with an awful cry" and starts to strangle him "with a wonderfully sublime joy" (17). They are saved by the appearance of their friend George and a couple of policemen who separate them. In short order we are told that "Damon, came, bewildered, to his senses, and helped to restore *his chum*" (17, my emphasis). The recuperation of the fraternal order is swift and unquestioned. The story ends with the police Sargent telling of the legendary game the two were re-enacting, but nothing more is said about Damon or Pythias. Like many supernatural tales, the greatest amount of space is taken up by the disintegration or transformation of the male self with the endings coming very quickly, giving only a short line to the protagonist's restoration to his former self. We are told of a recuperation but do not witness it, and we never see the effects of the experience on the men after their "normal" life resumes. The story, then, has been able to safely speak to male anxiety over competition, the limits of rationalism, physical vulnerability, virility and difference. However, in addressing these things through a supernatural experience *understood as psychological dissociation,* a class-bound homosociality remains in tact.

In 1910 Jack London published a tale that dealt more directly with the "primitive" side of white manhood. "When the World was Young" tells the story of James Ward, a successful businessman in San Francisco by day and a "savage and a barbarian living under the primitive conditions of several thousands of years before" by night.[26] Again, using theories of split personality, London sums up a central, post-Darwinian problem for the male subject at this time: "In himself he was two men, and chronologically speaking, these men were several thousand years or so apart" (128). Like Wanhope and the three young men in "Who Believes in Ghosts?!," Ward is well-versed in abnormal psychology, having "studied the question of dual personality probably more profoundly than any half dozen of the leading specialists in that intricate and mysterious psychological field" (128). Importantly, London makes his character fully aware of both personalities at all times. This gives James Ward a measure of self-control beyond your common hysteric. And, by being "both selves and both selves all the time" (128), it is harder to say which self is "wrong" or morbid and which is proper and healthy. The two, in other words, can exist inside one man. The problem, then, is not the primitive savage himself, but his successful negotiation in the modern world.

Despite the fact that doctors label him "a mental monstrosity and a de-generate" (129), Ward becomes a successful businessman and buys an estate, where he spends his nights roaming his land, letting out his more primitive self. We are told that after a kill, or in "moments of happiness, exaltation, or battle, he was prone to burst out in wild barbaric songs and chants" (129). This is explained as "some quirk of atavism, a certain portion of that early self's language had come down to him as a racial memory" (129). Crucially, when Ward gives a professor of languages a sampling of his songs and chants, we learn that he is speaking an early form of German. In other words, he is racially pure. Ward may be primitive, but he is not, in the words of William James, speaking any "Central African mumbo jumbo."[27] The *kind* of primitive you are, then, is important. Ward's "Teutonic" language perhaps best explains why the animalistic behavior of the night is not censored by the civilized day self.[28]

As it turns out, Ward's only real problem—not surprisingly—is women. The one thing that his civilized self cannot condone is the sexuality of his primitive self, a problem mirrored in the general culture of the middle and upper classes. Sports, war, imperialism are all acceptable forms of primitive masculinity, while sexuality had to be held in strict control—as part of an important set of racial distinctions among other things. Ward decides that "afternoon love-making could be prosecuted successfully; but. . . . found it appalling to imagine being married and encountering his wife after dark" (131). Despite his best intentions, though, Ward falls in love, and after proposing to his beloved, ventures to host a weekend house party.

On the last night of the party, Ward is awakened by the sound of his dogs in a desperate fight with a bear. Ward rushes out to battle the bear and does so successfully, clubbing it to death. Unfortunately, this spectacle unfolds in front of the eyes of his houseguests. Once the bear is dead, his guests rush to him, "but James Ward suddenly looking out of the eyes of the early Teuton, saw the fair frail Twentieth Century girl he loved, and felt something snap in his brain. . . . Inside his brain was an intolerable agony. It seemed as if the soul of him were flying asunder" (134). After this incident Ward becomes a "wholly . . . modern" man (135) and knows "in all its bitter fullness the curse of civilized fear. He is now afraid of the dark, and a night in the forest is to him a thing of abysmal terror." On the other hand, "he evinces a great interest in burglar-proof devices. His home is a tangle of electric wires. . . . [and] he has invented a combination keyless door-locks that travelers may carry in their vest pockets and apply immediately and successfully under all circumstances" (135). Ward has gained a wife but lost his primitive self. London exaggerates the effeminacy this loss induces in order to confirm the validity of a (racially pure) primitive self. The tale not only shows well a new connection being made between psychological concepts such as the alter ego or the split personality and primitive masculinity, but also reveals the fear that women have the power to change something very deep within this newly discovered subconscious, so recently masculinized by psychology.

Jack London's 1906 story "Planchette"[29] also deals with two young lovers, Chris and Lute. For reasons Chris will not disclose, however, he cannot marry. His haunting and eventual death at the spectral hands of his lover's long-dead father reveal some of the disparate and contentious ideals embedded in the definition of dominant manhood and primitive masculinity.

When we meet Chris and Lute, we are privy to Lute thoughts on her lover's personality—a personality that becomes a primary focus and source of mystery in the story. In Lute's estimation, Chris "could not express himself by word nor look nor touch without weaving into the expression, subtly and *occultly*, the feeling as of a hand that passed and that in passing stroked softly and soothingly. Nor was this all-pervading caress a something that cloyed with too great sweetness. . . . It was vigorous, compelling, masculine. . . . It was part of him, the breath of his soul as it were, involuntary and unpremeditated" (192–3, my emphasis). Later Lute remarks to Chris that he seems "to draw affection from all living things, as the trees draw moisture from the ground" and that this comes to him as his "birthright" (195). Finally, she tells him: "every animal loves you" (230). All these characteristics are aspects of the modernist conception of primitives. As Torgovnick argues, this construction viewed primitives as "mystics, in tune with nature, part of its harmonies" and, also like Chris, with personalities that displayed a noticeably "evocative power."[30] Fittingly, then, Chris's magnetism is the sum of his possessions. He and Lute are staying at a "summer camp of city-tired people" in California, though the lovers are both healthy natives of the state. It is a liminal environment. But unlike Chris, Lute is grounded by her family and past. She is at the camp with her Aunt Mildred and Uncle Robert, who raised her from infancy and whom she consistently refers to as "my people" (195). We are also told that Lute had a dream of becoming a great pianist and was about to go study in Germany when she met Chris (four years prior to the events of the story) and decided to stay in California. Chris seems to have no "people," nor does he have a job, past, or interests beyond Lute. Chris has no part in the professionalization that at this time is key part of the ongoing project to construct a particular— that is white and middle-class—national manhood. Chris's rootlessness and lack of profession, along with the "primitive" characteristics, help define his racial otherness. Specifically, they code him as Native American.

This argument is greatly substantiated by the ghost of Lute's dead father, a captain in the United States army who, we soon find out in a convoluted vision of his daughter's, spent most of his career as a solider fighting in the Indian wars. Communication with the dead father is achieved through planchette writing, introduced suitably by a Boston woman whose "frigid" magnetism is contrasted with Chris' warmer allure and Lute's healthiness. When Chris takes his turn, his hand writes out a message from the Captain. It is a letter of intent, telling Chris that he has already made two attempts on his life and will not stop until he "destroys" him (240).

Chris and the Captain represent two kinds of masculinity popularized at the turn of the century. Lute's father is associated with the planchette, a thing that "smacks of medievalism" (242). When Lute begins thinking of her father after his message is read, she imagines his great war horse, "his bravery, his quick temper, his impulsive championship, his madness of wrath in a righteous cause, his warm generosity and swift forgiveness, and his chivalry that epitomized codes and ideals primitive as the days of knighthood" (245). This characterization participates in the intensified interest in the medieval dating from this period, which played an important part in the cult of strenuosity.[31] At the same time, however, Chris displays many of the manly attributes celebrated in the pages of popular heroic adventure novels. He is healthy, strong, brave and magnetic. In fact, London is at pains to contrast him with another man staying at the camp, a capitalist, significantly, who is described by Lute as "obtuse and stupid like the ox . . . [and who] will follow you [Chris] about . . . like a little dog" (231).

"When the World Was Young" implies that specific characteristics are embedded in race and can be transmitted over ages genetically. In "Planchette," many of Chris's characteristics support this fantasy and connect him to popular images of the Native Americans. The story, then, can be read as a sort of purification ritual in which the white male solider—on whose shoulders a certain national identity rests—kills the man who is incapable of becoming the proper (white) husband. In killing Chris, a racial status quo is re-established. But, I would argue, it is done so without reaffirming that status quo. Indeed, the way London characterizes a romantic union between Chris and Lute compellingly criticizes a system that would break them up. In the moments before the "spectral blow" that throws Chris and his new horse "Comanche" to their death, London writes of the connection between Lute and Chris in dramatically glowing terms. As they ride together before the fall,

> All things tended to key them to an exquisite pitch—the movement of
> their bodies, at one with the moving bodies of the animals beneath them;
> the gently stimulated blood caressing the flesh through and through with
> the soft vigors of health; the warm air fanning their faces . . . permeating

them and bathing them, subtly, with faint, sensuous delight; and the
beauty of the world . . . flowing upon them and bathing them in the delight that is of the spirit and is personal and holy, that is inexpressible yet
communicable by the flash of an eye and the dissolving of the veils of the
soul (268–9).

But while on some level it is heterosexual love that places Chris in danger,
London offers another compelling reason for Chris's death, one that has a
great deal to do with a dominant form of white masculinity: excessive faith in
the use of science and rational thought to answer all the riddles of the uni-
verse. Lute becomes nervous after the reading of her father's planchette message and tries to get Chris to wait on buying the new horse. When he expresses
surprise at her fear, she cogently argues that "Science may be too dogmatic in
its denial of the unseen. The forces of the unseen, of the spirit, may well be
too subtle, too *sublimated,* for science to lay hold of. . . . Don't you see, Chris,
that there is rationality in the very doubt?" (252, my emphasis). Her position
does not dismiss science, only asks like William James if it is not too simplis-
tic. Interestingly, London, in the next instant, genders the argument by having Lute suddenly stereotype herself as an irrational woman: "Besides" she
says, "I am a woman, and that should in itself fully account for my predisposition toward superstition" (253). It is at this point that Chris dismisses her
argument. He believes that it is only the subconscious mind that manifests itself through planchette writing. Like so many supernatural tales from this period, the language of psychology is put to crucial work by men. Chris explains
that "We are playing with the subjective forces of our own being, with phenomena which science has not yet explained, that is all. Psychology is so
young a science. The subconscious mind has just been discovered. . . . the laws
of it are yet to be formulated" (257–8). His theorizing leads to a fatal arro-
gance: "The dead?" he says to Lute before their last ride, "I laugh at the dead.
They do not exist. They are not. I defy the powers of the grave" (256). Lute's
father, whose actions in life, we are told, were guided by "his spiritual nature"
(245) show the limits of masculinity based on rationalism alone. In the end,
Lute's double vision of both "the real happening" and "also the vision of her
father dealing the spectral blow" (271) is most accurate.

Chris is an interesting figure throughout the story because his different
characteristics are so richly connotative. While his manliness is secured somewhat traditionally in his athleticism, health and bravery, his detachment from
commercial or familial signifiers make his masculinity somewhat more original. The ending of the story, however, seems to square off two different kinds
of manhood, each polarized by the other. Finally, Chris stands (too) firmly in

one tradition, and ironically for a character coded as Native American, he loses his life because of his devotion to rationalist thought, one of the most important characteristics of white manhood.

Like London's tale, Henry James's "Owen Wingrave" (1892) takes on the cult of heroism and the celebration of strenuosity that mark this historical moment through revisiting an earlier generation of men who adhered blindly to traditions of heroic manhood. Owen Wingrave is a young man of great mental and physical talent who desires to pursue a life of the intellect. He comes, however, from a long line of soldiers and the story focuses on his attempt to free himself from this military inheritance. Owen disputes his family legacy on the grounds of its out-moded behavior. To his mind, war is a form of "crass barbarism."[32] Paradoxically, however, Owen's refusal to become a solider, his desire to move out of what he considers to be a more primitive culture and live a different kind of life, place him more solidly than ever in the past.

After refusing to continue with his military training, Owen is sent home to be re-indoctrinated into the ways of the family. His refusal has "'started up all the old ghosts'" (336), in particular, the ghost of his great-great-grandfather, Colonel Wingrave, who in a fit of rage killed his own son and was then himself found dead the following morning in the room where the boy had been laid out for burial. The oppressive domestic scene Owen returns to, then, becomes as contentious and, as it turns out, as life-threatening as any battlefield. As is the case in "Planchette," a woman provides a precipitating factor in the battle between men. It was generally understood, before his revolt against the military life, that Owen would marry Kate Julian, an impoverished family friend, whose own family history is littered with dead soldiers. She is angry at Owen for his turn against the family's long-standing tradition and ferociously teases him about his courage to try to shame him into returning to the fold, and thus to her. The haunted room where Colonel Wingrave was found dead becomes the proving ground. On a dare, Kate locks Owen in the room for the night. At some point in the early dawn, however, she regrets her decision and goes to let him out. She finds him lying dead "on the spot on which his ancestor had been found" looking "all the young solider on the gained field" (352).

Once again the more primitive powers of the past cannot be denied. No matter how scientifically knowledgeable, psychologically or intellectually modern, the return of these "past men" overwhelm the protagonist's selfhood. This is not to say that the authors do not have sympathy for their modern men. Owen has qualities of the best Jamesian characters: intellect and imagination. And while Owen's ancestors, like Lute's father, are somewhat romanticized for their unflinching commitment to a militaristic ideal, they are lacking qualities that both London and James clearly admire. Indeed, the narrator of James's story describes Owen as "of a substance too fine to be handled with [the] blunt fingers" of his relatives (327). Still, in many ways, the visits from violent men of the past emphasize the uncertainty of selfhood and/or the social dislocation that we have come to view the mark of the modern male, especially in literature. In all four tales we see personalities transformed or completely demolished. The vulnerability of these personalities stands in direct contrast to the ghostly presence which is strong, violent and unchanging. But while these stories draw a comparison between the ghosts and the more intellectual men of the present, the use of psychological theories draws a line of connection between them by, in essence, depositing a primitive masculinity into the subconscious of the protagonist. In so doing, these experiences reinvest modern white manhood with primitive power.

## BRINGING IT ALL BACK HOME: NATIONAL MANHOOD IN JAMES'S "THE JOLLY CORNER"

Henry James's "The Jolly Corner" (1908),[33] one of the writer's most complicated supernatural tales, is an excellent example of the connection between the supernatural and new psychological principles of consciousness at the turn of the century. Moreover, it shows the usefulness of the supernatural for exploring both male sexuality and multiple forms of masculinity. Put as simply as possible, "The Jolly Corner" is the story of a fifty-four year old bachelor, Spencer Brydon, who after a thirty-three years of living in Europe returns to America to inspect his properties and simultaneously re-ignites an intimate but romantically ambiguous relationship with his old friend, Alice Staverton. Over the course of the tale Brydon encounters his "ghostly double,"[34] a signifier (or embodiment) that shifts and mutates in spectacularly obfuscating ways. The "other" in this tale is complicated. Fundamentally, this "other" is nothing more (or less) than "the alter ego of his stifled opportunities"[35] or more specifically an "unlived American life"[36] As such, however, it not only brings up Spencer's difficulty in establishing a clear (hetro)sexual relationship with Alice, but also, more generally, Spencer's inability to embrace a specific type of masculinity. While many have commented on the "ambivalences of sexual alignments" that energize the story,[37] there has been little discussion of the ways Spencer's ghostly double speaks to issues of "primitive masculinity" and the effect this has on the, mostly failed, reconstruction of masculinity that is the central event of the story.

Appropriately, this troubling double resides in Spencer's childhood home, which lies empty but intact. The domestic setting, a staple of ghost stories, is an important signifier here, especially because it is Spencer's *childhood* home. The decisive dichotomy between home and community life, which resulted in "the equation of home life with the development of individual character"[38] sets up the possible psychological dimensions of the story immediately. Moreover, the fact that this home still exists for Spencer to compulsively return to night after night to engage with his other, less developed, self is an important class marker. After all this time, Spencer can still return to a place outside of productive life and the demands of adult manhood.

That Spencer is engaging in some form of regression is made clear fairly early on in the story. Importantly, James connects this regression to the formation of masculinity. Spencer's early relation to his "other" is filled with a kind of fanciful antagonism that is reminiscent of games like Cowboys and Indians and boyhood fictions like *Tom Sawyer* or *Huckleberry Finn;* it is clear that Spencer is fully enjoying the "stalking," as he puts it, of his phantom double:

> The terms, the comparisons, the very practices of the chase positively came again into play; there were even moments when passages of his occasional experiences as a sportsman, stirred memories, from his younger time, of moor and mountain and desert, revived for him—and to the increase of his keenness—by the tremendous force of analogy. He found himself in moments . . . stepping back into the shelter or shade, effacing himself behind a door or in an embrasure, as he had sought of old the vantage of rock and trees; he found himself holding his breath and living in the joy of the instant, the supreme suspense created by big game alone. (741)

As Richard Lowry points out in "Domestic Interiors: Boyhood Nostalgia and Affective Labor in the Gilded Age," boyhood fiction created a separate "psychic geography—that served both as a therapeutic retreat from the demands of an adult masculinity *and* as a space in which that masculinity could best be formed."[39] The male-centered *supernatural* tale supplies something similar.

At this fairly early point in the story, Spencer feels in control, that *he* is the one hunting the "other." And as a hunter (or an hysteric experiencing hyperaesthesia) his senses grow more keen. He has "to an extraordinary degree the power to penetrate the dusk at distances" to "visually project for his purpose a comparative clearness" (742). This "acquired faculty" makes him feel like "some monstrous stealthy cat" (742). Spencer has, in his own mind, become a more "primitive" man—the hunter—and he proudly wonders to himself "what it mightn't verily be, for the poor hard-pressed *alter ego*, to be confronted with such a type" (742) as himself. At the same time, while Spencer feels like he has regressed, he also feels he is "enjoying a consciousness, unique in the experience of man" by having "formed a relation" with his alter ego. He feels "he could 'cultivate' his whole perception" (743), and "bring . . . to perfection" his conscious self. In this way, Spencer's "primitive" behavior as a hunting animal in a primitive setting—where doors and other tricks of architecture mutate back into rocks and trees—can be seen as part, but only part, of an evolutionary movement. He is also "cultivating" his perceptions to new heights of sensitivity. Evolutionist language runs throughout the story, but it does so in both directions, recalling William James's dual conception of the subconscious as both progressive and primitive. In "The Jolly Corner" this dualism gets increasingly confusing as evolution/devolution, seer/seen, hunter/hunted shifts between the two selves.

For instance, at the moment Spencer's perception reaches its height of sensitivity, what he perceives is the fact that he is no longer in complete control. Rather than shadowing the other, he perceives "of his being definitely followed, tracked at a distance carefully taken and to the express end that he should be the less confidently, less arrogantly, appear to himself merely to pursue" (743–4). Spencer tells himself, "'He's there, at the top, and waiting—not, as in general, falling back for disappearance. He is holding his ground, and it's the first time—which is a proof, isn't it? that something has happened for him'" (744). This turn of events provokes exquisite feelings of contradiction. The certainty with which Spencer feels this change "made a single mouthful, as it were, of terror and applause" (745). Applause "since, if it was his other self he was running to earth, this ineffable identity was thus in the last resort not unworthy of him" (745), and terror at his new position of hunted: "he was already trying to measure by how much more he himself might now be in peril of fear" (745).

This highly charged moment is marked "by a prodigious thrill, a thrill that represented sudden dismay, no doubt, but also represented, and with the selfsame throb, the strangest, most joyous, possibly the next minute almost the proudest, *duplication of consciousness.* . . . Brydon at this instant tasted probably of a sensation more complex than had ever before found itself consistent with sanity" (745, my emphasis). This duplication of self is expressed, importantly, through the subject of courage; Spencer is *both* "rejoicing that he could, in another form, actively inspire that fear, and simultaneously quaking for the form in which he might passively know it" (745). Nelson has argued that "fraternal enactments are haunted by the simultaneously challenging and barred other."[40] In this complicated instant Spencer is perhaps momentarily free from this conundrum by actually experiencing doubleness. It is, however, a balancing act that cannot sustain itself. Spencer soon feels a "vivid impulse, above all, to move, to act, to charge, somehow and upon something—to show himself, in a word, that he wasn't afraid" (745–6).

Spencer's double conveys particular questions about nation and sexuality. Specifically, what kind of man America would have made out of Spencer, and, in connection, if that American manhood would have led him into marriage with Alice and a hetero-normative lifestyle in place of the liminal bachelor lifestyle Europe afforded. But the racial assumptions imbedded in Spencer's early encounters with his alter ego crucially inform heterosexual American masculinity, though it has received little critical attention. Eric Savoy argues that Brydon "returns to America as a *self-knowing* 'gay' bachelor—closeted, to be sure but with a sexual affiliation richly and connotatively established—whose provisional identity is contested and unraveled by his encounter with his hypothetical and rather differently closeted double" (3, my emphasis). This hypothetical double, according to Savoy, is the *heterosexual* Spencer, and his repressed desires are those for hetero-normativity and a way to finally explain "his long attachment to Alice Staverton" (9). Certainly the interaction between Spencer and his double reenacts normative masculine behavior, complete with Spencer's overwhelming fear that he will not display enough "courage." But there is more. In a story all about the fluid boundaries of a national and sexual identity, issues of race are crucial.

In turn-of-the-century America, the promise of both white manhood and heterosexual masculinity is "the promise of material privilege combined with privileged association."[41] As *National Manhood* amply proves, such a fraternity, because it is both white and heterosexual, is an "attenuated humanity" (200) that can never deliver on its promise of "rich emotional mutuality" (19). Spencer's proudest and most joyous moment in the story comes with his "duplication of consciousness," but it is really only in that one moment that he can live in a state of "radical equality" (18) with his other self. Through most of the tale this self is constructed as "other."

Theories of split personality and race were intertwined at the turn of the century. William James published an article in *Scribner's* in 1890 entitled "The Hidden Self." In it, James talks about a submerged self, one that is "fully conscious yet sealed off from normal consciousness, that preserves and represses memories of guilt or trauma."[42] Pauline Hopkins found James's ideas about the split self so useful to the lived experience of race in America that she used "The Hidden Self" as the subtitle to her novel *Of One Blood*, which began serial publication in 1902. In Hopkins's novel, one's race—specifically one's African blood—is the submerged part of the self. The novel is in some sense the story of that self coming to the surface and being "therapeutically . . . reconfigured" and then, like a Freudian tale, "racial difference [is] . . . acknowledged and its threatening qualities diffused."[43] In his article "Pauline Hopkins and the Hidden Self of Race," Thomas Otten argues that Hopkins's use of James's concepts speaks to the fact that for "many in the age of Jim Crow, the hidden self is not a racially a-specific construct but instead equated with the regressed, the brute, the African" (231).

Thus the references Spencer makes to his double, I would argue, are not only based on patent ideas of hetero-normative masculinity, but make use of racial constructs as well. For instance, he describes his double as "cautious and shifty" (741), as a "creature" who is "perhaps more formidable than any beast of the forest" (741) and he likens his own stalking to hunting "big game" (741). At another point, when Spencer takes the reader through the house, he notes that in the upper rooms the big windows let in "the world he had lived in, and he was more at his ease" (743). This "support" as he calls it, however, "failed him considerably" in the back part of the house. The "rear of the house affected him as the *very jungle of his prey.* The place was there more subdivided; a large 'extension' in particular, where small rooms for servants had been multiplied" (743, my emphasis). This area of the home, "the very jungle of his prey," where servants lived is indeed so "other" that it isn't even part of the original house, but rather an "'extension.'" Finally, when Spencer feels the double has "turned," that is, been provoked into action by Spencer's stalking, it takes on what is called a "menaced interest" and is described as "the fanged or the antlered animal" (744), implying a sexually aggressive or "brute" masculinity that is specifically associated with the African-American male.

Soon after the above descriptions, Spencer has an opportunity to meet his double when "the opposed projections of him" were both "in presence" on opposite sides of a closed door. He decides, however, that he will not open the door. Jumping at the idea of "Discretion!" (749), Spencer refuses to "accept the world of merged unlikenesses." [44] There are obvious issues of masculinity in choosing "Discretion" over the challenge Spencer feels coming from "the blank face of the door," which seemed to say "'Show us how much you have!'" (749). But in refusing the challenge, it is not only a certain type of masculinity, the brave hunter, being forfeited. He is also forfeiting the possibility of a more fully realized self. Spencer tells his alter ego: "you convince me that for reasons rigid and sublime—what do I know?—we both of us should have suffered. I respect them then, and though moved and privileged as, I believe, it has never been given to man, I retire" (750). So is it some sort of respect for the other that stops him? Perhaps not. Earl Rovit has persuasively argued that "discretion" in this case should be read in its secondary meaning, "as an act of separating or making sharp distinction between" (165). What, then, Spencer has retained in this moment of discretion is in fact, "the narrowly exclusive construction of his personality" (165). Indeed, despite his attempt at casting the experience as one of mutual respect, Spencer's own emotions change rapidly after his retreat. He feels a "vague anguish" (751), an absolute defeat in not being able to meet his shadowy double. The other now is not just "the agent of his shame" but shame itself "for his shame *was the deep abjection*" (752, my emphasis).

There are many ways to read this shame. With the issue of manliness or strenuous masculinity coming up again and again, the shame seems most compellingly to be Spencer's inability to conquer (become?) the other, and thus the Rooseveltian heterosexual American man. In fact, in this particular story, and for this particular author, what happens to Spencer should be seen in the context of Roosevelt's statements about the American male who goes abroad: "it is for the undersized man of letters," Roosevelt argued "who flees his country because he, with his delicate, effeminate sensitiveness, finds the conditions of life on this side of the water crude and raw; in other words, because he finds he cannot play a man's part among men, and so goes where he will be sheltered from the winds that harden stouter souls."[45] If not exactly buying into this idea, James certainly makes use of it, for it is in his American house that Spencer feels, through his stalking of the other, "a rigor to which nothing in his life had been comparable" (741). So it is perhaps the failure of these feelings to translate into a showdown and ultimate victory over his prey that is his shame. He has taken the measure of his manhood and found it wanting.

But perhaps it is not about conquering his prey so much as simply meeting his other. Spencer may not want so much to vanquish his hidden self as bring it to the surface, and, like the protagonist of Hopkins' novel, who has repressed his African blood, diffuse its "threatening qualities."[46] If Spencer is, in fact, a "self-knowing 'gay' bachelor"[47] it makes little sense to claim that the threatening qualities of his repressed self are homosexual desires. Indeed, the return to America, the re-kindled relationship with Alice Staverton, the language of the hunt and bids for bravery, all make it far more likely that Spencer is indulging in his repressed desires for hetero-normative masculinity itself. However, given the racial implications embedded in the idea of the hidden self, and the language Spencer uses to characterize his alter ego, I suggest that the threatening qualities of the repressed self are also, at least to some degree, about a racial other. The most utopian reading of the story would allow that Spencer's actions, his decision not to look, coupled with the obvious pleasure he gets from interacting with his double early on in the story, show a desire to extend the "attenuated humanity" of the white male fraternity. In his "proudest moment," when he is able to achieve double consciousness, he is both self and other. At the very least, the characteristics Spencer chooses to give his other, the evolutionary language that runs throughout the story, the connection being made between the subconscious and primitivism, the suffering Spencer concedes to the invisible presence and, finally, the shame that "was the deep abjection" make it important to include race as part of the otherness that Spencer is experiencing.

Upon leaving the house, however, Spencer does come in contact with a visible presence, one he has not sought. What he focuses on when he sees this image at the bottom of the stairs is "his vivid truth, his grizzled bent head and white masking hands, his queer actuality of evening-dress, of dangling double eye-glass, of gleaming silk lappet and white linen, of pearl button and gold watch-guard and polished shoe" (187). This is a complete image with a certitude of style and modernity that Spencer, I would argue, was never after. And, as we soon find out, this particular image fits exactly the description of the man *Alice Staverton* has seen in her dreams. She too, of course, has a stake in the man Spencer might have become had he stayed in America. For Spencer himself, the most exciting moments in the house are those spent sparring with his "primitive" double. When faced with the decision to look, he emphatically chooses not to. He does not want, it seems, a fully realized other, "hard and acute" (755) like the figure he ultimately sees, but rather a doubled self that brings him back, both problematically and tellingly, to a less "civilized" time. The fully actualized "intruder" at the bottom of the stairs has "a life larger than his own" (756), and one in front of which Spencer literally collapses.

Spencer regains consciousness with his head resting on Alice Staverton's lap. When he asks how she managed to save him, she kisses him and only replies "And now I keep you" (759). Spencer remains physically passive for the rest of the story, literally leaning on Alice; and there is a sense that Alice has managed to end things, to "foreclose any further disclosures"[48] through the certitude of her apparition. Spencer's engagement with his alter ego is first rejected by Spencer himself and then displaced by Alice's projection and, ultimately, by Alice herself. But, regardless of Spencer's own desire to be saved by Alice, "O keep me, keep me" is his reply to her statement of possession, the most idealized moment in the story comes not when Spencer is coupled with Alice, but rather at the moment of Spencer's "proudest duplication of consciousness," when he is coupled with his "other" self.

## CONCLUSION

Questions about white male virility appear, in some form, in every story discussed here. Even Howells's tales, while not presenting primitive masculinity, show an anxiety about the "fitness" of white men and their ability to form healthy unions with women. Theories about the subconscious as both primitive and possessing acute powers provide a way of connecting the supernatural tale and primitive masculinity. While most stories place their protagonists in situations that render them, for a time, powerless and/or irrational, this lack of control and irrational behavior is made up for by the space it creates to display a version of manliness unscathed by "over civilization." The ultimate achievement, however, would be the ability to create and control this powerfully fit and virile male. In these insistently homosocial stories it should not be surprising, then, that there exists a common fantasy about men, usually occult scientists, who can create or produce this primitive masculinity at will.

Jack London's "The Rejuvenation of Major Rathbone" (1899)[49] is one such tale. The tale's narrator and his friend Dover are scientists. Major Rathbone is Dover's aged uncle and the male object of their experiment. Rathbone takes on the problem of the split self—one part of which fulfills the requirements of strenuous masculinity while the other meets the needs of "civilization" through heterosexual marriage. Like other male characters in supernatural fiction, he fulfills both while simultaneously highlighting their mutual exclusivity.

The story begins with a discussion between the two scientists, one of whom claims to have developed an elixir that restores lost vitality. London is careful to characterize the liquid as "ordinary" with "none of the brilliant iridescence one would so naturally expect of such a magic compound" (28) and to ground the idea in experiments performed by famous doctors from the period, like the bacteriologist Robert Koch (1843–1910). Scientific authority in stories that use occult knowledge is always on the verge of collapsing. At the end of one Wanhope story the psychologist states that "though all psychology is in a manner dealing with the occult . . . I am shy of its grosser instances, as things that are apt to brings one's scientific poise into question."[50] This story is as much about the two scientists maintaining their claim to a rationalist discourse as it is about restoring lost vitality in men. The trick here is to do both. Given this problem, the tension between the two scientists is productive. The narrator is characterized early in the story as the more conservative. Indeed, the other scientist, Dover, calls him "ossified" and claims that he has "always hung back at the coat-tails of science" (28). The narrator responds that his conservatism has saved science "from breaking its neck" (28). As the more restrained scientist, however, he is the perfect person to help Dover, who at this juncture has become scared of his own success. He tells his scientific brother: "I have grown afraid of myself, and need another mind to hold me in check" (30).

The "heavy, almost colorless fluid" (28) that Dover has isolated as the elixir of youth is produced in all humans. Dover has simply succeeded in isolating the specific compounds that make up the "lymph" that transports nutrients and oxygen to cells. Dover's new lymph infusion, however, does not come from humans. Rather it is an "animal derivative" that "stay[s] and re-move[s] the effects of senility by acting upon the stagnated life-cells" (29). The fact that the particular lymph compound used to restore vitality comes from an animal resonates with contemporary evolutionary theories. As is the case with many London tales, idealized masculinity is partially regressive. While it was argued that primitive races were frozen at a lower level of the evo-lutionary scale, characterized by its closeness to animals and generalized ag-gression, white men were thought only to pass through such a stage in their youth. *Returning* youth for white men, then, would have to come from with-out, in this case, in the guise of an animal extraction.

The injections are administered by the two scientists and soon enough Major Rathbone recovers a good deal of his youth. The story highlights his physical strength and the return of his athleticism: one scene details him breaking in a colt none of the stablemen could control; another has him thrashing union leaders during a labor dispute. But for a man to remain an object of experimentation, he must remain problematic. At the beginning, his problem is simply old age. This adequately distances him from the two scien-tists. After regaining youth, however, something else is needed. The Major's "critical difference" comes in the form of "old man" traits, which remain alongside his youthful energy and strength; the narrator complains that "the irascibility which has come with advancing years still remained. And this, al-lied with the natural stubbornness and truculency of his disposition, became a grievous burden to us" (31). Out of the control of the two scientists, the Major renews his interest in (pointedly conservative) politics and becomes the mayor of the town. But while his success "only stimulated him to greater ac-tivity" (33), the narrator notes that "such activity . . . in one of his advanced years . . . seemed so inconsistent and inappropriate that his friends and rela-tives were shocked beyond measure" (33).

Things reach a crisis point when Major Rathbone, in a move that mir-rors Theodore Roosevelt's the year before this story was written, quits public office and applies for a commission to fight in the Spanish-American war. The two scientists have created a bit of a monster—or at any rate, an imperialist (this is a Jack London story, after all). Like so many of the stories discussed here, the supernatural brings out, or brings about, a specific kind of masculin-ity: vigorous, athletic, animalistic, combative. And in this tale, again like so many others, this is somewhat problematized at the same time that it is val-orized. For instance, while the Major's "tremendous vitality" is called, at one point, "an edifying spectacle" (32), the two scientists are scared, and perhaps threatened, by the *level* of vitality they have created, or possibly the depth of the regression. In discussing this problem, their language is instructive: "'It seems that before we can foist this rejuvenator upon the world, we must also discover an antidote for it—a sort of emasculator to reduce the friskiness attendant upon the return to youth. . . . You see,' Dover went on, 'after revivifying an aged person, that person passes wholly out of our power'" (34).

The scientists themselves do not create a chemical emasculator. Their antidote is an "intangible and abstract" *idea*—to have the Major fall in love. The emasculator, then, is a woman, specifically, the narrator's Aunt Debby. Due to their work with the Major, the two scientists are able to rejuvenate Aunt Debby "with the utmost dispatch" (35). As she grows younger the Major's romantic interest increases, while his "interest in war abated" (36). A woman, it seems, is the perfect "remedy for excessive spirit and strength" (34), something ultimately presented in most of these stories. For their part, the scientists decide that important "contingencies . . . must be seen to before we electrify the sleepy old world with the working formula of our wonderful discovery" (30). Despite their difficulties however, the fact that the narrator's aunt saves Dover's uncle underlines the pleasant homosociality within the scientific community. Fellow scientists can and must save each other—men like Dover push the envelope and scientists like the narrator save his profession's metaphorical neck.

Theories of "vitality" and the bizarre and often telling attempts to make occult scientific theories seem rational are also crucial. Both the topic of vitality and the ways in which it is dealt with betray specific bio-psychological fantasies of male power. Interestingly, unlike the mid–nineteenth-century supernatural tales, such as Poe's "Bernice" or Hawthorne's "The Birthmark," that power is exercised primarily over males, not females.[51] Turn-of-the-century supernatural tales are unique in their undisguised interest in the male body and their willingness to use it as a place of experimentation. (London has another tale, "A Thousand Deaths" in which a mad-scientist father repeatedly kills his son and brings him back to life.) Like all the supernatural stories investigated here, "The Rejuvenation of Major Rathbone" attempts to prove something about the white middle-class male psyche, something that can only safely come out when that male subject is made the object of forces not fully explainable by the model of single consciousness.

Many of the stories make no real effort to distinguish between a supernatural event and a psychological one. But given the characterization of the subconscious at the turn of the century, this makes sense. Supernatural tales can be read as forums in which multiple gendered identities, especially those concerned with male virility, can be safely played out. They offer a stage on which rationality can be pushed to its limits, and where homosociality can be expanded in ways that would be unacceptable outside of the space of the irrational. They consistently problematize heterosexual union and show how preoccupied men were with themselves and their relationships with other men; socially and, at times, erotically. These white male writers and their protagonists betray a deep fascination with the possibility of their own primitivism and, at the same time, a pride and intense identification with the power of rationalism and science. If this contradiction becomes too difficult, the stories also show how easy it is to import women to solve the problem. Still, it is important that, in these narratives, the "other" is not female but male—whether hidden within the self, or manifested as another presence. Within the confines of the supernatural, the tales manage to reconfigure the irrational in ways that actually relieve gender anxieties, especially fears about the effeminacy induced by "over-civilization." Importing racial, psychological, and evolutionary theories, supernatural fiction—like physical education, naturalist novels and psychological research—submits white masculinity to important and often violent re-formations. While at times these discourses reveal the vulnerability of their male subjects, they ultimately work to reinforce white male power.

# Notes

## NOTES TO INTRODUCTION

1.  There are a number of books that overstate (and overuse) the idea of a "crisis in mas-
    culinity." A partial list includes both Kimmel and Rotundo's books, David Leverenz,
    *Manhood and the American Renaissance* (Ithaca, NY: Cornell University Press, 1989);
    Calvin Thomas, *Male Matters: Masculinity, Anxiety and the Male Body on the Line*
    (Chicago: University of Chicago Press, 1996); David Pugh, *Sons of Liberty: the
    Masculine Mind in Nineteenth-Century America* (Westport, CT: Greenwood Press,
    1983); Scott Derrick, *Monumental Anxieties: Homoerotic Desire and Feminine
    Influence in 19th-Century U.S. Literature* (New Brunswick, NJ: Rutgers University
    Press, 1997). Gail Bederman's *Manhood and Civilization: A Cultural History of
    Gender and Race in the United States, 1880–1917* (Chicago: Chicago University
    Press, 1995) is notable for the fact that it avoids this pitfall. She makes the point,
    quite strongly, that while men might be in crisis, patriarchy stayed intact. Judith
    Kegan Gardiner also discusses the problems with "crisis" theory in masculinity stud-
    ies, noting that it often "implicates feminism" and is used as code for the idea that
    changes is the culture have "undermined" "men's masculinity" and thus "social sta-
    bility [is] therefore imperiled." *Masculinity Studies and Feminist Theory: New
    Directions* (New York: Columbia University Press, 2002) 6.
2.  I owe a great deal to Bryce Traister's article, "Academic Viagra: the Rise of American
    Masculinity Studies" *American Quarterly* 52:2 (June 2000), for organizing my
    thoughts around the vague uneasiness I had with the politics and possible conse-
    quences of writing about white manhood for the study of gender. For a more upbeat
    assessment of the ways in which the projects of masculinity studies and women's
    studies and feminism can positively interact with each other, see *Masculinity Studies
    and Feminist Theory: New Directions*. Ed, Judith Kegan Gardiner (New York:
    Columbia University Press, 2002).
3.  Shane Phelan, *Getting Specific: Postmodern Lesbian Politics* (Minneapolis: University
    of Minnesota Press, 1994) 90.
4.  See Robin Wiegman, "Unmaking: Men and Masculinity in Feminist Theory" and
    Calvin Thomas, "Reenflishing the Bright Boys; or How Male Bodies Matter to
    Feminist Theory." *Masculinity Studies and Feminist Theory: New Directions*.
5.  I am thinking specifically here of Judith Butler, *Gender Trouble* (New York:
    Routledge, 1990) and *Bodies That Matter: On the Discursive Limits of "Sex"* (New

York: Routledge, 1993); Diane Elam, *Feminism and Deconstruction: ms. en abyme* (New York: Routledge, 1994) and Diana Fuss, *Essentially Speaking: Feminism, Nature & Difference* (New York: Routledge, 1989).

6.  Judith Butler's early work, *Gender Trouble,* is a good example of this problem. It seemed to some that her celebration of drag and the performative aspects of gender underestimated how entrenched the sexed body is. As Moira Gatens points out: "It is not masculinity per se that is valorized in our culture but the masculine male." (*Imaginary Bodies* 15). In Butler's later book, *Bodies that Matter,* however, she argues that one can see gender as a discursive demarcation without claiming that there is no connection between sex and gender. And, further, that "Constructivism needs to take account of the domain of constraints without which a certain living and desiring being cannot make its way"—cannot, in other words, "matter" (94).

7.  Moria Gatens, *Imaginary Bodies: Ethics, Power and Corporeality* (New York: Routledge, 1996) 13, my emphasis. See also Elisabeth Grosz, *Volatile Bodies: Toward a Corporeal Feminism* (Bloomington: Indiana University Press, 1994).

8.  Rosi Braidotti, *Nomadic Subjects: Embodiment and Sexual Difference in Contemporary Feminism* (New York: Columbia University Press, 1994). 4

9.  Matthew Frye Jacobson, *Whiteness of a Different Color: European Immigrants and the Alchemy of Race* (Cambridge: Harvard University Press, 1998) 5.

10. See, for instance, Tom Pendergast, *Creating the Modern Man: American Magazines and Consumer Culture, 1900–1950* (Columbia: University of Missouri Press, 2000) 14–15; and Bryce Traister's "Academic Viagra: The Rise of American Masculinity Studies."

11. Pendergast, 14.

12. Jim Perkinson, "The Body of White Space: Beyond Stiff Voices, Flaccid Feelings and Silent Cells." *Revealing Male Bodies.* Eds. Nancy Tuana, William Cowling, et al. (Bloomington: Indiana University Press, 2002) 174.

13. Perkinson, 174.

14. Perkinson, 174.

15. In *Nomadic Subjects,* for instance, Rosi Braidotti argues, with Foucault, that by the modern period the body became the center of theoretical attention but insists, unlike Foucault, that "the body to be studied, comprehended, and intellectually possessed is also the woman's." *Nomadic Subjects: Embodiment and Sexual Difference in Contemporary Feminist Theory* (New York: Columbia University Press, 1994) 63. While this work does not aim to refute that female bodies have been "comprehended" more regularly than white men's, it does reveal moments when male bodies are objects of a reformative or authoritative gaze.

16. Judith Butler, *Bodies That Matter* 7

17. Butler, *Bodies That Matter* 187.

18. Mary Ann Doane, "Women's Stake: Filming the Female Body" *Feminism and Film Theory.* Ed. Constance Penely (New York: Routledge, 1988) 217.

19. Luce Irigaray, *This Sex Which Is Not One* (Ithaca: Cornell University Press, 1985) 180.

20. See for example, John Ringnall, *Realist Fiction an the Strolling Spectator* (London: Routledge, 1992); *Spectacles of Realism: Gender, Body, Genre.* Eds. Margaret Cohen and Christopher Prendergast (Minneapolis: University of Minnesota Press, 1995); *American Realism: New Essays.* Ed. Eric Sundquist (Baltimore: Johns Hopkins University Press, 1982).

21. John Rignall. *Realist Fiction and the Strolling Spectator* (London: Routledge, 1992) 2.

22. See Amy Kaplan, *The Social Construction of American Realism* (Chicago: University of Chicago Press, 1988) Chapter 6; Philip Fisher, "Acting, Reading, Fortune's Wheel: Sister Carrie and the Life History of Objects," *American Realism: New Essays.* Ed Eric Sundquist; and Walter Benn Michaels, *The Gold Standard and the Logic of Naturalism: American Literature at the Turn of the Century* (Berkeley: University of California Press, 1987).

23. There has been some wonderful work recently on male hysteria. See Mark Micale, *Diagnostic Discriminations: Jean-Martin Charcot and the Nineteenth-Century Idea of Masculine Hysterical Neurosis* (Yale: Ph.D. Dissertation, 1987); Micale, *Approaching Hysteria: Disease and Its Interpretation* (Princeton: Princeton University Press, 1995) and *Traumatic Pasts: History, Psychiatry, and Trauma in the Modern Age, 1870–1930.* Eds. Mark Micale and Paul Lerner. (New York: Cambridge University Press, 2001). In connecting James's work in psychical research to the French School, See Eugene Taylor, *William James on Exceptional Mental States* and *William James on Consciousness Beyond the Margin.*

24. See Kim Townsend, *Manhood at Harvard: William James and Others* (New York: W.W. Norton, 1996) for textual evidence of changing ideas about what kind of man was ideal.

25. See for instance Townsend, *Manhood at Harvard;* Michael Kimmel, "Consuming Manhood: The Feminization of American Culture and the Recreation of the Male Body 1832–1920," *The Male Body: Features, Destinies, Exposures.* Ed. Lawrence Goldstein (Ann Arbor: University of Michigan Press, 1994); E. Anthony Rotundo, *American Manhood: Transformations in Masculinity from the Revolution to the Modern Era* (New York: Basic Books, 1993); Gail Bederman, *Manliness and Civilization: A Cultural History of Gender and Race in the United States, 1880–1917* (Chicago: Chicago University Press, 1995); Kristin L. Hoganson, *Fighting for American Manhood: How Gender Politics Provoked the Spanish-American and Philippine-American Wars* (New Haven: Yale University Press, 1998); Melissa Debakis "Douglas Tilden's *Mechanics Fountain:* Labor and the 'Crisis of Masculinity' in the 1890s" *American Quarterly* 47:2 (June 1995); *Meanings For Manhood,* Mark Carnes and Clyde Griffen, eds. (Chicago: Chicago University Press, 1990); Harvey Green, *Fit For America: Health, Fitness, Sport and American Society* (New York: Pantheon Books, 1986)

26. Judith Kegan Gardiner, "Introduction." *Masculinity Studies and Feminist Theory: New Directions,* 14.

27. Laura Briggs, "The Race of Hysteria: 'Overcivilization' and the 'Savage' Woman in Late Nineteenth-Century Obstetrics and Gynecology." *American Quarterly* 52:2 (June 2000) 266.

## NOTES TO CHAPTER ONE

1. See for instance, E. Anthony Rotundo, *American Manhood: Transformations in Masculinity from the Revolution to the Modern Era* (New York: Basic Books, 1993); Michael Kimmel, "Consuming Manhood: The Feminization of American Culture and the Recreation of the Male Body, 1832–1920," *The Male Body: Features, Destinies, Exposures.* Ed. Lawrence Goldstein (Ann Arbor: University of Michigan Press, 1994); Gail Bederman, *Manliness and Civilization: A Cultural History of*

*Gender and Race in the United States, 1880–1917* (Chicago: The University of Chicago Press, 1995). John F. Kasson, *Houdini, Tarzan and the Perfect Man: The White Male Body and the Challenge of Modernity in America* (New York: Hill and Wang, 2001).

2. For an interesting discussion on the terms "manliness" and "masculinity" see Bederman *Manliness and Civilization* 7–20.

3. Most recently, Kasson's *Houdini, Tarzan and the Perfect Man* (2001) underestimates the role of class in shaping discourses on the body. While I agree with him that the male body was interesting to all classes at the turn of the century, that interest was not uniform. As this chapter will show, class crucially informed the different "ideal" male bodies being shaped in this transitional period.

4. For the working classes, scientific management was one such regime. For middle-class women, the popular treatments for neurasthenia provide a good example. See, of course, Carroll Smith-Rosenberg, *Disorderly Conduct: Visions of Gender in Victorian America* (New York: Oxford University Press, 1985) and more recently Michele Birnbaum, "Racial Hysteria: Female Pathology and Race Politics in Frances Harper's *Iola Leroy* and W.D. Howells's *An Imperative Duty*," *African American Review* 33:1 (1999); Laura Briggs' "The Race of Hysteria: 'Overcivilization' and the 'Savage' Woman in Late Nineteenth-Century Obstetrics and Gynecology," *American Quarterly* 52:2 (June 2000).

5. Stuart Blumin, "The Hypothesis of Middle-Class Formation in Nineteenth-Century America: A Critique and Some Proposals," *American Historical Review* 90: 2 (1985) 299–338.

6. Such a critique of Foucault comes predominantly from feminist theorists who, while finding much of his work useful, are critical of his "blind-spot" around sexual difference. This leads them to charge him with not paying enough attention to how the bodies themselves *inform* ideological inscription. Which is, importantly, *not* to say that they charge Foucault with seeing the body as "powerless" in the face of social inscription. See for instance, Rosi Braidotti, *Nomadic Subjectivities: Embodiment and Sexual Difference in Contemporary Feminist Theory* (New York: Columbia University Press, 1994); Elizabeth Grosz, *Volatile Bodies: Toward a Corporeal Feminism* (Bloomington, Indiana University Press, 1994); Donna Harraway, *Simians, Cyborgs and Women: The Reinvention of Nature* (New York: Routledge, 1991).

7. See for instance, Allan Sekula, "The Body and The Archive," *October* 39 (Winter 1986): 3–64; Michel Foucault, *Discipline and Punish: The Birth of the Prison*, trans, Alan Sheridan (New York: Vintage Books, 1995); Sander Gilman, *Seeing The Insane* (New York: J. Wiley, 1982) and *Disease and Representation: Images of Illness From Madness to AIDS* (Ithaca: Cornell University Press, 1988); Madeline Stern, "Mathew Brady and the *Rationale of Crime*," *The Quarterly Journal of the Library of Congress* 31: 3 (July 1974): 128–135; Carlo Ginzburg, "Morelli, Freud, and Sherlock Holmes: Clues and Scientific Method," *History Workshop* 9 (Spring 1980) 5–29; David Green, "Veins of Resemblance: Photography and Eugenics," *The Oxford Journal*, 7: 2 (1984): 2–16; Brian Wallis, "Black Bodies, White Science: Louis Agassiz' Slave Daguerreotypes," *American Art* 9: 2 (Summer 1995): 35–59; Ysabel Rennie, *The Search for Criminal Man: A Conceptual History of the Dangerous Offender* (Lexington: Lexington Books, 1978); Maren Stange, "Jacob Riis and Urban Visual Culture: The Lantern Slide Exhibition as Entertainment and

Ideology," *Journal of Urban History,* 15 :3 (1989): 274–303; Griselda Pollock, "Feminism/Foucault-Surveillance/Sexuality," *Visual Culture: Images and Interpretations.* Eds. Norman Bryson, Michael Ann Holly and Keith Moxey (Hanover, NH: University Press of New England, 1994) 1–29; John F. Kasson, *Rudeness and Civility: Manners in Nineteenth-Century Urban America* (New York: Hill and Wang, 1990) 70–111. Laura Briggs, "The Race of Hysteria: 'Overcivilization' and the 'Savage' Woman in Late Nineteenth-Century Obstetrics and Gynecology," *American Quarterly* 52:2 (June 2000); Lisa Cardyn, "The Construction of Female Sexual Trauma in Turn-of-the-Century American Mental Medicine," *Traumatic Pasts: History, Psychiatry, and Trauma in the Modern Age, 1870–1930.* Ed. Mark Micale and Paul Lerner (New York: Cambridge University Press, 2001) 172–201.

8. See Bederman, introduction to *Manliness and Civilization.*
9. George Chauncey, *Gay New York: Gender, Urban Culture and the Making of the Gay Male World, 1890–1940* (New York: Basic Books, 1994) 111.
10. See for instance, Daniel T. Rodgers, *The Work Ethic in Industrial America, 1850–1920* (Chicago: University of Chicago Press, 1974); Alan Trachtenberg, *The Incorporation of America: Culture and Society in the Gilded Age* (New York: Hill and Wang, 1982); Bruce Laurie, *Artisans into Workers: Labor in Nineteenth-Century America* (New York: Noonday Press, 1989); Nicholas Bromell, *By the Sweat of the Brow: Literature and Labor in Antebellum America* (Chicago: University of Chicago Press, 1993).
11. Dudley Sargent, *Physical Education* (Boston: Ginn & Company, 1906) 125.
12. Sargent, preface, *Health, Strength, and Power* (New York: H.M Caldwell and Co., 1904).
13. See, for instance, Ann Fabian, "Making a Commodity of Truth: Speculations in the Career of Benarr Macfadden." *American Literary History.* 1993 5(1): 51–76; Michael Anton Budd, "Every Man a Hero: Sculpting the Homoerotic in Physical Culture Photography." *The Passionate Camera: Photography and Bodies of Desire,* Ed. Deborah Bright (New York: Routledge, 1998): 41–57; Kasson, *Houdini, Tarzan and the Perfect Man.*
14. I refer to Macfadden's work throughout this chapter as popular or populist. Macfadden is hard to place. He is not solidly within a working-class discourse. Indeed, for him, physical culture had a great deal to do with social mobility. However, his lack of concern for efficiency as well as the quality of writing in his magazine places him outside the middle-class discourse as well. I label him populist because he consistently asked his readers to send in pictures of themselves or write articles about their experiences for the magazine, thereby inviting them to become part of the making of popular culture—to be producers as well as consumers. He also repeatedly used his own private experience as proof of the efficacy of his suggestions and constantly reminded his readers he had once been "like them." This is in complete contrast to middle-class physical educators who never stepped down from their separate and authoritative positions.
15. William Blaikie, *How to Get Strong and How To Stay So* (New York: Harper, 1884) 3.
16. Luther Gulick, *The Efficient Life* (New York: Doubleday, Page & Co., 1907) 35.
17. This underlying concern with sexual virility connects the physical culture discourse to that very special middle-class preoccupation, race suicide. With both the working-class and the immigrant populations growing and the birth rate of the middle class dropping, there was a general fear the middle and elite classes would be overwhelmed.

The physical culture discourse then was never simply about exercise. In addition to its connection to industrialism and work, which I am here primarily concerned with, physical culture was certainly also part of a white supremacist project to promote reproduction in the middle- and upper-class populations.

18. Sargent, *Health Strength and Power* 6.
19. Philip Hubert, "The Wheel of Today," *The Out-Of-Door Library* (New York: Charles Scribner's Sons, 1897) 183–184.
20. Melissa Dabakis "Douglas Tilden's Mechanics Fountain: Labor and the 'Crisis of Masculinity' in the 1890s" *American Quarterly* 47: 2 (June 1995) 204.
21. Sargent, *Physical Education* 134–5.
22. Sargent,*Physical Education*138.
23. Sargent, *Physical Education* 22–3.
24. Sargent, *Health, Strength and Power* 9.
25. Sargent, "The Physical Proportions of the Typical Man" *The Out-of-Door Library* 5.
26. Sargent, "The Physical Proportions" *The Out-of-Door Library* 12.
27. Sargent, *Health* x.
28. Gulick, *The Efficient Life* xv.
29. Sargent, "The Physical Proportions of the Typical Man," *The Out-of-Door Library* 24.
30. Andrew Draper, "Physical Training and Athletics in Schools," 60th Annual Meeting of the Massachusetts Teacher's Association, (Boston, 24 Nov. 1904.)
31. Francis Walker, "College Athletics" 278.
32. Jay W. Seaver, *Anthropometry and Physical Examination: A Book For Practical Use in Connection with Gymnastic Work and Physical Education* (New Haven, Conn., 1909) 8.
33. Seaver, *Anthropometry* 14.
34. Gulick, *Manual For Physical Measurements in connection with the Association Gymnasium Records* (New York: The International Committee of Young Men's Christian Associations, 1892) 6.
35. Gulick, *Manual* 4–5, my emphasis.
36. Sargent, *Physical Training: A Full Report of the Papers and Discussion of the Conference Held in Boston in November, 1889. Ed.* Isabel Barrows (Boston: Press of George H. Ellis, 1890) 65–66.
37. Sargent, *Physical Training* 96.
38. Sargent, "Physical Proportions of a Typical Man," *The Out-of-Door Library* 42.
39. Macfadden's feelings about doctors are another clue as to his class affiliations. According to Ann Fabian, "Making a Commodity of Truth: Speculations on the Career of Benarr Macfadden," the famous editor "filled his pages with medical advice designed to appeal to the poor who might be leery of the costs and class allegiances of professional doctors" (58).
40. Macfadden, *Physical Culture* 1:1 (1899): 5.
41. Macfadden, *Physical Culture* 2:2 (1899): 71.
42. Macfadden, *Physical Culture* 2:1 (1899): 4.
43. Macfadden, *Physical Culture* 2: 2 (1899): 78.
44. Some of these pictures of men are highly homoerotic. For an interesting discussion on this see Michael Anton Budd, "Every Man a Hero: Sculpting the Homoerotic in Physical Culture Photography." *The Passionate Camera: Photography and Bodies of Desire*. Ed. Deborah Bright (New York: Routledge, 1998): 41–57.

45. Macfadden, *Physical Culture* 1:3 (1899): 49.
46. Sargent, "Physical Characteristics of an Athlete, " *The Out-of-Door Library* 95.
47. Sargent, "Physical Characteristics of an Athlete," *The Out-of-Door Library* 100.
47. See Kasson's *Houdini, Tarzan and the Perfect Man* 51–2.
48. Alan Sekula, "The Body and the Archive." *October* 39 (1986): 7.
49. Marcus Aurelius Root. *The Camera and the Pencil* (1864). Qtd. in Sekula 9.
50. Foucault. "Body/Power," *Power/Knowledge: Selected Interviews and Other Writings, 1972–1977.* Ed. Colin Gordon. (New York: Pantheon Books, 1980) 55.
51. Sargent, *Physical Education* 254.
52. Sargent, "The Physical Proportions of the Typical Man," *The Out-Of-Door-Library* 15.
53. Jay W. Seaver, *Anthropometry and Physical Examination: A Book for Practical Use in Connection with Gymnasium Work and Physical Education* (New Haven, Conn., 1909) 58.
54. Sekula, "The Body and The Archive" 58.
55. For studies that focus on this, see Bederman, *Manliness and Civilization* and Tim Armstrong, *Modernism, Technology and the Body: A Cultural Study* (Cambridge: Cambridge University Press, 1998).
56. For a discussion of the connection between criminology and scientific management see Sekula, "The Body and the Archive."
57. Both the physical education manuals written by members of elite universities and scientific management tracts produced by and through the American Society of Engineers were written in similar tones and vocabularies. Both also assumed an educated reader.
58. Terry Mulcaire, "Progressive Visions of War in *The Red Badge of Courage* and *The Principles of Scientific Management*," *American Quarterly* 43.1 (1991): 51.
59. Taylor, "The Principles of Scientific Management," *American Magazine* 71:5 (1911): 580.
60. Ray Stannard Baker, "Frederick W. Taylor–Scientist in Business Management," *American Magazine* (1911): 565.
61. For a good discussion on this see Armstrong, introduction, *Modernism, Technology and The Body.*
62. See for instance, Armstrong, *Modernism,* Bederman, *Manliness and Civilization,* Harvey Green, *Fit For America: Health, Fitness, Sport and American Society* (New York: Pantheon Books, 1986) and Tom Lutz, *American Nervousness 1903: An Anecdotal History* (Ithaca: Cornell University Press, 1991).
63. See Mary Poovey, "'Scenes of an Indelicate Character': The Medical 'Treatment' of Victorian Women" in *The Making of the Modern Body.* Ed. Catherine Gallagher and Thomas Laqueur (Berkeley: University of California Press, 1987) 137–168.

## NOTES TO CHAPTER TWO

1. Realism's preoccupation with looking, and especially with looking at the body is discussed in numerous books. Here I am quoting from Christopher Prendergast, "Introduction: Realism, God's Secret, and The Body" *Spectacles of Realism: Gender, Body, Genre.* Eds. Margaret Cohen and Christopher Prendergast (Minneapolis: University of Minnesota Press, 1995) 5.

2.  Jann Matlock, "Censoring the Realist Gaze," *Spectacles of Realism* 49. See also Jennifer
    Scanlon, *Inarticulate Longings: The Ladies' Home Journal, Gender, and the Promises of
    Consumer Culture* (New York: Routledge, 1995); Ellen Gruber Garvey, *The Adman in
    the Parlor: Magazines and the Gendering of Consumer Culture, 1880s to 1910s* (New
    York: Oxford University Press, 1996); *The Sex of Things: Gender and Consumption in
    Historical Perspective*. Eds. Victoria de Grazia and Ellen Furlough (Berkeley: University
    of California Press, 1996). Many of the articles in *The Sex of Things* explore the "di-
    chotomized relationship between Mr. Breadwinner and Mrs. Consumer" that this
    chapter is trying to complicate. See for instance Jennifer Jones, "Coquettes and
    Grisettes: Women Buying and Selling in the Ancien Regime Paris," *The Sex of Things*
    33.

3.  See Mark Seltzer, *Bodies and Machines* (New York: Routledge, 1992); Alan
    Trachtenberg, "Experiments in Another Country: Stephen Crane's City Sketches"
    and Seltzer, "*The Princess Casamassima*: Realism and the Fantasy of Surveillance"
    *American Realism: New Essays*. Ed. Eric Sundquist (Baltimore: Johns Hopkins
    University Press, 1982).

4.  Anne Higonnet, "Real Fashion: Clothes Unmake the Working Woman," *Spectacles
    of Realism* 154.

5.  Diana Knight, "S/Z, Realism and Compulsory Heterosexuality," *Spectacles of
    Realism* 133.

6.  John Rignall argues that Walter Benjamin saw the flaneur's existence as "a precari-
    ous one, balanced as he is on the brink of the alienating system of commodity ex-
    change into which he will eventually be absorbed." Thus his "masterful control" will
    "prove in the end to be illusionary." John Rignall, *Realist Fiction and the Strolling
    Spectator* (London: Routledge, 1992) 3.

7.  William Dean Howells, *My Literary Passions, Criticism and Fiction*. 1895 (New York:
    Kraus Reprint Corp., 1968).

8.  All references to the novels will be from the following editions: Theodore Dreiser,
    *The Financier* (New York: Meridian Press, 1995); *The Titan* (New York: Meridian
    Classic Press, 1984). All page references in-text.

9.  Louis J. Zanine, *Mechanism and Mysticism: The Influence of Science on the Thought
    and Work of Theodore Dreiser* (Philadelphia: University of Pennsylvania Press, 1993).
    See especially Chapter Two.

10. The arguments in this chapter owe a great debt to the approach and insights of these
    first three authors. Howard Horowitz, *By the Law of Nature: Form and Value in
    Nineteenth-Century America* (New York: Oxford University Press, 1991) 192–217;
    Robert Shulman, *Social Criticism and Nineteenth Century American Fictions* (New
    York: Columbia University Press, 1987); Walter Benn Michaels, *The Gold Standard
    and The Logic of Naturalism: American Literature at the Turn of the Century* (Berkeley:
    University of California Press, 1987). See also Clare Eby, *Dreiser and Veblen, Saboteurs
    of the Status Quo* (Columbia: University of Missouri Press, 1998) chapter two;
    William Moddelmog, *Reconstructing Authority: American Fiction in the Province of the
    Law, 1880–1920* (Iowa City: University of Iowa Press, 2000) introduction and chap-
    ter six; Michael Tratner, *Deficits and Desires: Economies and Sexuality in Twentieth-
    Century Literature* (Stanford: Stanford University Press, 2001).

11. F.O. Matthiessen, *Theodore Dreiser* (William Sloane Associates, 1951) 112. See also
    Philip Gerber, *Theodore Dreiser*, revised edition (New York: Twayne Publishers,

1992); James Lundquist, *Theodore Dreiser* (New York: Frederick Ungar Publishing Co., 1974).

12. Lundquist, 65. My emphasis.

13. Dreiser has never fit comfortably in American letters, despite the now canonical status of *Sister Carrie* and *An American Tragedy.* He battled censorship to a far greater degree than most American authors. Not only was *Sister Carrie* all but dismissed when its publisher refused to advertise it, but *The Titan* and *The Genius* were also banned. *An American Tragedy* was the only novel to gain immediate praise. Beginning with Stuart Sherman's 1915 review of Dreiser for *The Nation,* his ethnic heritage as a German-American was deemed important. Sherman calls Dreiser "representative of a new . . . 'ethnic' element" that he sarcastically notes is supposed to "redeem *us* from *our* Puritanism. . . ." Reprinted in *The Stature of Theodore Dreiser,* eds. Alfred Kazin and Charles Shapiro (Bloomington: Indiana University Press, 1955) 5, my emphasis.

14. Gerber, 52, my emphasis.

15. Lundquist, 63.

16. Stephan Brennan, "The Financier: Dreiser's Marriage of Heaven and Hell" in *Studies in American Literature* 63; and Louis J. Zanine, *Mechanism and Mysticism* 66. Donald Pizer, also, when speaking of Dreiser comments, "He is of course Cowperwood himself." From *The Novels of Theodore Dreiser: A Critical Study* (Minneapolis: University of Minnesota Press, 1976) 185.

17. Pizer, for example, argues that a "significant weakness of *The Titan* is that its two plots do not cohere fictionally. Their primary connection, of course, is that Cowperwood applies a similar ethic of 'I satisfy myself' to love and business. But this connection fails to support the otherwise tenuous relationship between Cowperwood's two major interests." *The Novels of Theodore Dreiser* 198. See also Matthiessen's *Theodore Dreiser* 146. He agrees with Stuart Sherman's club-sandwich metaphor; and James Lundquist, *Theodore Dreiser,* especially chapter three, which generally echoes Matthiessen's argument about Cowperwood.

18. See Clare Eby, *Dreiser and Veblen, Saboteurs of the Status Quo;* William Moddelmog, *Reconstructing Authority: American Fiction in the Province of the Law;* and Michael Tratner, *Deficits and Desires: Economies and Sexuality in Twentieth-Century Literature.*

19. Alan Trachtenberg, *The Incorporation of America: Culture and Society in the Gilded Age* (New York: Hill and Wang, 1982) 3.

20. Gerber, *Theodore Dreiser* 48; Lundquist, *Theodore Dreiser* 64.

21. William Dean Howells, *Criticism and Fiction,* qtd in Horowitz, *By the Law of Nature,* 195. Moddelmog does comment, in passing, that Dreiser's use of detail was part of a bid for authority, placing "his own narrative in opposition to those more sensationalistic journalistic accounts of reality, suggesting that literature might relate stories that were, in a sense, more 'true'" (215).

22. In this time of transition, scholars have noted the "disappearance of traditional forms of private property and their transformation into immaterial kinds of wealth accessible only to those who knew how to manipulate it" (Moddelmog 193). Cowperwood straddles this line uncomfortably through both novels. But ultimately, I think (unlike Moddlemog) that Cowperwood's understanding of the new order—that is, in Veblen's terms, business over industry, is solid. He understands, as did men like Carnegie, that business controlled industry. The space Dreiser gives over to business dealings in his narrative suggests that he understood that such dealings, and not the

actual street railways or property of any kind, were the new links to successful masculinity. James Catano makes a similar point about Carnegie. See *Ragged Dicks: Masculinity, Steel, and the Rhetoric of the Self-Made Man* (Southern Illinois University, 2001) 73–74.

23.  Robert Shulman, *Social Criticism and Nineteenth Century American Fictions* (New York: Columbia University Press, 1987) 285.

24.  Thomas Strychacz, *Modernism, Mass Culture, and Professionalism* (New York: Cambridge University Press, 1993) 5.

25.  Strychacz, 23.

26.  Struchacz, see Introduction.

27.  *Theodore Dreiser: The Critical Reception,* ed. Jack Salzman (New York: David Lewis, 1972) 97.

28.  Thomas Stychacz, *Modernism, Mass Culture and Professionalism,* 3.

29.  Qtd in Stychacz, 15.

30.  *Theodore Dreiser: The Critical Reception* 98.

31.  Qtd in Stychacz, 10.

32.  Philip Fisher, *Hard Facts: Setting and Form in the American Novel* (New York: Oxford University Press, 1985) 134.

33.  Matthiessen, Gerber, Lundquist, and, to some extent Pizer. Eby makes a nice point in *Dreiser and Veblen* when she writes that "Recently, critics have stressed . . . the complicity of Dreiser's works with capitalism. This emphasis . . . disregards his self-perception and reputation during his lifetime as an imposing cultural critic" (9).

34.  Trilling comments on Parrington's use of this word to describe Dreiser and argues that critics like Parrington want us to like Dreiser, despite what, to Trilling's mind, is dreadful writing *because* he is a peasant and thus patently anti-bourgeois. See Trilling's "Reality in America" *The Liberal Imagination* (New York: Viking, 1950).

35.  See, for instance, Mark Seltzer, *Bodies and Machines* (New York: Routledge, 1992) as well as his essay "*The Princess Casamassima:* Realism and the Fantasy of Surveillance," and Alan Trachtenberg, "Experiments in Another Country: Stephen Crane's City Sketches," *American Realism: New Essays.* Ed. Eric Sundquist (Baltimore: Johns Hopkins University Press, 1982); also Jonathan Crary, "Unbinding Vision," *October* 68 (1994): 21–44.

36.  Michel Foucault, *Discipline and Punish: The Birth of the Prison* (New York: Vintage, 1979 edition) 199.

37.  Foucault, 202.

38.  Foucault, 200.

39.  Foucault, 217.

40.  Foucault, 216.

41.  Foucault, 221.

42.  See, for instance, John J. Conder, *Naturalism in American Fiction* (Kentucky: The University of Kentucky Press, 1984) chapter four.

43.  Hillel Schwartz *Never Satisfied: A Cultural History of Diets, Fantasies and Fat* (New York: The Free Press, 1986) 81. See especially chapters 3–6.

44.  Schwartz, *Never Satisfied,* 96.

45.  See Trilling, "Reality in America," *The Liberal Imagination* (1950).

46.  Schwartz, *Never Satisfied,* 93.

47. Critics like Benn Michaels and Horowitz talk well on the importance of dissembling in a market economy. Cowperwood's business success clearly rests on his show of placidity in times of economic panic. Less has been made of the fact that Cowperwood, while liking to see himself as unapologetic of his sexual behavior, and in fact criticizes other men in *The Titan* for their hypocrisy in carrying on affairs while preaching the sanctity of marriage, is not himself above dissembling affection: "By now also Cowperwood was so shrewd that he had the ability to simulate an affection and practice a gallantry which he did not feel, or, rather, was not backed by real passion. He was the soul of attention . . . and yet, at the same moment, perhaps, he would be looking cautiously about to see what life might offer in the way of illicit entertainment" (*T* 184).
48. See Robert Shulman, *Social Criticism and Nineteenth Century American Fiction* and Michael Tratner, *Deficits and Desires.*
49. Horowitz, 198.
50. Anne Higonnet, "Real Fashion: Clothes Unmake the Working Woman," *Spectacles of Realism: Gender, Body, Genre,* 154.
51. Christopher Prendergast, "Introduction: Realism, God's Secret, and The Body," *Spectacles of Realism: Gender, Body, Genre,* 7.
52. Cowperwood is so troubling as a character that champions of Dreiser have had a hard time accepting the fact that the author does not condemn him. Interestingly, this is another connection between Cowperwood and Carrie. Many have argued that seeing Carrie as getting off easily, despite her "immoral" behavior, is missing the point—that she is, in fact, a tragic character because she will never know the enjoyment of contentment and has lost any real interiority. I think a similar argument can be made for Cowperwood. Still, Cowperwood's actions are constructed by the author as more self-conscious than Carrie's, and perhaps, herein lies the difference between men and women in the new culture of desire. As mentioned earlier, men have more control over the process of mystification that results in a consumerist culture. This control, however, is shown to be limited in these books and Cowperwood is not immune to falling prey to its tangled webs—even if they are of his own making. Is Dreiser exonerating him on the count of his vulnerability to what he creates?
53. Prendergast 5.

## NOTES TO CHAPTER THREE

1. Eric Caplan, *Mind Games: American Culture and the Birth of Psychotherapy* (Berkeley: University of California Press, 1998).
2. See Tom Lutz, *American Nervousness*; Townsend, *Manhood at Harvard*; Mark Micale, *Diagnostic Discriminations: Jean-Martin Charcot and the Nineteenth-Century Idea of Masculine Hysteria Neurosis.* (Yale University Dissertation, 1987); Micale, *Approaching Hysteria: Disease and Its Interpretation* (Princeton: Princeton University Press, 1995); *Traumatic Pasts: History, Psychiatry, and Trauma in the Modern Age,* 1870–1930. Eds. Mark Micale and Paul Lerner (New York: Cambridge University Press, 2001).
3. Lisa Cardyn, "The Construction of Female Sexual Trauma." *Traumatic Pasts,* 180–181.
4. Jill Kress, *The Figure of Consciousness* (New York: Routledge, 2001) 2–3.

5.  See Anita Clair Fellman and Michael Fellman, *Making Sense of Self: Medical Advice Literature in Late Nineteenth-Century America* (Philadelphia: University of Pennsylvania Press, 1981); Eric Caplan, *Mind Games: American Culture and the Birth of Psychotherapy*; In *Traumatic Pasts: History, Psychiatry, and Trauma in the Modern Age*, 1870–1930 see Paul Lerner and Mark S. Micale, "Trauma, Psychiatry, and History: A Conceptual and Historiographical Introduction"; Ralph Harrington, "The Railway Accident: Trains, Trauma, and Technological Crisis in Nineteenth-Century Britain"; and Eric Caplan, "Trains and Trauma in the American Gilded Age." For a different take on the power of the somatic paradigm, see F.G. Gossling, *Before Freud: Neurasthenia and the American Medical Community, 1870–1910* (Urbana: University of Illinois Press, 1987).

6.  See Eric Caplan, *Mind Games* 7. See also introduction.

7.  Caplan, *Mind Games* 14.

8.  Caplan, *Mind Games* 14.

9.  Ralph Harrington, "The Railway Accident: Trains, Trauma, and Technological Crisis in Nineteenth-Century Britain." *Traumatic Pasts* 47.

10. Harrington 48.

11. See Harrington, "The Railway Accident" and Caplan, "Train and Trauma" in *Traumatic Pasts* and Caplan, *Mind Games,* chapter one.

12. See Caplan, "Trains and Trauma in the American Gilded Age." *Traumatic Pasts.*

13. Caplan, "Trains and Trauma" 63

14. See for instance William Hammond, *On Certain Conditions of Nervous Derangement* (New York: Putnam's Sons, 1881).

15. Mark Stephen Micale, *Diagnostic Discriminations: Jean-Martin Charcot and the Nineteenth-Century Idea of Masculine Hysterical Neurosis* (Yale University Dissertation, 1987) 25.

16. *The Encyclopedia Britannica* (New York: The Encyclopedia Britannica Company, 1910). Eleventh edition, Vol. XIV, 211.

17. Micale, *Diagnostic Discriminations* 23

18. Quoted in Eugene Taylor's *William James on Exceptional Mental States: The 1896 Lowell Lectures* (New York: Scribner, 1983) 55.

19. Micale, *Diagnostic Discriminations* 96.

20. Janet, *The Major Symptoms of Hysteria* (New York: The Macmillan Company, 1907) 15, my emphasis.

21. Micale, *Diagnostic Discriminations,* 119. This is not the case with Janet who devotes half of his third lecture to a form of hysteria he calls "Fugues." This form of hysteria is described as a "mania of running away" (Janet 44). Basically what happens is that another personality takes over for a period of days or even months, during which time the person leaves his present life behind and embarks on another, which usually involves extensive travel. Though he remains functional, he cannot remember what he has done upon the return to normal consciousness. Sometimes hypnosis is the only way to bring such hysterics back to their former self. Not surprisingly, every subject reported on by Janet for this particular kind of hysteria is male. Obviously, this has something to do with the considerable traveling involved. Interestingly, in this male form of hysteria, the hysteric remains functional, and does not completely shut out things going on in the real world. But perhaps the most important aspect of this type

of hysteria is that, according to Janet "the restoration of the normal self is much more complete." Janet, *The Major Symptoms of Hysteria* 60.

22. Micale, *Diagnostic Discriminations* 55–56.

23. Micale, *Diagnostic Discriminations* 119.

24. For lists of symptoms found in hysteria see Micale, *Diagnostic Discriminations* and *Approaching Hysteria: Disease and Its Interpretation* (Princeton: Princeton University Press, 1995); J.M. Charcot, *Lectures of the Diseases of the Nervous System* (Philadelphia: Henry C. Lea, 1879); William Hammond, *On Certain Conditions of Nervous Derangements* (New York: Putnam's Sons, 1881); Pierre Janet, *The Major Symptoms of Hysteria*. For symptoms of neurasthenia see F.G. Gossling *Before Freud*; Anita and Michael Fellman, *Making Sense of Self*; Tom Lutz, *American Nervousness*, Kim Townsend, *Manhood at Harvard*; George Beard, *American Nervousness: Its Causes and Consequences* (New York: G.P. Putnam's Sons, 1881); Albert Abrams, M.D., *The Blues (Splanchnic Neurasthenia): Causes and Cure* (New York: E.B. Treat and Company, 1904); J.W. Courtney, M.D., *The Conquest of Nerves: A Manual for Self-Help* (New York: Macmillan Company, 1911); J.H. Kellogg, *Neurasthenia or Nervous Exhaustion* (Battle Creek, Michigan: Good Health Publishing, 1915).

25. Trauma alone, however, would not necessarily result in hysteria. As Mark Micale argues in a recent article, "In Charcot's medical thinking, traumatic stimuli acted on . . . prior constitutional susceptibility" that is, a hereditary predisposition. Micale, "Jean-Martin Charcot and *les nevroses traumatiques:* From Medicine to Culture in French Trauma Theory of the Late Nineteenth Century," *Traumatic Pasts* 119.

26. Gossling, *Before Freud* x.

27. Lutz, *American Nervousness* 31.

28. See, for instance, Lisa Cardyn, "The Construction of Female Sexual Trauma." *Traumatic Pasts*.

29. Fellman & Fellman, *Making Sense of Self* 5.

30. Albert Abrams, M.D., *The Blues (Splanchnic Neurasthenia): Causes and Cure* (New York: E.B. Treat and Company, 1904) 20.

31. *Encyclopedia Britannica*, eleventh edition, Vol.14, 211.

32. For a more detailed discussion of the disseminations of Charcot's ideas see Micale, *Diagnostic Discriminations* 125–198.

33. Eugene Taylor, *William James on Consciousness Beyond the Margin* (Princeton: Princeton University Press, 1996) 5.

34. Ann Braude, *Radical Spirits: Spiritualism and Women's Rights in Nineteenth-Century America* (Boston, Mass.: Beacon Press, 1989).

35. See cases presented in Myers' *Human Personality and its Survival of Bodily Death*. Ed and abridged by Leopold Hamilton Myers (New York: Longmans, Green, and Co., 1909); Edmund Gurney, F.W.H. Myers and Frank Podmore, *Phantasms of the Living* (New York: E.P. Dutton and Co., 1918) and William James, *Essays in Psychical Research* in *The Works of William James* (Cambridge: Harvard University Press, 1986).

36. S.E.D. Shortt, "Physicians and Psychics: The Anglo-American Medical Response to Spiritualism, 1870–1890." *The Journal of the History of Medicine and Allied Sciences* (Vol. 39, July 1984) 346.

37. Shortt 348.

38. Shortt 355.

39.  William James, *Essays in Psychical Research. The Works of William James* (Cambridge: Harvard University Press, 1986) 22.

40.  See for instance Janet, *The Major Symptoms of Hysteria.*

41.  Hammond, for instance, refers to hysteria in his book *On Certain Conditions of Nervous Derangement* as a "paralysis of the will" 39.

42.  Myers, *Human Personality and its Survival of Bodily Death* xiii-xviii.

43.  Myers, *Human Personality* xvii.

44.  Myers, *Human Personality* 37–38. James and Janet characterized the subliminal in similar ways. But all three men seemed to have been far more fascinated with the "strengths" of this region than its weaknesses. This is a definite shift from mid–nineteenth-century conceptions of hysteria.

45.  Janet, *The Major Symptoms of Hysteria* 9, my emphasis.

46.  Myers, *Human Personality* 54, 52.

47.  Cesare Lombroso, *The Man of Genius,* (London: Walter Scott Publishing Co.,1905) 138.

48.  Lombroso vii.

49.  John F. Nisbet, *Insanity of Genius and the General Inequality of Human Faculty, Physiologically Considered* (London: Ward & Downey, 1891) xv.

50.  See for instance, George Beard, *American Nervousness.* Also, see Max Nordau's *Degeneration* (New York: D. Appleton, 1905). Nordau specifically paired genius with hysteria.

51.  Nisbet, *Insanity of Genius* xv.

52.  Eugene Taylor, *William James on Exceptional Mental States* (New York: Scribner, 1983) 150.

53.  Taylor, *William James on Exceptional Mental States* 151.

54.  Lombroso 149.

55.  Boris Sidis, *Philistine and Genius* (New York: Maffat, Yard and Company, 1911) 93, 95.

56.  Myers, *Human Personality* 76.

57.  Janet, *The Major Symptoms of Hysteria* 295.

58.  In many ways, this is like James's idea that true geniuses are highly effective people and that "'Even though geniuses are liable to obsession, they work it off through their socially constructive efforts.'" Qtd. in Taylor, *William James on Exceptional Mental States* 161.

59.  Myers, *Human Personality* 56.

60.  Quoted in Taylor, *William James on Exceptional Mental States* 5.

61.  Taylor, *William James on Exceptional Mental States* 53.

62.  Taylor, *William James on Exceptional Mental States* 60, my emphasis.

63.  Myers, *Human Personality* 76.

64.  Myers, *Human Personality* 115.

65.  James, for instance, described mediumship in *Principles* as a form of split or alternating personality as opposed to an ability to connect with spirits. Nonetheless, James repeatedly showed a willingness to test the validity of such communication. There is a story, perhaps apocryphal, that when Myers was on his deathbed, James fulfilled a promise to his long-time friend, by sitting outside Myers's door with a pad and pencil in the moments after his death with the understanding that he would try to com-

municate with James. Apparently nothing happened. See Axel Munthe, *The Story of San Michele*. (London: J. Murray, 1929) 331–372.

66. William James, *The Varieties of Religious Experience: A Study of Human Nature*, 1902 (New York: Collier Books, 1961) 198.
67. This interest in the body fits with James's oeuvre generally, from his theories on habit and emotions to his interest in the mind cure movement.
68. Eugene Taylor, *William James on Consciousness Beyond the Margin* (Princeton: Princeton University Press, 1996) 60.
69. William James, *Essays in Psychical Research* 95.
70. See Taylor, *Consciousness Beyond the Margin* 28–29.
71. William James, *Essays in Psychical Research* 204.
72. James, *Essays in Psychical Research* 207
73. Janet, *Major Symptoms of Hysteria* 137.
74. Myers, *Human Personality* 76.
75. William James, "On A Certain Blindness in Human Beings." *Talks to Teachers on Psychology and to Students on Some of Life's Ideals*, 1892 (New York: Dover Publications, Inc., 1962) 126, 129.
76. Hal Foster. Qtd in Michele Wallace, "Modernism, Postmodernism and the Problem of the Visual in Afro-American Culture." *Out There: Marginalization and Contemporary Cultures*. Eds., Russell Ferguson, et. al. (Cambridge: The MIT Press, 1990) 48.
77. James, "On A Certain Blindness." *Talks to Teachers* 128–129.
78. William James, *Essays in Psychical Research* 222.
79. James, *Essays in Psychical Research* 134.
80. James, "The Will to Believe," *Essays on Faith and Morals* (New York: Meridian Books, 1962) 38.
81. James, "The Will to Believe" 48.
82. James, "The Will to Believe" 49–50.
83. James, "The Will to Believe" 50.
84. James, "Reflex Action and Theism," *Essays on Faith and Morals* 132.
85. James, "The Will to Believe" 44.
86. James, "The Will to Believe" 41.
87. Myers, *Human Personality* 117
88. Myers, *Human Personality* 118.
89. James, *Varieties* 104.
90. Annie Payson Call, *Power Through Repose*, (Boston: Little Brown, 1917) 19.
91. Call 74.
92. James, *Varieties* 105.
93. James, *Essays in Psychical Research*, 204.
94. James, *Psychology: Briefer Course* (New York: Henry Holt and Company, 1893), 17.
95. James, *Varieties* 62.
96. James, *Varieties* 64.
97. James, *Varieties* 211.
98. See Townsend, *Manhood at Harvard*.
99. Myers, *Human Personality* 115.
100. Myers, *Human Personality* 115.
101. James, *Varieties* 289.
102. James, *Varieties* 290.

103.  James, *Varieties* 290.
104.  Qtd. in Eugene Taylor, *William James on Exceptional Mental States* 163.
105.  Myers, *Human Personality* 73, my emphasis.
106.  Carroll Smith-Rosenberg's term for women with neurasthenia.

## NOTES TO CHAPTER FOUR

1.   *Shapes that Haunt the Dusk* is the title of a collection of ghost stories edited by William Dean Howells and published in 1891.
2.   Dorothy von Mucke has recently argued that fantastic tales often focus on "an individual's problematic relationship to sensual pleasure and the individual's alienated relationship toward desire." *The Seduction of the Occult and the Rise of the Fantastical Tale* (Stanford: Stanford University Press, 2003) 3.
3.   Kathleen L. Spencer, "Purity and Danger: *Dracula,* the Urban Gothic, and the late Victorian Degeneracy Crisis" in *English Literary History* 59 (1992) 200.
4.   Qtd. in Spencer 201, 199.
5.   For an interesting discussion on the relationship between supernatural or fantastic literature and the preoccupation with the material world and "this form's surprising alliance with the practices of nineteenth-century realism," see Deborah A. Harter, *Bodies in Pieces: Fantastic Narrative and the Poetics of the Fragment* (Stanford: Stanford University Press, 1996) 8.
6.   See both Harter, *Bodies in Pieces* and, most recently, von Mucke, *The Seduction of the Occult.*
7.   Allan Gardner Lloyd-Smith, *Uncanny American Fiction: Medusa's Face* (1989) 134.
8.   From *The Writings of William James.* All page references in text.
9.   Collette Guillaumin, quoted in Dana Nelson. *National Manhood: Capitalist Citizenship and the Imagined Fraternity of White Men* (Durham: Duke University Press, 1998), 10.
10.  It was commonly agreed that men and women of color did not experience the kinds of nervous illness, like hysteria, whose symptomology these stories adopt as the earmarks of supernatural experiences. The racialist assumptions of nervous illness helped to re-cast the transitory experiences white men had with/as "others" as a kind of rehabilitory experience. For an interesting discussion on the tonifying effects of miscegenation for *women* in literature, see Michele Birnbaum, "Racial Hysteria: Female Pathology and Race Politics in Frances Harper's *Iola Leroy* and W.D. Howells's *An Imperative Duty*" *African American Review* 33.1 (1999). For a discussion of the medical discourses of race and hysteria in women, see Laura Briggs, "The Race of Hysteria: 'Overcivilization' and the 'Savage' Woman in Late Nineteenth-Century Obstetrics and Gynecology." *American Quarterly* 52:2 (June 2000).
11.  Dana Nelson, *National Manhood: Capitalist Citizenship and the Imagined Fraternity of White Men* (Durham: Duke University Press, 1998) 63.
12.  This emphasis on the body is another connection to the primitive. Torgovnick argues that "Within Western culture, the idiom 'going primitive' is fact congruent in many ways with to the idiom 'getting physical.'" Marianna Torgovnick, *Gone Primitive: Savage Intellects, Modern Lives* (Chicago: Chicago University Press, 1990) 228.
13.  Richard S. Lowery, "Domestic Interiors: Boyhood Nostalgia and Affective Labor in the Gilded Age." *Inventing the Psychological: Toward a Cultural History of Emotional*

*Life in America.* Eds. Joel Pfister and Nancy Schnog (New Haven: Yale University Press, 1997) 113.

14. Burton Bledstein, quoted in *National Manhood* 14.
15. Lubin, "Modern Psychological Selfhood" in *Inventing the Psychological,* 135. While this challenge is important and anticipates modernism, the narrative structure of these stories is fairly conventional. Indeed, while turn-of-the-century supernatural fiction shows us plenty of "crises of subjectivity" in the form of nervous illness and even split personality, this rarely extends to issues of form. As Joseph Karaganis has argued for naturalism generally, "anxiety about the hegemony of the self is *dramatized* in these works through the breakdown of agents, subjects, and grammatical relationships rather than *thematized* through an intentional break with linguistic and narrative conventions—a gesture that would be completed by modernism proper." "Naturalism's Nation: Toward An American Tragedy" *American Literature* 72.1 (2000) 158.
16. Nelson, *National Manhood* 158.
17. William Dean Howells "His Apparition" *Questionable Shapes* (New York: Harper & Brothers, 1903). All page references in text.
18. Von Muck, *The Seduction of the Occult* 3.
19. "The Eidolons of Brook Alford." *Between the Darkness and the Daylight* (New York: Harper & Brothers Publishers, 1907) 65. All other page references in text.
20. *"Henry James: Stories of the Supernatural.* Ed Leon Edel (New York: Taplinger Publishing Company, 1970) 159. All other page references in text.
21. See Martha Banta, *Henry James and the Occult* (Bloomington: Indiana University Press, 1972), especially chapter one.
22. Nelson, *National Manhood* 150.
23. G. Stanley Hall, for instance, argued in his 1904 book *Adolescence* that Africans are in fact an "adolescent race" in which an earlier stage of evolution is preserved.
24. Targovnick, *Gone Primitive* 46.
25. Jack London, "Who Believes in Ghosts?!" *Jack London: Fantastical Tales.* Ed. Dale L. Walker (Lincoln: University of Nebraska Press, 1998) 11. All other page references in text.
26. *Jack London: Fantastic Tales* 128. All other page references in text.
27. William James, *Essays in Psychical Research* 134.
28. London was probably well aware of the popular idea, dating from the studies of Dr Samuel Morton in the 1830s, that members of the "'Teutonic Family'" had a measurable "cranial superiority" to both Africans and African-American. See Nelson, *National Manhood,* 110.
29. Jack London, "Planchette" in *Moon-Face and Other Stories* (New York: Gosset & Dunlap Publishers, 1906). All page references in text.
30. Torgovnick, *Gone Primitive* 8, 94.
31. For a discussion on the turn-of-the-century interest in the medieval period and its relation to masculinity, see T. Jackson Lears's discussion of anti-modernism in *No Place of Grace: Antimodernism and the Transformation of American Culture, 1880–1920* (New York: Pantheon Books, 1981).
32. Henry James, "Owen Wingrave," *Henry James: Stories of the Supernatural.* Ed. Leon Edel (New York: Taplinger Publishing Company, 1970) 328.
33. Edel, *Henry James: Stories of the Supernatural.* All page references in text.

34. Eric Savoy, "The Queer Subject of 'The Jolly Corner.'" *The Henry James Review* 20.1 (1999) 1.
35. Earl Rovit, "The Language and Imagery of 'The Jolly Corner.'" *The Finer Thread, the Tighter Weave: Essays on the Short Fiction of Henry James.* Eds. Joseph Dewey and Brooke Horvath (Purdue University Press, 2001) 161.
36. Savoy 1.
37. Rovit 160. See also Savoy's "The Queer Subject"
38. John Demos, "Oedipus in America: Historical Perspectives on the Reception of Psychoanalysis in the United States." *Inventing the Psychological: Toward a Cultural History of Emotional Life in America.* Eds. Joel Pfister and Nancy Schnog (new Haven: Yale University Press, 1997) 67.
39. *Inventing the Psychological* 111.
40. Nelson, *National Manhood* 99.
41. Nelson, *National Manhood* 18.
42. Qtd. in Thomas J. Otten, "Pauline Hopkins and the Hidden Self of Race." *English Literary History* 59 (1992): 229.
43. Otten 229.
44. Rovit 165.
45. Qtd. in Kim Townsend, *Manhood at Harvard: William James and Others* (New York: W.W. Norton and Company, 1996) 149.
46. Otten 229.
47. Savoy 3.
48. Savoy 6.
49. Walker, *Jack London: Fantastical Tales.* All page references in text.
50. Howells, *Questionable Shapes* 215.
51. The majority of books on supernatural or fantastic fiction focus on women. See for instance, Dorothea E. von Mucke, *The Seduction of the Occult and the Rise of the Fantastic* and Deborah Harter, *Bodies in Pieces: Fantastic Narrative and the Poetics of the Fragment.* One work that does focus on the masculinity, though for mid–nineteenth-century texts, is Cyndy Hendershot, *The Animal Within: Masculinity and the Gothic* (Ann Arbor: The University of Michigan Press, 1998).

# Bibliography

Abrams, Albert. *The Blues (Splanchnic Neurasthenia): Causes and Cure.* New York: E.B. Treat and Company, 1904.

Allert, Beate, ed. *Languages of Visuality: Crossings Between Science, Art, Politics and Literature.* Detroit: Wayne State University Press, 1996.

Armstrong, Tim. *Modernism, Technology and the Body: A Cultural Study.* Cambridge: Cambridge University Press, 1998.

Banta, Martha, ed. *New Essays on The American.* New York: Cambridge University Press, 1987.

———. *Henry James and the Occult.* Bloomington: Indiana University Press, 1972.

Baron, Ava, ed. *Work Engendered: Toward a New History of American Labor.* Ithaca: Cornell University Press, 1991.

Barrows, Isabel, ed. *Physical Training: A Full Report of the Papers and Discussions of the Conference Held in Boston in November, 1889.* Boston: Press of George H Ellis, 1890.

Beard, George. *American Nervousness: Its Causes and Consequences.* New York: G.P. Putnum's Sons, 1881.

Bederman, Gail. *Manliness and Civilization: A Cultural History of Gender and Race in the United States 1880–1917.* Chicago: The University of Chicago Press, 1995.

Bell, Michael. *The Problem of American Realism: Studies in the Cultural History of Literary Idea.* Chicago: The University of Chicago Press, 1993.

Berger, John. *Ways of Seeing.* New York: Penguin, 1980.

Berlant, Lauren. "National Brands/National Body: *Imitation of Life.*" *Comparative American Identities.* Ed. Hortense Spillers. New York: Routledge, 1991.

Briggs, Laura. "The Race of Hysteria: 'Overcivilization' and the 'Savage' Woman in Late Nineteenth-Century Obstetrics and Gynecology." *American Quarterly* 52:2 (June 2000).

Birnbaum, Michele. "Racial Hysteria: Female Pathology and Race Politics in Frances Harper's *Iola Leroy* and WD Howells's *An Imperative Duty.*" *African American Review* 33.1 (1999).

Blaikie, William. *How to Get Strong and How to Stay So.* New York: Harper, 1884.

Blanchard, Mary. "Boundaries and the Victorian Body: Aesthetic Fashion in Gilded Age America." *American Historical Review.* 1995 100(1): 21–50.

Blumin, Stuart. "The Hypothesis of Middle-Class Formation in Nineteenth-Century America: A Critique and Some Proposals." *American Historical Review.* 1985 90(2): 299–338.

Bok, Edward. *The Americanization of Edward Bok.* New York: Charles Scribner's Sons, 1922.

Bowlby, Rachel. *Just Looking.* London: Mathuen, 1985.

Braidotti, Rosi. *Nomadic Subjects: Embodiment and Sexual Difference in Contemporary Feminist Theory.* New York: Columbia University Press, 1994.

Brand, Dana. *The Spectator and the City in Nineteenth-Century American Literature.* New York: Cambridge University Press, 1991.

Braude, Ann. *Radical Spirits: Spiritualism and Women's Rights in Nineteenth-Century America.* Boston: Beacon Press, 1989.

Brody, Miriam. *Manly Writing: Gender, Rhetoric, and the Rise of Composition.* Carbondale: Southern Illinois University Press, 1993.

Bromell, Nicholas. *By the Sweat of the Brow: Literature and Labor in Antebellum America.* Chicago: The University of Chicago Press, 1993.

Brown, Michael. "Imag(in)ing Mars: A Transformation in Nineteenth Century American Visual Culture." Diss. University of Utah, 1994.

Budd, Michael Anton. "Every Man a Hero: Sculpting the Homoerotic in Physical Culture Photography." *The Passionate Camera: Photography and Bodies of Desire.* Ed, Deborah Bright. New York: Routledge, 1998.

Burroughs, John. *Whitman: A Study.* Boston: Houghton, Mifflin and Company, 1902.

Butler, Judith. Gender Trouble: Feminism and the Subversion of Identity. New York: Routledge, 1990.

———. *Bodies that Matter: on the Discursive Limits of 'Sex.'* New York: Routledge, 1993.

Call, Annie Payson. *Power Through Repose.* Boston: Little Brown, 1917.

Cannon, Kelly. *Henry James and Masculinity: The Man at the Margins.* New York: St. Martin's Press, 1994.

Caplan, Eric. *Mind Games: American Culture and the Birth of Psychotherapy.* Berkeley: University of California Press, 1998.

Carnes, Mark and Clyde Griffen, eds. *Meanings for Manhood.* Chicago: University of Chicago Press, 1990.

Catano, James V. *Ragged Dicks: Masculinity, Steel, and the Rhetoric of the Self-Made Man.* Southern Illinois University, 2001.

Chauncy, George. *Gay New York: Gender, Urban Culture and the Making of the Gay Male World, 1890–1940.* New York: Basic Books, 1994.

Cohen, Margaret and Christopher Prendergast, eds. *Spectacles of Realism: Gender, Body, Genre.* Minneapolis: University of Minnesota Press, 1995.

Conder, John. *Naturalism in American Fiction.* Kentucky: The University of Kentucky Press, 1984.

Connell, R.W. *Masculinities.* Berkeley: University of California Press, 1995.

Cooley, Thomas. *The Ivory Leg in the Ebony Cabinet: Madness, Race and Gender in Victorian America.* Amherst: UMass Press, 2001.

Courtney, J.W. *The Conquest of Nerves: A Manual for Self-Help.* New York: MacMillan Company, 1911.

Debord, Guy. *The Society of the Spectacle.* New York: Zone Books, 1994.

Dember, William. *Visual Perception: The Nineteenth Century.* New York: John Wiley and Sons, Inc. 1964.

Doane, Mary Ann. *The Desire to Desire: The Woman's Film of the 1940s.* Bloomington: Indiana University Press, 1987.

Draper, Andrew. *Addresses and Papers.* Albany: New York State Educational Department. 1909.

Dreiser, Theodore. *Sister Carrie.* 1900. New York: Penguin Books, 1980.

————. *The Financier.* 1912. New York: Meridian Books, 1995.

————. *The Titan.* 1914. New York: Meridian Classic Press, 1984.

————. *The "Genius."* 1915. New York: Penguin Books, 1967.

Dutton, Kenneth. *The Perfectible Body: The Western Ideal of Male Physical Development.* New York: Continuum, 1995.

Eby, Virginia Clare. *Dreiser and Veblen, Saboteurs of the Status Quo.* Columbia: University of Missouri Press, 1998.

Edwards, Richard Henry. *Popular Amusements.* 1915. New York: Arno Press, 1976.

Elam, Diane. *Feminism and Deconstruction: ms. en abyme.* New York: Routledge, 1994.

Elkins, James. *The Object Stares Back.* New York: Simon & Schuster, 1996.

Ellmann, Richard. *Oscar Wilde.* New York: Alfred A. Knopf, 1988.

Erenberg, Lewis. *Steppin' Out: New York Nightlife and the Transformation of American Culture 1890–1930.* Westport: Greenwood Press, 1981.

Ernst, Robert. *Weakness is a Crime: The Life of Benarr Macfadden.* Syracuse: Syracuse University Press, 1991.

Fabian, Ann. "Making a Commodity of Truth: Speculations on the Career of Benarr Macfadden." *American Literary History.* 1993 5(1): 51–76.

Fellman, Anita and Michael. *Making Sense of Self: Medical Advice Literature in Late Nineteenth Century America.* Philadelphia: University of Pennsylvania Press, 1981.

Fisher, Philip. *Hard Facts: Setting and Form in the American Novel.* New York: Oxford University Press, 1985.

Foster, Kathleen. "The Making and Meaning of *Swimming.*" *Thomas Eakins and the Swimming Picture.* Eds. Doreen Bolger and Sarah Cash. Forth Worth: Amon Carter Museum, 1996.

Foucault, Michel. *Power/Knowledge: Selected Interviews and Other Writings.* Ed. Colin Gordon. New York: Pantheon Books, 1980.

————. *The History of Sexuality: Volume I: An Introduction.* 1978. New York: Vintage Books, 1990.

————. *Discipline and Punish: The Birth of the Prison.* New York: Vintage Books, 1995.

Fox, Richard Wightman and T.J. Jackson Lears, Eds. *The Culture of Consumption: Critical Essays in American History, 1880–1980.* New York: Pantheon Books, 1983.

Freud, Sigmund. "The Uncanny." *Standard Edition of the Complete Psychological Works.* Ed and trans. James Strachey. London: Hogarth Press, 1953. V17. 217–252.

Fuss, Diana. *Essentially Speaking: Feminism, Nature & Difference.* New York: Routledge, 1989.

Gallagher, Catherine and Thomas Laqueur, Eds. *The Making of the Modern Body: Sexuality and Society in the Nineteenth Century.* Berkeley: University of California Press, 1987.

Gardiner, Judith Kegan, ed. *Masculinity Studies and Feminist Theory: New Directions.* New York: Columbia University Press, 2002.

Gatens, Moira. *Imaginary Bodies: Ethics, Power, and Corporeality.* New York: Routledge, 1996.

Gerber, Philip. *Theodore Dreiser.* New York: Twayne Publishers, 1992. Revised edition.

Gilman, Sander. *Disease and Representation: Images of Illness from Madness to AIDS.* Ithaca: Cornell University Press, 1988.

Goldstein, Lawrence, ed. *The Male Body.* Ann Arbor: The University of Michigan Press, 1994.

Gorn, Elliott. *The Manly Art: Bare-Knuckle Prize Fighting in America.* Ithaca: Cornell University Press, 1986.

Gossling, F.G. *Before Freud: Neurasthenia and the American Medical Community, 1870–1910.* Urbana: University of Illinois Press, 1987.

Green, Harvey. *Fit for America: Health, Fitness, Sport and American Society.* New York: Pantheon Books, 1986.

Griffin, Susan. *The Historical Eye: The Texture of the Visual in Late James.* Boston: Northeastern University Press, 1991.

Grosz, Elizabeth. *Volatile Bodies.* Bloomington: Indiana University Press, 1994.

Grover, Kathryn, ed. *Fitness in American Culture: Images of Health, Sport, and the Body, 1830–1940.* Amherst: University of Massachusetts Press, 1989.

———. *Hard at Play: Leisure in America 1840–1940.* Amherst: University of Massachusetts Press, 1992.

Gulick, Luther H. *The Efficient Life.* New York: Doubleday, 1907.

———. *Manual for Physical Measurements in Connection with the Association Gymnasium Records.* New York: The International Committee of Young Men's Christian Associations, 1892.

———. *Physical Education by Muscular Development.* Philadelphia: P. Blakiston's Son & Co., 1904.

Haber, Samuel. *Efficiency and Uplift: Scientific Management in the Progressive Era 1890–1920.* Chicago: University of Chicago Press, 1964.

Haley, Bruce. *The Healthy Body in Victorian Culture.* Cambridge: Harvard University Press, 1978.

Hall, G. Stanley. *Adolescence.* New York: D. Appleton and Company, 1905.

Hammond, William. *On Certain Conditions of Nervous Derangement.* New York: Putnam's Sons, 1881.

Haraway, Donna. *Simians, Cyborgs, and Women: The Reinvention of Nature.* New York: Routledge, 1991.

Hatt, Michael. "Muscles, morals, mind: the male body in Thomas Eakins' *Salutat.*" *The Body Imaged: the Human Form and Visual Culture since the Renaissance.* Eds. Kathleen Adler and Marcia Pointon. New York: Cambridge University Press, 1993.

Hendeshot, Cyndy. *The Animal Within: Masculinity and the Gothic.* Ann Arbor: The University of Michigan Press, 1998.

Higham, John. *Writing American History.* Bloomington: Indiana University Press, 1970.

Horowitz, Howard. *By the Law of Nature: Form and Value in Nineteenth-Century America.* New York: Oxford University Press, 1991.

Howells, William Dean. *A Hazard of New Fortunes.* 1890. New York: Penguin Books, 1983.

———. *Shapes that Haunt the Dusk.* Ed. New York: Harper & Brothers, 1891.

———. *Questionable Shapes.* New York: Harper & Brothers Publishers, 1903.

———. *Between Darkness and Daylight.* New York: Harper & Brothers Publishing, 1907.

James, Henry. *The American.* 1877. New York: Penguin Books, 1995.

———. *The Bostonians.* 1886. New York: Vintage Books, 1991

———. *Stories of the Supernatural.* Leon Edel, Ed. New York: Taplinger Publishing Co., 1970.

James, William. *Psychology: Briefer Course.* New York: Henry Holt and Company, 1893.

———. *The Varieties of Religious Experience: A Study in Human Nature.* New York: Collier Books, 1961.

———. *Essays on Faith and Morals.* New York: Meridian Books, 1962.

———. "On a Certain Blindness in Human Beings." *Talks to Teachers on Psychology and to Students of Some of Life's Ideals.* 1892. New York: Dover Publications, 1962.

———. *Essays in Psychical Research* in *The Works of William James*. Cambridge: Harvard University Press, 1986.

Janet, Pierre. *The Major Symptoms of Hysteria: Fifteen Lectures Given in the Medical School of Harvard University.* New York: The Macmillan Company, 1907.

Jenks, Chris, ed. *Visual Culture*. New York: Routledge, 1995.

Johns, Elizabeth. "*Swimming:* Thomas Eakins, the Twenty-Ninth Bather." *Thomas Eakins and the* Swimming *Picture*. Eds. Doreen Bolger and Sarah Cash. Forth Worth: Amon Carter Museum, 1996.

———. "An Avowal of Artistic Community: Nudity and Fantasy in Thomas Eakins's Photographs." *Eakins and the Photograph*. Eds. Susan Danly and Cheryl Leibold. Washington: Smithsonian Institute Press, 1994.

———. *Thomas Eakins: The Heroism of Modern Life*. Princeton: Princeton University Press, 1983.

Kaplan, Amy and Donald Pease, eds. *Cultures of United States Imperialism*. Durham: Duke University Press, 1993.

Kaplan, Amy. *The Social Construction of American Realism*. Chicago: University of Chicago Press, 1988.

———. "Romancing the Empire: The Embodiment of American Masculinity in the Popular Historical Novel of the 1890s." *American Literary History* 2, no.4 (Winter 1990): 659–90.

Karaganis, Joseph. "Naturalism's Nation: Toward An American Tragedy." *American Literature* 72.1 (2000) 153–180.

Kasson, John F. *Rudeness and Civility: Manners in Nineteenth-Century Urban America*. New York: Hill and Wang, 1990.

———. *Houdini, Tarzan and the Perfect Man: The White Male Body and the Challenge of Modernity in America*. New York: Hill and Wang, 2001.

Kazin, Alfred and Charled Shapiro, Eds. *The Stature of Theodore Dreiser*. Bloomington: Indiana University Press, 1955.

Kellogg, J.H. *Neurasthenia or Nervous Exhaustion*. Battle Creek, Michigan: Good Health Publishing, 1915.

Kimmel, Michael. *Manhood in America: A Cultural History.* New York: Free Press, 1996.

———. "Baseball and the Reconstitution of American Masculinity, 1880–1920." *Sports, Men, and the Gender Order: Critical Feminist Perspectives*. Eds. M. Messner and D. Sabo. Champaign: Human Kinetics Books, 1990.

———. "Men's Responses to Feminism at the Turn of the Century." *Gender and Society.* 1 September 1987: 262–83.

———. "Consuming Manhood: The Feminization of American Culture and the Recreation of the Male Body, 1832–1920." *The Male Body: Features, Destinies, Exposures*. Ed. Lawrence     Goldstein. Ann Arbor: University of Michigan Press, 1994.

Kress, Jill. *The Figure of Consciousness*. New York: Routledge, 2001.

Laquer, Thomas. *Making Sex: Body and Gender from the Greeks to Freud*. Cambridge: Harvard University Press, 1990.

Leach, William. *Land of Desire: Merchants, Power, and the Rise of a New American Culture*. New York: Pantheon, 1993.

Lears, T.J. Jackson. *No Place of Grace: Antimodernism and the Transformation of American Cuture, 1880–1920*. New York: Pantheon Books, 1981.

Lloyd-Smith, Allan Gardner. *Uncanny American Fiction: Medusa's Face.* New York: St. Martin's Press, 1989.

Lombroso, Cesare. *The Man of Genius.* London: Walter Scott Publishing Co., 1905.

London, Jack. *Jack London: Fantastical Tales.* Dale L. Walker, Ed. Lincoln: University of Nebraska Press, 1998.

———. *Moon-Face and Other Stories.* New York: Gosset & Dunlap Publishers, 1906.

Lowery, Richard S. "Domestic Interiors: Boyhood Nostalgia and Affective Labor in the Gilded Age." *Inventing the Psychological: Toward a Cultural History of Emotional Life in America.* Eds. Joel Pfister and Nancy Schnog. New Haven: Yale University Press, 1997.

Lubin, David M. "Modern Psychological Selfhood in the Art of Thomas Eakins." *Inventing the Psychological.* Eds. Joel Pfister and Nancy Schnog. New Haven: Yale University Press, 1997.

Lundquist, James. *Theodore Dreiser.* New York: Frederick Ungar Publishing Co., 1974.

Lutz, Tom. *American Nervousness 1903: An Anecdotal History.* Ithaca: Cornell University Press, 1991.

MacAloon, John. *This Great Symbol: Pierre de Coubertin and the Origins of the Modern Olympic Games.* Chicago: The University of Chicago Press, 1981.

Macfadden, Benarr. *Manhood And Marriage.* New York: Physical Culture Publishing Co., 1916

———. *Physical Culture Magazine.* Vols 1 and 2. New York: Physical Culture Publishing Co., 1900.

Mangan, J.A. and James Walvin, eds. *Manliness and Morality: Middle-Class Masculinity in Britain and America, 1800–1940.* New York: St. Martin's Press, 1987.

Masteller, Richard N. "Western Views in Eastern Parlors: The Contribution of the Stereograph Photographer to the Conquest of the West." *Prospects.* 6 1981: 55–71.

Micale, Mark Stephen. *Diagnostic Discriminations: Jean-Martin Charcot and the Nineteenth Century Idea of Masculine Hysteria Neurosis.* Yale University Dissertation, 1987.

———. *Approaching Hysteria: Disease and Its Interpretation.* Princeton: Princeton University Press, 1995.

———, Paul Lerner, eds. Traumatic Pasts: History, Psychiatry, and Trauma in the Modern Age, *1870–1930.* New York: Cambridge University Press, 2001.

Michaels, Walter Benn. *The Gold Standard and the Logic of Naturalism: American Literature of the Turn of the Century.* Berkeley: University of California Press, 1987.

Moddelmog, William. *Reconstructing Authority: American Fiction in the Province of the Law, 1880–1920.* Iowa City: University of Iowa Press, 2000.

Muller, Jerry Z. *Adam Smith in His Time and Ours.* Princeton: Princeton University Press, 1993.

Myers, F.W.H. *Human Personality and Its Survival of Bodily Death.* New York: Longmans, Green, and Co., 1909.

———, and Frank Podmore. *Phantasms of the Living.* New York: E.P. Dutton and Co., 1918.

Nasaw, David. *Going Out: The Rise and Fall of Public Amusements.* New York: Basic Books, 1993.

Nelson, Dana. *National Manhood: Capitalist Citizenship and the Imagined Fraternity of White Men.* Durham: Duke University Press, 1998.

Nisbet, John F. *Insanity of Genius and the General Inequality of Human Faculty, Psychologically Considered.* London: Ward & Downey, 1891.

Nordau, Max. *Degeneration.* New York: D. Appelton, 1905.

Oliver, Phil. *William James's 'Springs of Delight': the Return toLife.* Vanderbilt University Press, 2001.

Otten, Thomas J. "Pauline Hopkins and the Hidden Self of Race." *English Literary History.* 59 (1992).

Peiss, Kathy. *Cheap Amusements: Working Women and Leisure in Turn-of-the-Century New York.* Philadelphia: Temple University Press, 1986.

Pendergast, Tom. *Creating the Modern Man: American Magazines and Consumer Culture, 1900–1950.* Columbia: University of Missouri Press, 2000.

Perchuk, Andrew and Helaine Posner, Eds. *The Masculine Masquerade: Masculinity and Representation.* Cambridge: MIT Press, 1995.

Phelan, Peggy. *Unmarked: The Politics of Performance.* New York: Routledge, 1993.

Phelan, Shane. *Getting Specific: Postmodern Lesbian Politics.* Minneapolis: University of Minnesota Press, 1994.

Pizer, Donald. *The Novels of Theodore Dreiser: A Critical Study.* Minneapolis: University of Minnesota Press, 1976.

Pollock, Griselda. "Feminism/Foucault–Sex/Surveillance." *Visual Culture: Images and Interpretations.* Eds. Norman Bryson, et. al. Hanover, NH: University Press of New England, 1994.

Poovey, Mary. *Uneven Developments: The Ideological Work of Gender in Mid-Victorian England.* Chicago: The University of Chicago Press, 1988.

———. "'Scenes from an Indelicate Character': The Medical 'Treatment' of Victorian Women." *The Making of the Modern Body.* Eds. Catherine Gallagher and Thomas Laqueur. Berkeley: University of California Press, 1987. 137–168.

Rabinbach, Anson. *The Human Motor: Energy, Fatigue, and the Origins of Modernity.* New York: Basic Books, 1990.

Rabinow, Paul. *The Foucault Reader.* New York: Pantheon Books, 1984.

Rignall, John. *Realist Fiction and the Strolling Spectator.* London: Routledge, 1992.

Rodgers, Daniel T. *The Work Ethic in Industrial America, 1850–1920.* Chicago: The University of Chicago Press, 1974.

Rotundo, Anthony. *American Manhood: Transformations in Masculinity from the Revolution to the Modern Era.* New York: Basic Books,1993.

———. "Boy Culture." *Meanings for Manhood.* Eds. Mark Carnes and Clyde Griffen. Chicago: The University of Chicago Press, 1990.

Rovit, Earl. "The Language and Imagery of 'The Jolly Corner.'" *The Finer Thread, the Tighter Weave: Essays on the Short Fiction of Henry James.* Ed. Joseph Dewey and Brooke Horvath. Purdue University Press, 2001.

Salzman, Jack, ed. *Theodore Dreiser: The Critical Reception.* New York: David Lewis, 1972.

Sargent, Dudley A. *Health, Strength and Power.* New York: H.M. Caldwell Co., 1904.

———. "Physical Characteristics of An Athlete." *The Out-of-Door Library.* New York: Charles Scribner's Sons, 1897. 183–184.

———. *Physical Education.* Boston: Ginn & Co., 1906.

Savoy, Eric. "The Queer Subject of 'The Jolly Corner.'" *The Henry James Review.* 20:1 (1999).

Schwartz, Hillel. *Never Satisfied: A Cultural History of Diets, Fantasies, and Fat.* New York: The Free Press, 1986.

Seaver, Jay W. *Anthropometry and Physical Examination: A Book for Practical Use in Connection with Gymnastic Work and Physical Education.* New Haven: O.A. Dorman Co., 1896.

Sedgwick, Eve Kosofsky. *Between Men: English Literature and Male Homosocial Desire.* New York: Columbia University Press, 1985.

———. *Epistemology of the Closet.* Berkeley: University of California Press, 1990.

Sekula, Allan. "The Body and The Archive." *October.*1986 39 (Winter). 3–64.

Seltzer, Mark. *Bodies and Machines.* New York: Routledge, 1992.

Sennett, Richard. *The Fall of Public Man.* New York: Knopf, 1977.

Shortt, S.E.D. "Physicians and Psychics: The Anglo-American Medical Response to Spiritualism, 1870–1890. *The Journal of the History of Medicine and Allied Sciences.* 39 (July 1984) 346.

Shulman, Robert. *Social Criticism and Nineteenth Century American Fictions.* New York: Columbia University Press, 1987.

Sidis, Boris. *Philistine and Genius.* New York: Maffat, Yard and Company, 1911.

Silverman, Kaja. *Male Subjectivity at the Margins.* New York: Routledge, 1992.

———. "Fragments of a Fashionable Discourse." *Theorizing Feminism: Parallel Trends in the Humanities and Social Sciences.* Eds. Anne Herrmann and Abigail Stewart. Boulder: Westview Press, 1994.

———. *The Threshold of the Visible World.* New York: Routledge, 1996.

Smith-Rosenberg, Carroll. *Disorderly Conduct: Visions of Gender in Victorian America.* New York: Oxford University Press, 1985.

Spencer, Kathleen L. "Purity and Danger: *Dracula,* the Urban Gothic and the Late Victorian Degeneracy Crisis. *English Literary History.* 59 (1992).

Strychacz, Thomas. *Modernism, Mass Culture, and Professionalism.* New York: Cambridge University Press, 1993.

Sundquist, Eric, ed. *American Realism: New Essays.* Baltimore: Johns Hopkins University Press, 1982.

Taylor, Eugene. *William James on Exceptional Mental States: the 1896 Lowell Lectures.* New York: Scribner, 1983.

———. *William James on Consciousness Beyond the Margin.* Princeton: Princeton University Press, 1996.

Taylor, Frederick Winslow. "The Principles of Scientific Management." *American Magazine* 1911 LXXI(V). 577.

Tester, Keith, Ed. *The Flaneur.* London: Routledge, 1994.

Thompson, Bertrand Clarence. "The Literature of Scientific Management." *Scientific Management: A Collection of the More Significant Articles Describing the Taylor System of Management.* Ed. b.c. Thompson. Cambridge: Harvard University Press, 1914.

Tichi, Cicelia. *Shifting Gears: Technology, Literature, Culture in Modern America.* Chapel Hill: The University of North Carolina Press, 1987.

Tinter, Adeline. *Henry James and the Lust of the Eyes.* Baton Rouge: Louisiana State University Press, 1993.

Todorov, Tzvetan. *The Fantastic.* Ithaca: Cornell University Press, 1975.

Torgovnick, Marianna. *Gone Primitive: Savage Intellects, Modern Lives.* Chicago: Chicago University Press, 1990.

Townsend, Kim. *Manhood at Harvard: William James and Others.* New York: W.W. Norton & Company, 1996.

Trachtenberg, Alan. *The Incorporation of America: Culture and Society in the Gilded Age.* New York: Hill and Wang, 1982.

Traister, Bryce "Academic Viagra: the Rise of American Masculinity Studies." *American Quarterly* 52: 2 (June 2000): 274–304.

Tratner, Michael. *Deficits and Desires: Economies and Sexuality in Twentieth-Century Literature.* Stanford: Stanford University Press, 2001.

Tuana, Nancy, William Cowling, Maurice Hamington, Greg Johnson and Terrance Macmullan, eds. *Revealing Male Bodies.* Bloomington: Indiana University Press, 2002.

Van Leer, David. "The Beast in the Closet: Homosociality and the Pathology of Manhood." *Critical Inquiry.* 15 Spring 1989: 578–605.

von Mucke, Dorothy E. *The Seduction of the Occult and the Rise of the Fantastical Tale.* Stanford: Stanford University Press, 2003.

Wallace, Michele. "Modernism, Postmodernism and the Problem of the Visual in Afro-American Culture." *Out There: Maginalization and Contemporary Cultures.* Eds. Russell Ferguson, et. al. Cambridge: The MIT Press, 1990.

Weigel, Sigrid. *Body- and Image-Space: Re-reading Walter Benjamin.* New York: Routledge, 1996.

Wharton, Edith. *The House of Mirth.* 1905. New York: Penguin Books, 1964.

Wiegman, Robyn. *American Anatomies: Theorizing Race and Gender.* Durham: Duke University Press, 1995.

Williams, Linda. *Hard Core: Power, Pleasure, and the "Frenzy of the Visible."* Berkeley: University of California Press, 1989.

Wolff, Janet. "The Invisible Flaneuse: Women and the Literature of Modernity." *Theory, Culture and Society.* 2.3 1985: 37–46.

Zanine, Louis J. *Mechanism and Mysticism: The Influence of Science on the Thought and Work of Theodore Dreiser.* Philadelphia: University of Pennsylvania Press, 1993.

Zimmerman, David A. "Frank Norris, Market Panic, and the Mesmeric Sublime" *American Literature* 75.1 (2003): 61–90.

# Index

For Product Safety Concerns and Information please contact our EU representative GPSR@taylorandfrancis.com Taylor & Francis Verlag GmbH, Kaufingerstraße 24, 80331 München, Germany

Printed and bound by CPI Group (UK) Ltd, Croydon, CR0 4YY
08/06/2025
01897001-0015